ENGLISH TEACHING FROM A TO Z

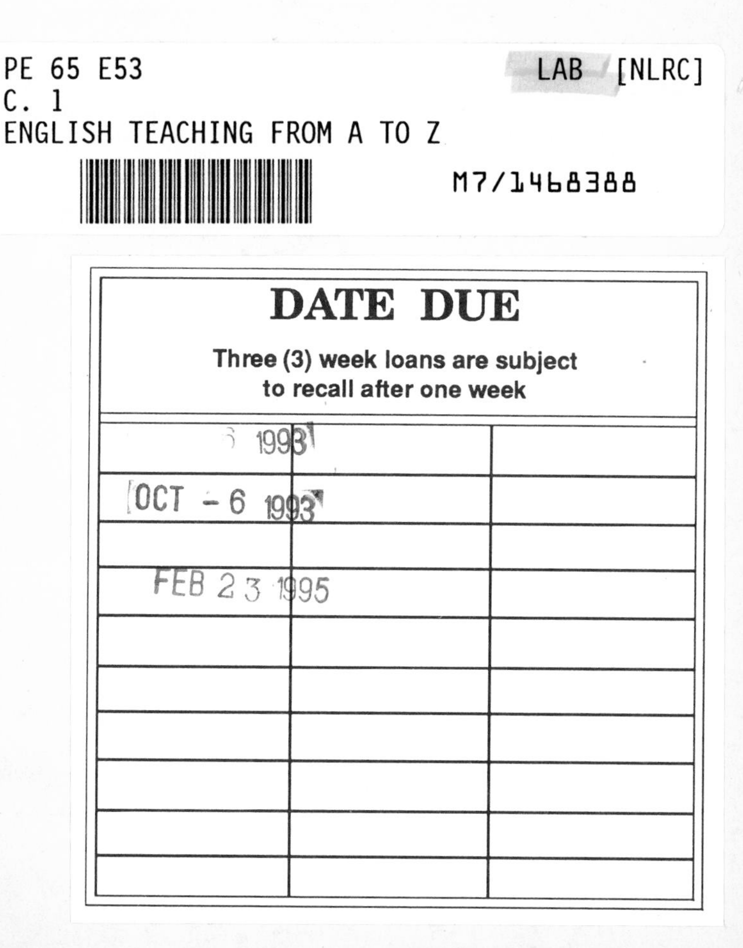

Open University Press

English, Language, and Education series

General Editor: Anthony Adams

Lecturer in Education, University of Cambridge

This series is concerned with all aspects of language in education from the primary school to the tertiary sector. Its authors are experienced educators who examine both principles and practice of English subject teaching and language across the curriculum in the context of current educational and societal developments.

TITLES IN THE SERIES

Time for Drama
Roma Burgess and Pamela Gaudry

Computers and Literacy
Daniel Chandler and Stephen Marcus (eds.)

Readers, Texts, Teachers
Bill Corcoran and Emrys Evans (eds.)

Developing Response to Poetry
Patrick Dias and Michael Hayhoe

The Primary Language Book
Peter Dougill and Richard Knott

Children Talk About Books: Seeing Themselves as Readers
Donald Fry

Literary Theory and English Teaching
Peter Griffith

Assessing English
Brian Johnston

Lipservice: The Story of Talk in Schools
Pat Jones

The English Department in a Changing World
Richard Knott

Oracy Matters
Margaret MacLure, Terry Phillips and Andrew Wilkinson (eds.)

Teaching Literature for Examinations
Robert Protherough

Developing Response to Fiction
Robert Protherough

Microcomputers and the Language Arts
Brent Robinson

English Teaching from A–Z
Wayne Sawyer, Anthony Adams and Ken Watson

English Teaching in Perspective
Ken Watson

The Quality of Writing
Andrew Wilkinson

The Writing of Writing
Andrew Wilkinson (ed.)

ENGLISH TEACHING FROM A TO Z

Edited by
Wayne Sawyer,
Ken Watson and
Anthony Adams

Open University Press
Milton Keynes · Philadelphia

Open University Press
12 Cofferidge Close
Stony Stratford
Milton Keynes MK11 1BY

and
242 Cherry Street
Philadelphia, PA 19106, USA

First Published 1983 by St Clair Press. Published in this edition by
Open University Press 1989

British Library Cataloguing in Publication Data

English teaching from A to Z. – (English,
language and education series).
1. Schools. Curriculum subjects. English
language. Teaching
I. Sawyer, Wayne II. Adams, Anthony, *1933*–
III. Watson, Ken IV. Series
420'.7'1

ISBN 0-335-15832-3

Library of Congress Cataloging in Publication Data

English teaching from A to Z
edited by Wayne Sawyer, Anthony Adams and
Ken Watson.
p. cm. – (English, language, and education series)
Includes index.
ISBN (invalid) 0-335-15832-3 (pbk.)
1. English philology—Study and teaching—Handbooks, manuals, etc.
I. Sawyer, Wayne. II. Watson, Ken (Ken D.) III. Adams, Anthony.
IV. Series.
PE65.E53 1988
428'.007—dc 19 88-1609 CIP

Typeset by Rowland Phototypesetting Limited
Bury St Edmunds, Suffolk
Printed in Great Britain by the Alden Press Limited, Oxford

General Editor's Introduction

As the following reprint of the original editors' Preface indicates, this book, like several in this series, has its origins in Australia and, especially, in the work of Ken Watson's St Clair Press which has done a great deal to develop progressive approaches to English teaching in that country. My own role here as General Editor is somewhat different to that in the other books of the series as here I was invited by Wayne Sawyer and Ken Watson to co-edit with them an international edition of their 1983 edition and I must, therefore, share with them total responsibility for the final outcome.

When Wayne and Ken edited their first edition they were both lecturing at the University of Sydney, where Ken is still. The book grew out of the everyday business of their teaching. The came to feel that what was needed was a vade-mecum which would contain all the key references and ideas to which a teacher of English needed easy access – an English teacher's 'desk book' in fact. This immediately struck a chord with me. My students had similar needs and I, together with my colleague, Esmor Jones, had pioneered in the UK the idea of a desk book for English teachers in our publication, *The World in Words* (1969) in the early days of Pergamon Press's *Pergamon English Library*. It is a great pleasure to see this idea return 20 years later into publishing over here.

Like my two co-editors I also share a commitment to what they call in their original Preface, the 'new English', although I am not so sure how new this remains nowadays. There is a danger that the 'new English' of the time when this book is published will be an arid, purely instrumental English, based upon the practice of skills with little of what Sawyer and Watson call the 'language as resource' approach. All three of us would certainly see language (in the widest sense of that word) as being at the heart of the English curriculum, while recognising the importance of literature as a major example of language in use. Indeed, Doughty, Pearce and Thornton's own research and publication, *Language in Use* (Edward Arnold, 1971) is one of the major influences behind the present volume. Interestingly enough, that publication grew out of a Schools Council Curriculum Development Project, directed by Professor M. A. K. Halliday, who was then based at University College, London and who has since moved to the Linguistics Department of the University of Sydney. This is a further indication, therefore, of the Anglo-Australian origins of the present work.

Readers of this series may already be familiar with Ken Watson's *English Teaching in Perspective* to which the present volume may be seen as something of a companion in its original edition. This revised international edition has been devised with a slightly different purpose: to act as a general reference work to accompany the *English, Language, and Education* series as a whole. As it was in preparation, Wayne left the University of Sydney to return to the secondary classroom and the other two of us handed over the 'lion's share' of the revisions to him. Although we all share equal responsibility for the achievements and demerits of the present volume Wayne's contribution to final outcome must remain paramount. I have, however, as both General Editor of the series and the only local editor, taken over a major responsibility for seeing the product through the Press and must take full responsibility for any editorial shortcomings and inconsistencies.

In practice, editing a reference book of this kind has proved an interesting and demanding task, especially when seen through the eyes of two very different cultures. I have been helped by several visits to Australasia which have given me both a theoretical and classroom awareness of practice in English teaching 'down under' and the book owes much to many conversations with Wayne and Ken in locations as diverse as Vancouver, London, Montreal and Sydney. We hope, therefore, that we have added a North American element to the original conception of the book. Even as the final copy has been seen through the Press we are only too well aware that the editing process is not yet complete. We have not really been able to take account, in the UK, of the impact of the report of the Kingman Committee or of the national curriculum guidelines for English, both of which are still (November 1987) to be published. What we have tried to do is to cover, with copious, if inadequate, references, all those areas of English teaching about which teachers, lecturers and students may need brief explanations and to provide this, in so far as the limited extent of the book may make possible. We would welcome from readers suggestions for areas not included as well as any corrections or additions to what has emerged from our several labours.

Inevitably, the book retains traces of its Australian origins in that it contains many more references to Australian practice and research than would normally be the case in a book published in the UK. This is partly the natural outcome of having two out of the three editors Australian themselves (one the senior editor) but it is also something that may be revealing for UK and North American readers. Whilst working on the book, I have been struck by the similarities in good practice between ourselves and the Australians, and (in many cases) the dissimilarities between UK and Australian usage of our common language. I refer the reader to the important 'note on the usage entries' in the original Preface which will indicate the standpoint from which Wayne and Ken began writing. To the references cited there must be added, in the UK, the important work of W. H. Mittins *et al.*, *Attitudes to English Usage* (Oxford University Press, 1970). In spite of its date of publication this remains one of the best surveys of current usage available in UK terms, though, on language as a whole, we would now wish also to add to the references David Crystal's *Cambridge Encyclopedia of Language* (Cambridge University Press, 1987), which appeared too late to be taken account of in our entries in the present volume. In our many discussions it was the usage entries that we found most difficult to finalise on an agreed basis and, even when we had finished, several of our entries were challenged (sometimes successfully) by our in-house editor. We have made no attempt in the present edition to take on board the even more difficult and intractable area of North American usage, or the differences between different parts of the United States and Canada, though we may seek to do this in a still later edition. All three editors, however, just as does the style of the whole series, recognize the significance and importance of our responsibility as English teachers to English as an international language and it is in this sense that the present volume is offered as an essential addition to the English teacher's reference shelf.

Anthony Adams

Introduction to original Australian edition (1983)

This handbook for primary and secondary teachers aims to provide, in handy reference form, information about many matters of daily concern to English teachers: explanations of literary and educational terms, assessments of commercial materials, notes on disputed items of usage, practical ideas for the classroom. Where appropriate, summaries of recent research are also given. We have not felt it necessary, however, to include some of the everyday terms used by English teachers, such as *simile* and *metaphor*.

The book is written from a viewpoint of acknowledged bias. The editors and contributors are united in a commitment to the principles which underlie what has come to be called the 'new English'. These principles include such things as a 'language as resource' approach to language use and development, a language-across-the-curriculum policy, a psycho-linguistic view of the reading process and a sense that literature, language and personal experience all have equal place in the English classroom.

A note on the usage entries

Apart from the present volume, there are, to our knowledge, only two Australian guides to usage. (The various Australian dictionaries are quite inadequate in this regard.) They are *Watch Your Language*, published by the Australian Broadcasting Commission, and pp. 223–50 of *Every Child Can Write!* ed. R. D. Walshe (PETA). These pages are a revision of Walshe's article in *Good Australian English*, ed. G. W. Turner (Reed) and his *Usage Update*, a pamphlet in the PEN series published by the Primary English Teaching Association.

It must be recognized that these works represent the *opinions* of the authors, opinions that are *not* based on extensive surveys of usage. Since usage is at bottom a *social* matter, the lack of such data must be considered a weakness. In this respect the entries on usage in the present volume are, we modestly believe, a step forward, in that our conclusions on some of the more controversial items are based on surveys of some hundreds of English graduates, mainly graduates of the University of Sydney. Such a sampling is, however, too narrow, and an Australian dictionary of usage, based on a comprehensive sampling, remains an urgent need.

At times we have referred to Fowler's *Modern English Usage*, Partridge's *Usage and Abusage* and Burchfield's *The Spoken Word*. While the first two are works of great erudition, they are guides to the United Kingdom rather than Australian usage, and all three rest, in the last analysis, on opinion. They must not, therefore, be seen as prescriptive.

Abbreviations used in usage entries:

BURCHFIELD – *The Spoken Word* by Robert Burchfield, London: BBC, 1981.

FOWLER – *Fowler's Modern English Usage*, 2nd edition, revised by Sir Ernest Gowers, Oxford: Oxford University Press, 1968. If the first edition is referred to, the date 1926 is cited.

PARTRIDGE – *Usage and Abusage* by Eric Partridge, London: Hamish Hamilton, 1947.

WALSHE – *Every Child Can Write!* ed. R. D. Walshe, Sydney: PETA, 1981.

Our thanks are due to the following people who helped to gather some of the data for the usage entries: Lisa Blackwell, Eric Bertuccio, Margaret Burke, Anne Castle, Jenny Emery, Therese English, Peter Fleming, Kerrie Green, Jane Hall, Therese Hawes, Karen Hedwards, Robyn Keegan, Robyn Keen, Cathy Lough, Michelle Munro, Margaret Norman, Marilyn Ramsey, Meriss Shenstone, Leanne Wake and Elizabeth Wyburn.

Ken Watson and Wayne Sawyer

Comparison of ages, stages, classes, years, grades and systems.

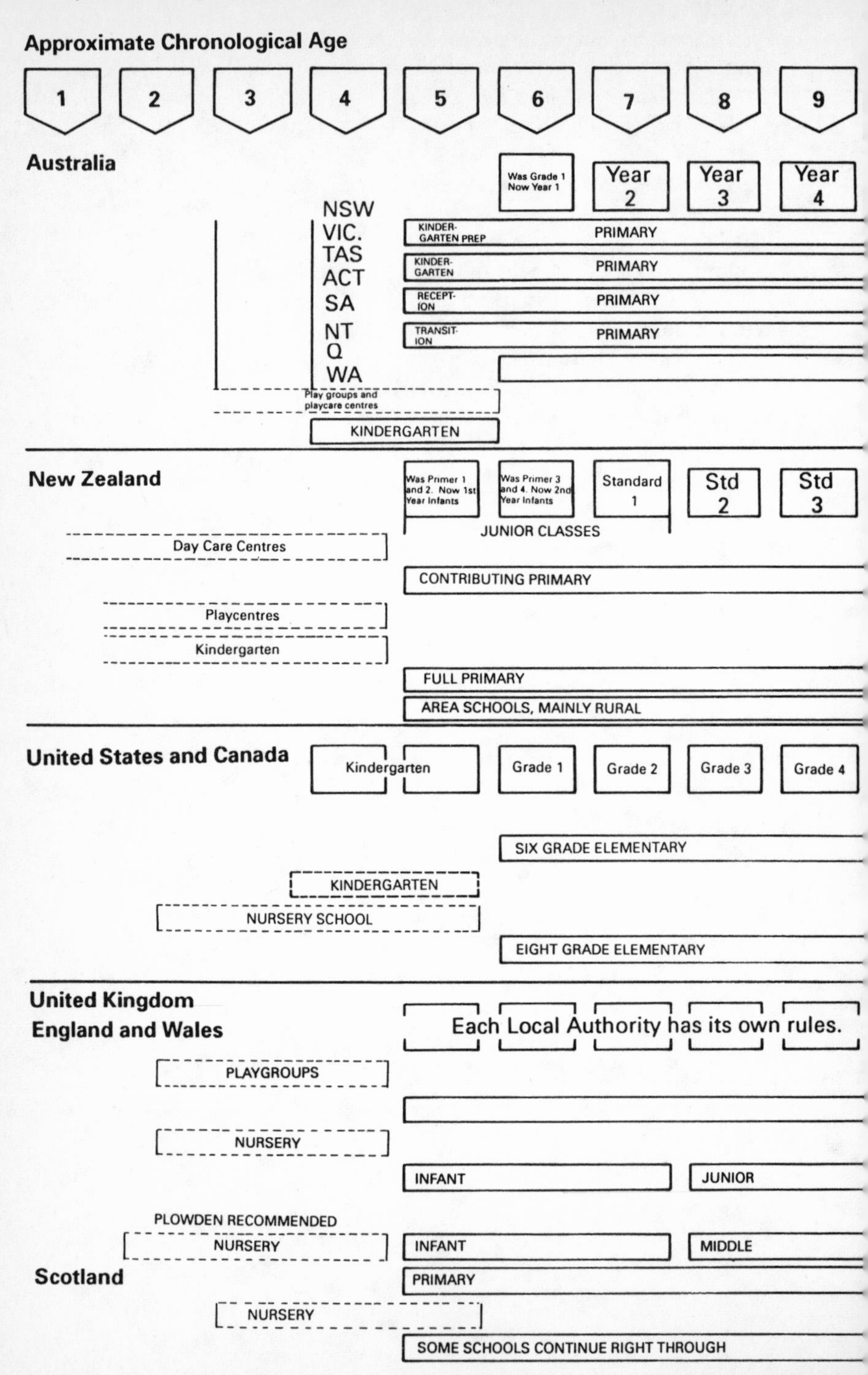

Note: This chart gives a rough guide only. All systems are changing and in all cases the chronological ages are approximate.

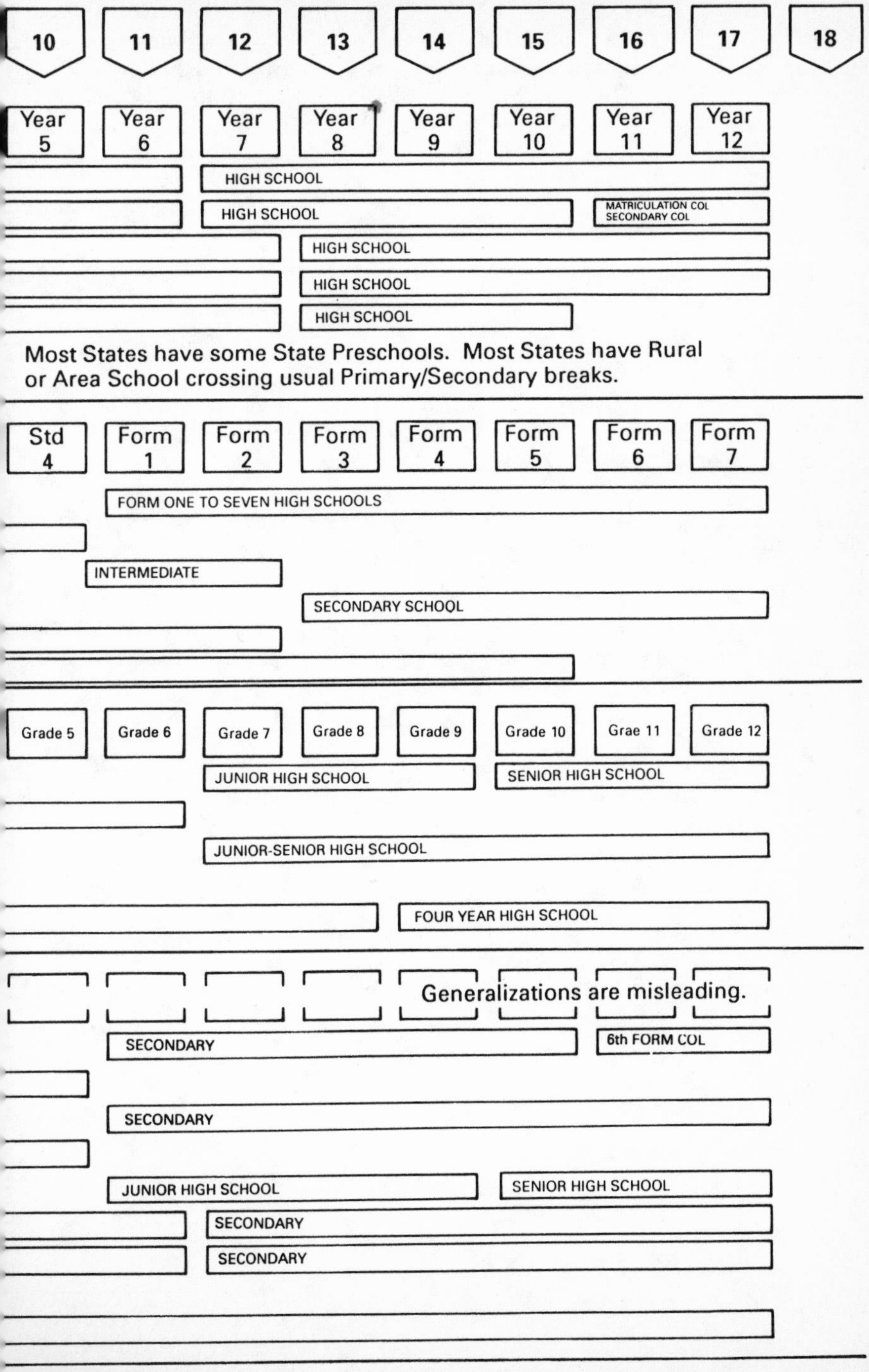

10 | 11 | 12 | 13 | 14 | 15 | 16 | 17 | 18

Year 5 | Year 6 | Year 7 | Year 8 | Year 9 | Year 10 | Year 11 | Year 12

HIGH SCHOOL

HIGH SCHOOL | MATRICULATION COL SECONDARY COL

HIGH SCHOOL

HIGH SCHOOL

HIGH SCHOOL

Most States have some State Preschools. Most States have Rural or Area School crossing usual Primary/Secondary breaks.

Std 4 | Form 1 | Form 2 | Form 3 | Form 4 | Form 5 | Form 6 | Form 7

FORM ONE TO SEVEN HIGH SCHOOLS

INTERMEDIATE

SECONDARY SCHOOL

Grade 5 | Grade 6 | Grade 7 | Grade 8 | Grade 9 | Grade 10 | Grae 11 | Grade 12

JUNIOR HIGH SCHOOL | SENIOR HIGH SCHOOL

JUNIOR-SENIOR HIGH SCHOOL

FOUR YEAR HIGH SCHOOL

Generalizations are misleading.

SECONDARY | 6th FORM COL

SECONDARY

JUNIOR HIGH SCHOOL | SENIOR HIGH SCHOOL

SECONDARY

SECONDARY

CONTRIBUTORS

Entries which do not bear the initials of the writer have been written by the editors.

Roslyn Arnold
Laurie Butterfield
Brian Cambourne
Len Cairns
John Collerson
W. D. Emrys Evans
Warwick Franks
Maria Gray-Spence
Brian Johnston
Peter Jones
Rod Leonarder
Macarthur Reading Team:
  Richard Parker
  Joan Mason
  Vivienne Nicoll
  Len Unsworth
Paul Richardson
Don Spearritt
Phil Stabback
Bob Walshe
Neil Whitfield
Geoff Williams

a

AATE *See* AUSTRALIAN ASSOCIATION FOR THE TEACHING OF ENGLISH.

ABILITY GROUPING *See* STREAMING.

ACCELERATED READING *See* READING MACHINES.

ACCENT *See* DIALECT.

ACCEPTABILITY *See* USAGE.

ACCIDENCE – That part of morphology (q.v.) dealing with inflection (q.v.).

ACCOMMODATION – A term employed by the psychologist Jean Piaget to describe an aspect of cognitive development. *Accommodation* relates to that reaction of the individual with his/her environment which causes the intellect to modify or reshape previous schemata (q.v.) so that they become in effect new structures. *Assimilation*, on the other hand, is the process whereby the individual incorporates new experiences into existing schemata in such a way that they remain essentially unchanged.

ACCOUNTABILITY MOVEMENT – Particularly in the United States, there is a growing insistence that educational programmes and indeed teachers themselves be scrutinized in terms of the progress of the learners and cost effectiveness.
See also MINIMAL COMPETENCY TESTING.

ACRONYM – A word usually formed from the initial letters of a group of words, for example UNESCO. An interesting exercise is to ask pupils to treat common words as if they were acronyms and expand into appropriate phrases, for example 'PASTE': 'Passes all sticky tape easily'.

ACTION RESEARCH – Small-scale research which involves diagnosing a problem in a specific context and attempting to solve it by a particular course of action. It is often undertaken by a single teacher in his/her classroom or by a group of teachers in a single school. Since there is usually no attempt to control all variables, the results of such research are only generalizable in so far as other teachers recognize that their own classrooms exhibit similar problems in similar contexts.

References
C. Adelman and R. Walker, *A Guide to Classroom Observation*, London: Methuen, 1975.
L. Cohen and L. Mannion, *Research Methods in Education*, London: Croom Helm, 1980.
See also the publications of the Ford Teaching Project published by the Centre for Applied Research in Education, University of East Anglia.

ACTIVITY LEARNING – A term used to describe learning methods involving active participation, such as simulations, group projects, role play. In reading, the method of surrounding children with interesting reading materials and allowing them to learn with a minimum of teacher intervention.

ADJUNCT – A kind of adverbial (q.v.) which is a major constituent of a sentence or clause, e.g. 'She is working indoors'.

ADOLESCENT LITERATURE *See* YOUNG ADULT LITERATURE.

ADVERBIAL – The Kingman Report (q.v.) makes use of this general term for that constituent of a sentence which is distinct from subject, object, verb and complement. There are three kinds of adverbials: adjuncts (q.v.), conjuncts (q.v.) and disjuncts (q.v.).

ADVERTISING – The study of the language of advertising is an important aspect of 'subject English'. Particularly at secondary level, classes can discuss:

(1) the pros and cons of advertising;
(2) the importance of connotation (q.v.) in advertising, for example in brand names;
(3) the ways in which particular advertisements make their appeal, for example:
  (i) snob appeal ('In all the best homes . . .', 'Men of judgement prefer . . .');
  (ii) capitalizing on the desire for security ('Get with the strength, bank Commonwealth') or the desire for ease and comfort ('miracle' cleaners; food that one simply 'Heats and eats');
  (iii) the appeal to authority ('University tests have shown . . .').

This could include a study of both the 'hidden persuasion' of advertising (as in the types of appeal already mentioned) and also the underlying assumptions (ask groups to find ads that seem to be saying 'good looks are the most important thing in relationships', 'the modern is better than the old', 'happiness depends on possessions').

It has been pointed out that the word 'cheap' is rarely used in advertising because it is considered to carry mainly unfavourable connotations (except, oddly, when it is used to refer to food). Marghanita Laski once made up the unlikely advertising slogan, 'Cheap clothes for old fat women' and then rewrote it in words that carry more favourable connotations: 'Limited income clothes for dignified maturity'. Pupils could be invited to try their hand at the same sort of thing.

Other aspects of the language of advertising that could be studied include the use of puns and ambiguity (Passport Scotch: 'If you haven't got a Passport you probably aren't going anywhere') slogans ('Coke adds life'), repetition and the tendency to use superlatives ('biggest', 'brightest', 'most satisfying').

A good activity which explores many facets of advertising involves dividing the class into groups, each of which becomes an advertising agency competing for the lucrative advertising contract for a new product, *Fringle*. Each group first decides what the Fringle is, and then designs display ads, writes advertising jingles, makes a storyboard for a TV advertisement, and so on. The class then decides which group deserves to win the contract.

A variation of this activity could be deliberately to design the ads for a specific medium and thus open the topic out into the area of media generally (what problems are brought up by advertising on radio and in newspapers that don't exist in TV advertising?). A further variation would be to nominate a target audience and open up the whole area of a product's image (why do Coke ads always feature young people, usually outdoors? What kind of people smoke Dunhill?).

AESTHETIC READING – Louise Rosenblatt, in her important book *The Reader, the Text, the Poem*, suggests that there are two kinds of reading: that in which the primary concern of the reader is with what she/he will carry away from the reading, and that in which the reader's primary concern is with what happens *during* the actual reading event. The first, more or less instrumental type of reading, she calls *efferent* reading (from the Latin *efferre*, 'to carry away'); the second she calls *aesthetic* reading: 'In aesthetic reading, the reader's attention is centred directly on what he is living through during his relationship with that particular text' (Louise Rosenblatt, *The Reader, the Text, the Poem.* Carbondale, Ill.: Southern Illinois University Press, 1978, p. 25.)

AFFECT, EFFECT – *Affect* is usually a verb, meaning 'to influence' or 'to touch the emotions'; *effect* can either be a noun ('a result') or a verb ('to bring about a result'). Understandably, the two words are frequently confused.

AFFECTIVE DOMAIN *See* BLOOM'S TAXONOMY.

AFFIX – A bound morpheme (q.v.), such as a prefix (placed at the beginning of a word to change its meaning, e.g. *in*hospitable, *dis*believe) or a suffix (placed at the end of a word, e.g. good*ness*, walk*ing*). One can make a distinction between a derivational affix, which when added to a root or stem forms another word (e.g. like*ness*) and an inflectional affix, which expresses plurality (dog*s*), tense (wait*ed*) or comparison (larg*est*).

AGREEMENT *See* PRONOUN AGREEMENT, VERB AGREEMENT.

AIMS AND OBJECTIVES – In educational writings a distinction is commonly made between *aims*, which are general or overarching statements of intent, and *objectives*, which relate to more specific goals. In the 1985 English syllabus (Years 7–10) in New South Wales, for example, the *aim* is stated as 'to enable students to strive towards personal excellence in using language', and the *objectives* are related to particular areas of the syllabus. The objective of 'Reading' is 'that students understand, enjoy and respond perceptively to what they read in a wide range of contexts'.

ALLEGORY – A (usually extended) narrative in which the characters and events symbolize some underlying idea, usually of an ethical nature. 'Allegory' can be considered from another viewpoint as a collective term which usually includes such literary genres as the fable, apologue, parable and exemplum (q.v.). Yelland, Jones and Easton in their *Handbook of Literary Terms* define these with their differences for the interested reader, though the term 'allegory' probably suffices for classroom use. Well-known examples include Aesop's fables, *The Faerie Queene*, *Arcadia*, *Pilgrim's Progress*, some of Chaucer and Dryden and, more recently, *Animal Farm* and Thurber's *Fables for Our Time.*

Students may need to look into the background of some allegorical works to appreciate the themes, much as they may need to do with satire (q.v.). This poses the problem of the intentional fallacy (q.v.) but may be a necessary starting point for some students, indeed for some works. Teachers need to be aware of the twin dangers in treating some allegorical works of making too specific a correspondence between the subject and its referent, or of over-universalizing the referent. For example, Orwell's remark in a non-specific context that 'throughout history, one revolution after another . . . has simply led to a change of masters, because no serious effort has been made to eliminate the power instinct' ('Catastrophic Gradualism', 1946) has such obvious application to *Animal Farm* that it has become a critical commonplace about the novel. Yet such a 'universalizing' view runs counter to Orwell's very specific writings on the novel: 'I thought of exposing the Soviet myth in a story that could be easily understood . . . I included events, for example the Teheran Conference, which were taking place while I was writing' (1947 Preface to Ukranian edition of *Animal Farm*).

Does the real *Animal Farm* lie in one of these views or in a view of the novel that sees its themes as universal but based on a specific model?

A good way into the idea of allegorizing for students is to have them write their own. James Moffett's programme, *Active Voice*, incorporates a series of parables and fables with the aim of gradually moving young writers into making generalizations about life and people. Thus, from the viewpoints of writing development and of gaining insight into the allegorizing process, the writing of allegories has its advantages.

Using nursery rhymes with underlying political purposes in their origins can be another way of studying the allegory – nursery rhymes such as 'Rock-a-Bye-Baby', 'Mary Mary Quite Contrary', 'Humpty Dumpty' are starters for this activity.

ALLITERATION – The repetition of initial consonants. An attractive example, excellent for verse speaking (q.v.), is W. S. Gilbert's chorus from *The Mikado*:

To sit in solemn silence
In a dull, dark dock,
In a pestilential prison,
With a life-long lock;
Awaiting the sensation
Of a short, sharp shock,
From a cheap and chippy chopper
On a big, black block!

ALLUSION – An indirect reference to something. In literature, the use of allusion often enriches the meaning; in T. S. Eliot's *The Waste Land*, for example, the allusion to a song, 'When lovely woman stoops to folly', in Oliver Goldsmith's *The Vicar Of Wakefield*, causes the reader to contrast the behaviour of modern woman with the behaviour of women in former times:

When lovely woman stoops to folly, and
Paces about her room again, alone,
She smoothes her hair with automatic hand,
And puts a record on the gramophone.

The three commonest sources of allusions are history, literature and myth. Pupils can be asked to track down and/or explain some of the commonest (given *in context*, of course):

Historical: a Pyrrhic victory, fifth column, crossing the Rubicon, a Beau Brummel.
Literary: a Scrooge, a Romeo, an Uncle Tom, a real Micawber, a Walter Mitty, a yahoo.
Classical: Achilles' heel, a Cassandra, a couple of Harpies.

T. S. Eliot was once described by a critic as a Prufrock who would dare to eat a peach – if he could find a socially acceptable way to peel it!

ALPHABET METHOD – This method of teaching reading (also known as the Alphabetic Method) was popular till well into the nineteenth century. John Locke and John Wesley both wrote of being taught to read by the alphabetic method (largely using the 'Horn book' – a thin oak board with the alphabet printed on it and covered with a thin layer of translucent horn). The alphabetic method taught the children the twenty-six letter names and they spelt their way to reading – e.g. 'see–ay–tee spells cat'. Children were usually slow to learn to read via this approach. **(LC)**

AMONG *See* USAGE: BETWEEN AND AMONG.

ANAGRAM – The letters of a word are transposed to form another word. Samuel Butler's *Erewhon* is an anagram of *nowhere.* Willard Espy, in his book *The Game of Words* (London, Wolfe, 1971), lists some brilliantly apt anagrams of the names of famous people:

Adolf Hitler – Hated for ill
Florence Nightingale – Flit on, cheering angel!
William Shakespeare – I ask me, has Will a peer?

Students, too, could be asked to do this, perhaps with their own names.

ANALYSIS OF VARIANCE, COVARIANCE –
Analysis of variance, as applied in educational research, is a statistical procedure for determining whether the mean post-treatment scores of different groups of students taught by different methods or subjected to different types of experimental treatment vary to a greater extent than can be attributed to chance variation. If the obtained differences among means are likely to occur by chance less than one in twenty, or one in one hundred, times, the means are said to differ significantly at the 5 per cent, or 1 per cent level, respectively.
Analysis of covariance is a procedure for determining whether the mean post-treatment scores of different groups of students subjected to different types of experimental treatment vary to a greater extent than can be attributed to chance, when allowance has been made for initial differences among the groups on variables such as ability levels or pre-test scores which are likely to be related to the post-treatment scores. **(DS)**

ANAPHORA – The process of referring to what has already been mentioned. In the sentence 'I read the newspaper and then threw it away', 'it' refers anaphorically to 'the newspaper'.

AND *See* USAGE.

ANIMAL COMMUNICATION – A unit on animal communication gives pupils plenty of scope for research and discussion and is likely to lead to greater insight into the uniqueness of human language. There is a very good unit on this topic in *Language and Communication I* by Forsyth and Woods (Longman). A useful starting point for such work could be the following account by Stuart Chase:

> I attended a party a few years ago at the home of Fredric March . . . My host took me across the room to a table on which was a large cage with a handsome myra bird on the perch. . . .
> 'Joe,' said Mr March, 'this is Mr Chase, who is interested in politics.'
> Joe cocked his head at a sharper angle and said smartly and clearly: 'Are you a Communist?'
> 'No,' I said. 'Are you?'
> 'Good boy, good boy,' Joe replied.
> 'Well,' said our host, 'What do you think about foreign affairs, Joe?'
> Joe had a strong comment ready: 'Such a situation! Such a situation!'
> This all sounded pretty lucid, but I noted that other arrivals were put through a similar dialogue. In due course I met . . . Thew Wright, who had brought Joe to the party. . . .
> 'How long did it take?' I asked.
> 'It took about a month, working every day,' he replied.

'What did you use?'
'Grapes,' he said, 'Cost me a fortune. The key word was "politics".'
(Stuart Chase, *Communicate*, McDougal Littell)

ANTHOLOGIES *See* POETRY ANTHOLOGIES, SHORT STORY COLLECTIONS, SOURCE BOOKS.

ANTI-CLIMAX – The effect achieved when a marked build-up occurs in the audience or reader's expectations only to be destroyed by a particular or an incident that destroys the expected climax. Any mock heroic work is usually full of such deliberate anti-climaxes, for example, Pope's *Rape Of The Lock*:

> To Fifty chosen sylphs, of special Note,
> We trust the important Charge, the Petticoat
> (II, 117–18)

> Here Britain's Statesmen of the Fall foredoom
> Of Foreign Tyrants, and of Nymphs at home,
> Here Thou, Great Anna! whom three Realms obey,
> Dost sometimes Counsel take – and sometimes
> Tea.
> (III, 5–8)

ANTI-HERO – The antithesis of the traditional courageous and resourceful hero of fiction. Examples of modern anti-heroes are Jim Dixon in Kingsley Amis's *Lucky Jim*, Yossarian in Joseph Heller's *Catch 22*, Willy Loman in Arthur Miller's *Death of a Salesman* and Holden Caulfield in J. D. Salinger's *Catcher in the Rye.*

ANTITHESIS – A literary device which places contrasting objects or ideas into close juxtaposition so as to make contrast effective or dramatic. For example, J. B. Priestley's essay 'Television' contains the sentence 'It can turn children into future scholars of Trinity and Girton or into gunmen and molls', and this brings the 'future scholars' into antithetical relationship with 'gunmen and molls'. A famous example is Keats' 'Heard melodies are sweet, but those unheard/Are sweeter. . . .'

APPLIED LINGUISTICS ASSOCIATION OF AUSTRALIA (ALAA) – Founded in 1976, ALAA aims to promote the application of linguistics to the teaching of mother tongue and foreign languages, to multicultural education and to other problems of language and society. Its journal is the *Australian Review of Applied Linguistics* (q.v.).

APOSTROPHE

(1) A figure of speech in which a personified object or a dead or absent person is addressed as if present and capable of understanding, for example:

> Milton! thou should's be living at this hour
> (Wordsworth, *London*, 1802)

Stern daughter of the voice of God!
(Wordsworth, *Ode to Duty*)

Death, be not proud . . .
(Donne, *Sonnet*)

(2) Orthographic symbol used to show possession (e.g. the boy's book).
(3) Orthographic symbol used to show omission (e.g. doesn't).

The use of the apostrophe to show possession causes writers both young and old so much trouble that there is a strong case for its abandonment. Already it has disappeared in such collocations as 'teachers college', 'girls school', and it is hard to think of any situation where its correct use is vital to understanding, except in 'the boys' books' and the like (and even here the context generally removes any ambiguity). Much more irritating than its omission is its frequent use with ordinary plurals (no new phenomenon, by the way). For those anxious that they and their pupils get it right, R. D. Walshe (*Every Child Can Write*, Sydney: PETA, 1981, p. 225) suggests the following three-step rule:

(1) Write the name of the owner/owners.
(2) Then add an apostrophe.
(3) Only add an *s* if it sounds right.

Thus if two princesses own rooms in the castle, the word *princesses* is written down, and an apostrophe added, but no *s* is added since the result would sound distinctly odd. Thus we end up with *the princesses' rooms.*

Alternatively, Barry Walters (*Groundwork in Plain English*, Sydney: Wiley, 1974, p. 64) offers a two-step rule:

(1) Ask yourself, 'To whom does the (   ) belong?'
(2) Place the apostrophe *immediately* after your reply.

APU *See* ASSESSMENT OF PERFORMANCE UNIT.

ARGOT – Originally referring to the jargon of thieves, this word has come in common usage to refer to the slang of any subculture. Many of the currently popular works used in schools contain a wealth of this material; S. E. Hinton's novels, for example. An interesting exercise for many of the other popular novels would be to have children create an argot for groups of characters in the novel, for example *A Wrinkle in Time, The Hobbit, The Silver Sword, The Chocolate War.*
See also SLANG.

AS . . . AS; THAN *See* USAGE.

AS . . . THAN *See* USAGE.

ASPIRATE – The speech sound associated with the letter *h*. The 'misplaced aspirate', associated with some non-standard dialects, was the subject of Thomas Hood's most celebrated pun. He wrote of Cleopatra, who

died, historians relate
Through having found a misplaced asp irate.

ASSESSMENT AND EVALUATION – These terms are often used interchangeably, but there is a tendency for *assessment* to be used in the more restricted sense of a measure of performance or achievement, while *evaluation* is becoming a much broader term, denoting concern not only with pupil performance but with the nature of the course itself and the quality of teaching and learning.

The confusion in terminology is symptomatic of a general state of uncertainty about assessment in English. Many current practices are manifestly invalid, and many teachers are acting on a model of evaluation that is at odds with their professed aims. This entry will concern itself with a model appropriate to all aspects of English teaching; the reader is referred to other entries (see below) which deal with specific problems and summarize relevant research.

The model outlined here is that given by Brian Johnston and Ken Watson in an article in *Developments in English Teaching* 2(1), 1983.

Johnston and Watson argue that in the space of a single unit of work the teacher is called upon to undertake four quite distinct tasks which can be grouped under the heading 'evaluation':

(1) *monitoring and describing* students' performance in order to help them overcome difficulties and enable them to articulate and understand what they *can* do;
(2) *reflecting* on the progress of the unit; determining, for example, whether the students have perceived content, audience, degree of abstraction in the way originally intended;
(3) *appreciating or judging* the quality of students' products;
(4) *determining*, in the light of both process and product, what should be undertaken next.

Their model demands that teaching be so organized that students know when (1) and (2) are going on and (3) isn't. It urges teachers to recognize that many of the students' experiments and mistakes are a necessary part of the learning process; that such things are confidential to the learning process and not the basis for judging the quality of the students' work. It reminds teachers that it is not necessary that the product of every unit be judged; sometimes it is sufficient that there be appreciation, by teacher and class. It also suggests that an important part of the teacher's role is to encourage the students to develop skills of self-evaluation (Fig. 1).

See also CRITERION-REFERENCED ASSESSMENT; EVALUATION OF ENGLISH PROGRAMMES; GOAL-BASED ASSESSMENT; MULTIPLE-CHOICE TESTS; NORM-REFERENCED ASSESSMENT; PEER ASSESSMENT; WRITING, ASSESSMENT OF; SELF-ASSESSMENT BY STUDENTS.

ASSESSMENT OF PERFORMANCE UNIT (APU) – A government funded Unit set up after the publication of the Bullock Report (q.v.) to provide regular monitoring of standards (q.v.) in a range of curriculum areas, including

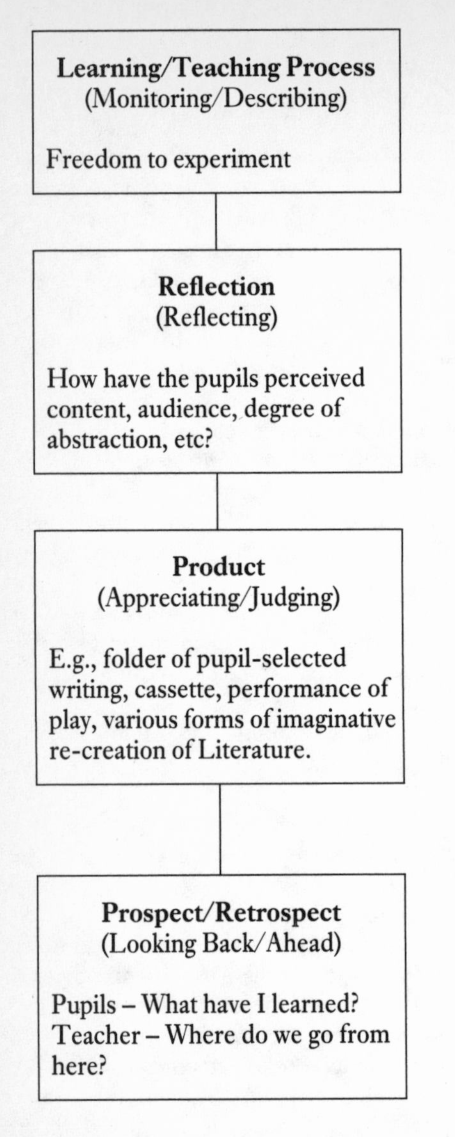

Teacher monitors descriptively to help individuals in their development, make available extra resources, etc.

Pupils must feel free to take risks without being judged on their success or failure.

Many products will be the subject of appreciation rather than judgement/assessment. If there is to be grading, pupils should be aware of this and should know the criteria upon which judgement will be made. Pupils should have control over what is presented for judgement.

Pupils should be encouraged to develop skills of self-evaluation. The teacher will have to decide whether to build further upon what has been achieved, or whether a change of direction is needed.

Figure 1 Model for assessment in English.

language. The Unit has devised tests to monitor national achievement in reading, writing, speaking and listening. Characteristic of its work had been the principle of 'light sampling' so that only a relatively small number of children are tested each year. There has been resistance to the idea of introducing a system of 'blanket testing' which it was felt would have an undesirable effect on the curriculum, leading teachers to teach to the tests. Generally the results of the sampling undertaken by the Unit give no credibility to the myth of declining standards. More recently (1987) the incoming Conservative government has announced its intention of introducing a system of national blanket testing at ages 7, 11, 14 and 16. It remains to be seen how this controversial proposal will operate and what will be its effects on the already established Assessment of Performance Unit.

ASSONANCE – The repetition of vowel sounds for a particular effect, e.g. T. S. Eliot's 'And th*e* afternoon, th*e* *e*vening, sl*ee*ps so p*e*acefull*y*' or Coleridge's 'He holds h*i*m w*i*th h*i*s gl*i*tter*i*ng eye'.

ATMOSPHERE – A somewhat overused term (often wrongly used interchangeably with 'setting'), this refers to a particular aura or mood which the writer may strive to create. The atmosphere of gloom and impending disaster in the opening scene of *Macbeth*, the unpleasant, dingy monotony of Eliot's *Preludes* or the degenerate horror of the 'hill's skull' lines from Lowell's *Skunk Hour*, are examples of the attempt to evoke a particular atmosphere. It is useful to help senior students particularly to build up a vocabulary to apply to 'atmosphere'.

AUDIENCE – One of the aspects of the Schools Council Project on the Written Language of 11–18 Year Olds (q.v.) was the allocation of 2,200 scripts into 'sense of audience' categories:

Self as audience
Child to self

Teacher as audience
Child to trusted adult
Pupil to teacher (general)
Pupil to teacher (particular relationship)
Pupil to examiner

Wider audience (known)
Expert to known lay person
Child to peer group
Group member to working group

Unknown audience
Writer to his/her readers

('Pupil to teacher, particular relationship', differs from 'pupil to teacher, general' in that frequently in secondary school children come to develop personal relationships with one or more of their teachers, relationships fed by their interest in the teacher's subject, and this will be reflected in their writing. 'Expert to known lay person' refers to the not infrequent situation where a child has a particular area of expertise which is not shared by the teacher or by the rest of the class.)

Sense of audience has emerged as one of the most crucial factors influencing children's writing development (and indeed their speaking development as well). A main line of language development in the 5 to 18 age group is the growing awareness of social context and the growing realization that the language one uses will vary with the situation. This important strand of language development is certainly susceptible to teacher intervention, and one of the most important things teachers can do for students is to provide a variety of contexts for speaking and as wide a range of audiences as possible. The Schools Council Project found, as surveys since have found, that the overwhelming bulk of school writing falls into the 'Pupil to examiner' category. A range of possibilities in speech and writing for different audiences is being neglected.

As far as possible, audiences should be *real* audiences who can make real responses. Walshe calls the search for *real* readers our 'key strategy in the future development of school writing'. His book (1981) suggests many of the possible readers that exist in schools (and this, of course, means listeners too) apart from teacher-as-examiner: other pupils in the class, oneself, principal and subject masters, other classes, parents, pen-friends, feeder primary schools. He also suggests appropriate publishing projects to reach these readers. Another publication edited by Walshe – *Better Reading/Writing Now!* – lists 100 ways to publish children's writing.

Leslie Stratta has also given a sample of the kinds of writing tasks that can emerge when teachers actively strive to give pupils experience in writing for different audiences:

Child to self
Notes written by pupil for own purposes. Personal diary/record book. Tentative first drafts.

Child to trusted adult
Writing from personal experiences where the pupil feels free to tell the truth. Writing of any task where the pupil knows that the teacher will respond humanely to anything the pupil writes.

Pupil to teacher, general
Any writing which is 'educational' where the pupil expects a response (not an evaluation) but where the relationship is such that the pupil may or may not be prepared to chance his or her arm, or reveal what he or she really thinks or feels.

Pupil to teacher, particular relationship
(Writing related to a growing interest in the subject – a professional relationship based on shared interest and expertise.) Essays which have a literary critical emphasis (e.g. in the senior secondary school). Writing which in some way either informs the teacher of a pupil's understanding of literature, or asks the pupil to respond to a work of literature (as in junior secondary).

Pupil to examiner
Writing which is specifically set as practice for examinations. A variety of writing which may be set in class for any age group, which is marked by the teacher as if it were an examination. Writing which offers back what the pupil has been told/taught.

Expert to known lay person
Pupils writing on a topic or hobby about which they are knowledgeable, or

where they have become knowledgeable during the course of school/out of school investigation, but where the teacher/other pupils may be less knowledgeable (e.g. fishing; provision for the old in the locality; cars through the ages, and so on).

Child to peer group
Letters to pupils in another school. Form magazine. Writing which will be read/presented to other pupils in the school (e.g. playscript for presentation).

Group member to working group
(A known audience which may include the teacher.) Pupil is a member of a group composing a joint piece of writing (e.g. drama script; topic of thematic work; exploring a work of literature for presentation; writing a newspaper, and so on).

Writer to readers (or public)
Writing which reaches out to a somewhat, or wholly unknown audience (e.g. for publication in a magazine; entry to a competition; or where the pupil is attempting to write as a professional writer).

References
James Britton *et al.*, *The Development of Writing Abilities (11–18)*, London: Macmillan, 1975.
Leslie Stratta, 'Sense of audience and writing tasks that can emerge', *Issues and Ideas* 3(1), March 1981.
R. D. Walshe, *Every Child Can Write*, Sydney: PETA, 1981.
R. D. Walshe (ed.), *Better Reading/Writing Now!* Sydney: PETA, 1980.

AUDITORY DISCRIMINATION – This term may be used in two ways. The first is the ability to discriminate the differences between sounds, and the second is the learnt ability to consciously segment speech into print-related units.

In relation to the former, children as young as 2 years of age are naturally able to distinguish and to use speech sounds. Therefore, those pre-reading exercises designed to teach such skills to children are a waste of time, particularly as far as reading is concerned. A number of studies investigating prerequisite reading skills have revealed that a large percentage of children are able to perform the various auditory discrimination skills activities involved in such pre-reading exercises before they have received any training.

In relation to the latter, many kindergarten children's only experience is with oral language which is a continuous flow that they segment into 'chunks' of meaning – usually phrases or clauses – and not with the discrete units of language as represented in print. Elkonin (1973) believes that drilled word analysis procedures are the most effective means of making the phoneme a concrete entity for young children, and that this should be achieved before written language is introduced. However, while it has been found that the ability to *perceive* sound units in words is highly correlated with reading achievement (Clark, 1976), investigators have found that this ability does not necessarily need to be developed prior to learning to read, but rather, it normally occurs as the result of interaction with written language and continues to be developed and refined over a period of time in the early reading stages (Ehri and Wilce,

1985; Pick, 1978). Experiences involving matching spoken words to the printed representation of well-known rhymes, songs or stories; activities such as listening for and identifying similar beginnings or rhyming sounds in words which are well known to the children; and encouraging children to write using their own 'invented' spellings (q.v.), are useful and appropriate means of facilitating this development. **(MRT)**
See also READING READINESS; CONCEPTS ABOUT PRINT; PRE-READING; LANGUAGE EXPERIENCE APPROACH.

References

M. M. Clark, *Young Fluent Readers*, London: Heinemann, 1976.
L. C. Ehri, and L. S. Wilce, 'Movement into reading: is the first stage of printed word learning visual or phonetic?' *Reading Research Quarterly* 20(2), 1985: 163–78.
D. B. Elkonin, 'USSR, in J. Downing (ed.), *Comparative Reading*, New York: Macmillan, 1973.
A. D. Pick, 'Perception in the acquisition of reading', in F. B. Murray and J. J. Pikulski (ed.), *The Acquisition of Reading*, Baltimore: University Park Press, 1978.

AUSTRALIAN ASSOCIATION FOR THE TEACHING OF ENGLISH (AATE) – The national association of English teachers, having on its council representatives from the affiliated English teachers' associations of the six States and the two Territories. There is no provision for individual membership of AATE. The journal of AATE is *English in Australia* (q.v.).

AUSTRALIAN CHILDREN'S BOOK AWARDS – The Children's Book Council of Australia (q.v.) makes three annual awards. They are:

(1) Australian Book of the Year:
1984 – *A Little Fear* by Patricia Wrightson
1985 – *The True Story of Lilli Stubeck* by J. Aldridge
1986 – *Green Wind* by Thurley Fowler
(2) Australian Junior Book of the Year:
1984 – *Bernice Knows Best* by Max Dann
1985 – *Something Special* by Emily Rodda
1986 – *Arkwright* by Mary Steele
(3) Australian Picture Book of the Year:
1984 – *Bertie and the Bear* by Pamela Allen
1985 – Not awarded
1986 – *Felix and Alexander* by Terry Denton

AUSTRALIAN CHILDREN'S TELEVISION FOUNDATION – A national, non-profit organization created in 1982 to encourage the development, production and transmission of high-quality children's television programmes. It is supported by the Commonwealth Government and the governments of New South Wales, Victoria, South Australia, Western Australia and the Northern Territory. Address: 22–4 Blackwood Street, North Melbourne, Victoria 3051.

AUSTRALIAN JOURNAL OF READING – Journal of the Australian Reading Association (q.v.). Subscription inquiries: *Australian Journal of Reading*, School of Education, Flinders University, Bedford Park, SA 5042.

AUSTRALIAN READING ASSOCIATION (ARA) – A national association of all whose concern is to improve the quality of reading instruction at all levels. Its journal is the *Australian Journal of Reading* (q.v.). Inquiries: Margaret Routh, ARA Treasurer, 1 Garfield Drive, Paddington Qld 4064.

AUSTRALIAN REVIEW OF APPLIED LINGUISTICS – Journal of the Applied Linguistics Association of Australia (q.v.). Inquiries should be directed to the Editor, Mark Garner, Victoria College (Rusden Campus), Blackburn Road, Clayton, Victoria 3168.

AUTOBIOGRAPHY –

(1) Autobiography deserves a place in English studies, particularly in the middle and upper section of the secondary school, but the difficulty is to find autobiographies that are wholly readable. Here are some suggestions:

Years 6, 7, 8

Marga Minco, *Bitter Herbs* (Second World War).

Years 9, 10

Eugenie Crawford, *A Bunyip Close Behind Me* (Australia at the end of the nineteenth century).

Anne Frank, *The Diary of Anne Frank* (Second World War).

Esther Hautzig, *The Endless Steppe* (Second World War).

Ilse Koehn, *Mischling, Second Degree* (Second World War).

Years 10, 11, 12

A. B. Facey, *A Fortunate Life.*

Maxim Gorky, *My Childhood* (nineteenth-century Russia).

Anne Hobbs, *Tisha: A Young Teacher in Alaska.*

Mary Rose Liverani, *The Winter Sparrows* (growing up in Scotland and Australia).

Patsy Adam Smith, *Hear the Train Blow* (growing up in Australia in the 1930s).

Margaret Tucker, *If Everyone Cared* (being Aboriginal in the first half of the twentieth century).

Richard Wright, *Black Boy* (growing up black in the United States).

See also BIOGRAPHY.

(2) Having students write their autobiographies is a valuable activity. Many teachers make such a unit the first one undertaken when pupils arrive in secondary school. Pupils' accounts can be illustrated with photographs, and as well as telling of their lives up to the time of entering secondary school they can attempt answers to the questions: What sort of person am I? What are my likes and dislikes?

Reference

Peter Abbs, *Autobiography in Education*, London: Heinemann, 1974.

'A child is essentially learning how to mean: that is, [s/he] is constructing a semantic system, and this implies, of course, that [s/he] is also at the same time constructing a lexico-grammatical and a phonological system as the way of 'realising' [his/her] meaning potential.'

(M. A. K. Halliday,
'How children learn language')

b

BAAL *See* BRITISH ASSOCIATION OF APPLIED LINGUISTICS.

BACK FORMATION – The reverse of normal word formation, e.g. *edit* from *editor*; *televise* from *television*; *sedate* (verb) from *sedative*.

BACK TO BASICS *See* BASICS.

BALANCE – Another of those blanket literary terms that will occur occasionally in this book. It can be reasonably used as a blanket term covering such devices as antithesis (q.v.) chiasmus, contrast, parallelism, the balanced sentence or even juxtaposition. Yelland, Jones and Easton (*A Handbook of Literary Terms*) even include inversion and oxymoron as among the terms that could be included under the blanket label 'balance'.

As a blanket term, it is a useful one for senior students to have at their fingertips (after all, no literature course ought to become a course on labelling or on making the most pedantic distinctions – and this is especially so at the school level). Further, it is a term that is easily applied by students to any situation where some sort of obvious balancing is being striven for – be it for contrast or simple comparison. Shakespeare juxtaposes the end of Act I Scene 1 with the opening of Act I Scene 2 in *Henry IV Part I*. Eleanor Spence's *A Candle for St Antony* contrasts a number of episodes in Chapter 1 with very similar episodes in Chapter 2. These are both works studied in Australian schools currently and the kind of balancing that occurs in them is typical of the kind of structural features of which senior students especially need to be aware.

Perhaps the balanced sentence needs a word to itself. This is a device that can be defined as widely as 'balance' itself, except that its features occur within one sentence and for that reason the balanced sentence tends to be treated as a separate literary device. The eighteenth century, of course, was the age of balance and the most oft-quoted exponent of the balanced sentence is Dr Johnson:

> The notice which you have been pleased to take of my labours, had it been early, had been kind; but it has been delayed till I am indifferent and cannot

enjoy it, till I am solitary and cannot impart it, till I am known and do not want it.

(Letter to Lord Chesterfield, February 1755)

As can be seen, the balanced sentence may include any of the other aforementioned devices such as antithesis, contrast and parallelism.

BALLAD – A poem that tells a story simply and economically, often through dialogue and the use of a refrain. Famous traditional ballads include *The Twa Corbies*, *Sir Patrick Spens*, *Edward*; the best-known Australian example is *The Wild Colonial Boy*. Of the many modern poets who have made use of the ballad form, two – the Englishman Charles Causley and the Australian John Manifold – deserve to be better known in schools.

BALLAD METRE – A four-line stanza with alternating four-stress and three-stress lines, for example:

There lived a wife at Usher's Well
And a wealthy wife was she;
She had three stout and stalwart sons,
And sent them o'er the sea.

Not all ballads make use of this metre.

BANDING – A modified form of streaming (q.v.). For example, instead of placing 200 Year 7 pupils in seven graded classes, a school might decide to create two bands, the top one to include those who would have been graded into the top four classes. Within each band the classes are either parallel or randomly grouped.

BARNES, DOUGLAS – Reader in Education at the University of Leeds. His seminal research into communication and learning in small groups has had a profound influence on English teaching. Co-author (with James Britton and Harold Rosen) of *Language, the Learner and the School* (Harmondsworth: Penguin, rev. edn, 1971), author of *Language in the Classroom* (Milton Keynes: Open University Press, 1973) and *From Communication to Curriculum* (Harmondsworth: Penguin, 1976). With Frankie Todd, he has produced a report of a study of 13 year olds learning in small groups funded by the Social Science Research Council (UK) and entitled *Communication and Learning in Small Groups* (London: Routledge & Kegan Paul, 1977). With his wife, Dorothy, and Stephen Clarke he conducted a major study of the English courses offered to 15–17 year olds, published as *Versions of English* (London: Heinemann, 1984).

BARTHES, ROLAND – French literary theorist – sometimes structuralist, (q.v.) or post-structuralist (q.v.), sometimes not – and semiologist. Barthes' work is wide-ranging, but possibly of most immediate relevance to the English teacher is his argument that literary texts can be divided into a system of interlocking codes, namely:

(1) The hermeneutic code: the code of puzzles and mysteries which lead the reader forward through the text.
(2) The proairetic code: the code of actions and behaviour which organizes events in a logical manner.
(3) The semic code: the code which organizes characters in a narrative through using linguistic devices such as adjectives and so on.
(4) The symbolic code: the code of patterns of images, of themes or symbols.
(5) The cultural code: this code identifies the numerous references which texts constantly make to particular bodies of knowledge.

Reference

Roland Barthes, *S/Z*, London: Cape, 1975.

BASAL READERS – A term used to refer to books created specifically for training beginning and early readers often as part of a wider programmed 'reading scheme'. Basal readers are marked by a controlled vocabulary that usually includes repetition of a few phonic elements. Their real intent is drilling in such repeated structures. The psycholinguistics (q.v.) school of reading argues that meaning-making is at the centre of reading and that prediction is the strategy for making meaning. Hence to be meaningful, language must be predictable. The irony of many basal reading programmes and materials is that the language structures are so artificial and unfamiliar as to be unpredictable and hence difficult for beginning readers to read.

Also, despite being obstensibly 'stories', there is generally little real attempt to create stories likely to generate reader interest. Recent research into the connections between literature and literacy has increasingly shown that an interest in the story will encourage many readers to overcome the handicaps of supposedly 'difficult' language in order to get at meaning. **(MRT)**

References

J. Graham, 'Reading literature with a slow learner', in J. Miller (ed.), *Eccentric Propositions*, London: Routledge & Kegan Paul, 1984.
Aidan Warlow, 'Alternative worlds available', in Margaret Meek *et al.* (eds), *The Cool Web*, London: Bodley Head, 1977.
Geoff Williams and David Jack, 'The role of story: learning to read in a special education class', in *Revaluing Troubled Readers*, Occasional Paper No. 15, Programme in Language and Literacy, College of Education, University of Arizona, n.d.

BASICS – The slogan 'back to the basics' has been for some years popular with those who claim that standards (q.v.) are declining. Rarely, however, is the term 'basics' defined. (When a definition *is* offered, it is often bizarre: Ronald Reagan, for example, has urged the schools to return to 'those endless grammar drills; stuffing [heads] with rules and exceptions-to-rules . . . singsong recitations of *Evangeline* or *The Rhyme* [sic] *of the Ancient Mariner*'!)

As far as one can judge from the contexts in which the term appears, there seem to be two distinct meanings given to the term. Sometimes it appears to relate to those skills seen as essential to survival in our society; sometimes to those elements fundamental to the mastery of a subject. Elsewhere, I have labelled those using the term in its first meaning 'survivalists', and the others 'fundamentalists'.[1]

When the survivalists talk of the basics they tend to refer to broad competencies such as 'a reading level sufficient to cope with everyday demands in an industrial society'; if they attempt to be more specific, they refer to such 'skills' as 'the ability to write a business letter' or 'the ability to fill out an income tax return'. There is, of course, an element of commonsense in this approach: schools should operate with one eye on the outside world. But too great an emphasis on the skills of survival would lead to a dangerous narrowing of the goals of education. There are textbooks offering courses in 'survival English', and sterile things they are, for imagination, creativity and critical thinking play no part in them, and literature is dismissed as a frill.

The fundamentalists begin from much more dubious premises. Their stock-in-trade is misleading metaphor and false analogy: 'the building blocks of language', 'learning language is like learning to play the piano', 'using language is like putting the pieces of a Meccano set together'. They break down reading and writing into a set of discrete skills which they advocate should be taught separately, leaving the learner to resynthesize them. (*See* SKILLS MODEL OF ENGLISH and LANGUAGE ACQUISITION for the weaknesses of this approach.) Not only do the fundamentalists put forward a model of language learning that is at odds with the evidence, but many of the so-called 'basic skills' they stress – the difference between *their* and *there*; the difference between *lay* and *lie* – are not basic to communication at all.[2] The model of English offered by the fundamentalists leads to a concentration upon the forms of language divorced from human purposes, even though real language cannot exist apart from meaning and function.

Finally, there is a sense in which the 'new English' and its founding fathers (Britton, Moffett, Dixon *et al.*) *never* moved away from the basics; and it is a misrepresentation by the 'back to basics' school to claim that they did. Britton and Moffett are concerned with nothing if not with reading, writing and speaking.

Notes

1. In R. D. Walshe (ed.), *101 Questions Primary Teachers Ask, Sydney*: PETA, 1980, pp. 29–31.
2. See Judy Stephen, 'Basic skills – fundamentals or frills?', in K. Watson and R. Eagleson (eds), *English in Secondary Schools: Today and Tomorrow*, Sydney: ETA of NSW, 1977.

See also DUMMY-RUN EXERCISES; SKILLS MODEL OF ENGLISH; STANDARDS.

BATHOS – is a term that covers three related areas: false pathos (q.v.), unintentional anti-climax (q.v.) and the more general fall from the sublime to the commonplace. Tennyson usually gets a bad press in relation to the first two areas – Eliot, for example, referred to his limited capacity for expressing 'complicated, subtle, and surprising emotions'. Certainly the nineteenth century seems a period rife for this sort of criticism (and perhaps the secondary teacher of Dickens needs to keep an eye open for false pathos). One of our favourite examples of the fall from the sublime to the ordinary occurs in Arnold:

O easy access to the hearer's grace
When Dorian shepherds sang to Proserpine!
For she herself had trod Sicilian fields,
She knew the Dorian water's gush divine,
She knew each lily white which Enna yields,
Each rose with blushing face;
She loved the Dorian pipe, the Dorian
strain.
But ah, of our poor Thames she never heard!
Her foot the Cumnor cowslips never stirr'd

BAY AREA WRITING PROJECT – The Bay Area Writing Project began at Berkeley, California, in the mid-1970s, developed by James Gray and a team of primary, secondary and tertiary teachers. The concept of the Project has spread across the United States and overseas.

The BAWP consists of a five-week summer course in which teachers discuss writing and, most importantly, write themselves. Teachers attending the Project are paid an allowance and then paid for providing inservice courses later on in their own schools and local regions. The BAWP originators believed that 'If teachers are ever going to teach writing more and teach it better, they will have to practise writing more themselves', and further, that the 'best people to teach teachers are other teachers'.

The BAWP has continued to receive unqualified praise. James Moffett (who has an article on BAWP in his *Coming on Center*, from which all quotations in this entry are taken), calls it 'the most positive development in English education during the '70s – indeed, during the whole period since World War II'. This is, he argues, because writing together helps teachers 'learn as they never could otherwise what are the most useful ways to respond to others' writing'.
See also NATIONAL WRITING PROJECT.

BEHAVIOURISM – The school of psychology, closely identified with the Americans J. B. Watson and B. F. Skinner, that studies only observable and measurable behaviour. It is associated particularly with stimulus–response techniques, and its psychology of learning is based on evidence gathered in laboratory experiments with rats and pigeons. Behaviourism's influence on English teaching can be seen in the proliferation of textbooks which drill pupils in the correct response, using language without regard for meaning and context. An example of behaviourism applied to the teaching of reading is Distar (q.v.).

BETWEEN, AMONG *See* USAGE.

BERNSTEIN, BASIL *See* ELABORATED AND RESTRICTED CODES.

BETWEEN YOU AND I/ME *See* USAGE.

BIAS – Bias is the expression of an author's frame of reference with respect to issues such as sexism, racism, ageism.

Because responses to written material are partly determined by cultural and sociopolitical attitudes, the detection of bias is dependent upon readers developing the ability to recognize their own frame of reference as well as that of the author in relation to issues such as those mentioned above.

See also CRITICAL READING.

BIBLIOTHERAPY – The humanizing, civilizing value of literature is widely attested to and in a general sense most English teachers are convinced that the reading of fiction, poetry and drama can powerfully affect children's development. Bibliotherapy takes such a belief one step further by arguing that a particular child experiencing an emotional difficulty or having problems adjusting to a new situation will be helped by being given books in which the fictional characters are shown overcoming similar difficulties. For example, a child who is failing to come to terms with the divorce of his or her parents and the appearance on the scene of a step-parent will be helped by a novel which shows a child adjusting to such changed circumstances. The theory is a beguiling one, but it fails to take account of recent developments in research into reader response (q.v.), which have demonstrated that different readers can read the same book in quite distinct ways. Indeed, it is not even necessary to go to the pages of research journals for evidence of this: that highly moral book *To Kill a Mockingbird* has been withdrawn from some Queensland schools because of its alleged immorality, and C. S. Lewis's *The Lion, the Witch and the Wardrobe*, which most readers interpret as a Christian allegory, has been condemned in some parts of the United States as being blasphemous and anti-Christian.

For a positive view of bibliotherapy, see Mary R. Jalongo, 'Bibliotherapy: literature to promote socio-emotional growth', *The Reading Teacher*, April, 1983.

BILDUNGSROMAN – The *Concise Oxford Dictionary* defines this term as a novel 'dealing with one person's early life and development' and it is a useful term for students to have at their fingertips when discussing such novels as *Sons and Lovers*, *Huckleberry Finn* or *A Portrait of the Artist as a Young Man*.

BIOGRAPHY – Like autobiography (q.v.), biography deserves a place in the English curriculum, particularly at secondary school level. Here are a few suggestions:

Years 7, 8 Paul Brickhill, *Reach for the Sky* (Douglas Bader); Eleanor Doorly, *The Radium Woman* (Marie Curie).
Years 9, 10 Alan Burgess, *The Small Woman* (Gladys Aylward); Laurence Meynell, *Builder and Dreamer* (Isambard Brunel).
Years 10,11 Douglas Lockwood, *I, the Aboriginal*; Elfrida Vipont, *A Little Bit of Ivory* (Jane Austen).

BLANK VERSE – A term sometimes mistakenly applied to free verse (q.v.). Properly used, it applies to the unrhymed iambic pentameters used by Shakespeare and other poetic dramatists. An iambic pentameter is a line of five feet, each of which consists of an unstressed syllable followed by a stressed syllable:

She gáve / me fór / my páins / a wórld / of sighs:
She swóre, / in fáith, / 'twas stránge, / 'twas páss/ing stránge
(*Othello*)

BLENDS – The telescoping of two words to form a new word which shares or combines their meaning, for example *smog*, *chortle*, *motel*. Pupils can be invited to invent their own blends, for example *grismal*.

BLOOM'S TAXONOMY – Benjamin Bloom and his associates in the United States have suggested that educational objectives can be classified hierarchically within three domains: the cognitive domain (concerned with knowledge, intellectual abilities and skills), the affective domain (concerned with emotional responses, attitudes and values), and the psycho-motor domain (concerned with physical and manipulative skills). The subdivisions in the cognitive domain, widely used when objective tests are being prepared, are (from lowest to highest) knowledge (i.e. recall), comprehension, application, analysis, synthesis and evaluation. The subdivisions in the affective domain are receiving or attending, responding, valuing, organization of value system, generalization or characterization of value system. A hierarchy for the psycho-motor domain has not been developed.

There has been much criticism of Bloom's taxonomy, particularly when applied to curriculum development. It is argued that the separation into three domains is artificial, since in practice all three are closely related, and that it is not applicable to all areas of the curriculum. As far as English is concerned, the most serious objection is that it leads to a concentration upon measurable behaviour, for much of what goes on in the English classroom cannot be measured.

Reference

B. S. Bloom, D. R. Krathwohl *et al.*, *Taxonomy of Educational Objectives*, Handbooks 1 and 2, New York: McKay, 1956.

BOOKS FOR KEEPS – The magazine of the School Bookshop Association which is published six times a year and contains a great deal of valuable material on children's books, including news of awards, profiles of authors, and up-to-date reviews. Details are available from: School Bookshop Association, 1 Effingham Road, London SE12 8NZ, England.

BOUND MORPHEME – A morpheme (q.v.) that cannot stand alone as an independent word, for example *-ness* as in *goodness*, *-ly* as in *brightly*.

BREAKTHROUGH TO LITERACY – *Breakthrough to Literacy* in an initial reading method utilizing the philosophy of the language-experience approach. The materials and teachers manual were developed in the United Kingdom.

When implemented in the spirit of the manual, this scheme represents an ideal application of the language-experience approach, while the provision of a range of prepared materials relieves the teacher of some of the mechanical effort of implementing such a programme. Unfortunately, implementation of the scheme is often attempted independently of the manual, and the materials become the dominant and therefore a limiting feature of the classroom programme. Published by Longman-Cheshire.

See also READING SCHEMES, LANGUAGE EXPERIENCE APPROACH. **(MRT)**

BRITISH ASSOCIATION OF APPLIED LINGUISTICS – An influential body that has sought to find ways of making linguistic theory more accessible to teachers and more relevant to the work of English departments in schools.

BRITTON, JAMES – One of the most influential figures in English Curriculum, James Britton was formerly head of the English Department at the University of London's Institute of Education. He was a member of the committee which produced the Bullock Report (q.v.). His *Language and Learning* (1970) is a seminal work on language development at home and at school. He headed the Schools Council Project on the Written Language of 11–18 Year Olds (q.v.), the findings of which are reported in *The Development of Writing Abilities (11–18)*, London: Macmillan, 1975.

Reference

J. Britton, *Prospect and Retrospect*, Montclair, USA: Boynton-Cook, 1982.

BULLOCK REPORT – In response to claims of falling standards, particularly in reading, the Minister for Education and Science in Britain set up, in 1972, a committee of inquiry under the chair of Sir Alan (later Lord) Bullock. The Committee's report, entitled *A Language for Life*, appeared in 1975, and has since exerted considerable influence on English teaching throughout the English-speaking world. Two of the Committee's main recommendations were:

- Each school should have an organized policy for language across the curriculum, establishing every teacher's involvement in language and reading development throughout the years of schooling.
- A substantial course in language in education (including reading) should be part of every primary and secondary teacher's initial training.

Other important conclusions of the Committee were:

- Language competence grows incrementally, through an interaction of writing, talk, reading and experience, and the best teaching deliberately influences the nature and quality of this growth. (1.10)
- Language has a unique role in developing human learning; the higher processes of thinking are normally achieved by the interaction of a child's language behaviour with his/her other mental and perceptual powers. (4.1–4.7)
- Children learn as certainly by talking and writing as by listening and reading. (4.8–4.10)
- There is no one method, medium, approach, device . . . that holds the key to the process of learning to read. (6.1)
- Exercises in English textbooks or kits of one kind or another are inadequate for developing comprehension. (8.14)

- There is a strong association between voluntary reading and reading attainment. Teachers should devise various ways of extending their pupils' interest in fiction and of increasing the amount and range of their voluntary private reading. (9.3ff)
- The demands of examinations should not be allowed to distort the experience of literature. (9.16–9.17)
- Oral work should take place in both large and small group situations, with an emphasis on the latter. (10.11–10.12)
- Competence in language comes above all through its purposeful use, not through the working of exercises divorced from context. (11.19–11.20; 11.25)
- The majority of the Committee . . . believe that . . . mixed ability grouping offers most scope for English teaching, provided it receives a great deal of thought and planning. (15.10; 15.12)

See also LANGUAGE ACROSS THE CURRICULUM; LANGUAGE, CONSCIOUS STUDY OF.

'Some kind of transformation must be imposed on experience. Life does not exist as a vast anthology of unedited narratives. We impose narrative on it . . . and make it something whole and ordered.'

(Connie and Harold Rosen,
The Language of the Primary School Children)

C

CAI (Computer-Assisted Instruction) *See* MICROCOMPUTERS IN ENGLISH.

CAL (Computer-Assisted Learning) *See* MICROCOMPUTERS IN ENGLISH.

CALDECOTT MEDAL – Named in honour of Randolph Caldecott, the famous English illustrator of children's books, the medal is awarded each year to the artist of 'the most distinguished American picture book for children'. Maurice Sendak won the medal in 1964 for *Where the Wild Things Are*. Recent winners have been:

1978 – Peter Spier for *Noah's Ark*
1979 – Paul Goble for *The Girl Who Loved Wild Horses*
1980 – Donald Hall for *The Oxcart Man*
1981 – Arnold Lobel for *Fables*
1982 – Chris Von Allsberg for *Jumanji*
1983 – Marcia Brown for *Shadow*
1984 – Alice and Martin Provensen for *The Glorious Flight*
1985 – N. Hodges for *St George and the Dragon*
1986 – C. Van Allsburg for *Polar Express*.

CAMBRIDGE LANGUAGE ARTS SOFTWARE SERVICES LTD (CLASS) – A software house which specializes in materials for work in English Language Arts and Humanities. It has published material suitable for language development programmes in primary and secondary English as well as a number of computer-based simulations. Details from CLASS, 2 Howard Court, Howard Road, Cambridge, England.

CAN, MAY *See* USAGE.

CANADIAN COUNCIL OF TEACHERS OF ENGLISH – The national association of English teachers publishing *English Quarterly* and *Canadian Journal of English Language Arts*. Address: PO Box 3382, Postal Station B, Calgary, Alberta, Canada T2M 4M1.

CARNEGIE MEDAL – Awarded annually by the British Library Association for a children's book of outstanding merit. The first winner was Arthur Ransome's *Pigeon Post* in 1936; since then winners have included Mary Norton's *The Borrowers* (1952), Philippa Pearce's *Tom's Midnight Garden* (1958), Rosemary Sutcliff's *The Lantern Bearers* (1959), Alan Garner's *The Owl Service* (1967), Ivan Southall's *Josh* (1971), Richard Adams's *Watership Down* (1972). Recent winners have been:

1975 – *The Machine Gunners* by Robert Westall
1976 – *Thunder and Lightnings* by Jan Mark
1977 – *The Turbulent Term of Tyke Tiler* by Gene Kemp
1978 – *The Exeter Blitz* by David Rees
1979 – *Tulku* by Peter Dickinson
1980 – *City of Gold* by Peter Dickinson
1981 – *Scarecrows* by Robert Westall
1982 – *The Haunting* by Margaret Mahy
1983 – *Handles* by Jan Mark
1984 – *The Changeover* by Margaret Mahy
1985 – *Storm* by Kevin Crossley-Holland
1986 – *Granny was a Buffer Girl* by Berlie Doherty

CASE STUDY – A method of research which is becoming more and more important in education. The case study researcher makes detailed observations of an individual unit, be it a child, a class, an English Department, a school.

Critics of the case study approach claim that the results obtained are not generalizable, but it does seem that teachers are more inclined to take note of case studies than of research based on the scientific paradigm, since case studies are usually reported in such a way as to make it easy for teachers to identify those elements of the studies which parallel their own classroom situations.

CASSETTE RECORDER *See* TAPE RECORDER.

CATHARSIS – Literally, 'a purging'. The term was coined by Aristotle to refer to emotion afforded to the audience witnessing dramatic tragedy. But since, the literary use of the term has come to refer to the purging effect on the writers themselves of writing about some aspects of their own lives, either directly or by identification with a fictional character. Hence the term has been applied in autobiography to such works as Gosse's *Father and Son* and sections of John Stuart Mill's and Gibbon's autobiographies, and in fiction to Lawrence's *Sons and Lovers*.

Of course, the extent to which any piece of writing may be regarded as cathartic can only be a matter of speculation, perhaps even to the writer. Of the works mentioned above, the cathartic effect and relation to their own lives have been attested to by either the authors themselves, close friends or revealing studies of early drafts.

David Holbrook in his *English for the Rejected* speculates about the cathartic qualities of the writing of his students and (though the English teacher should always avoid the temptation to play amateur psychologist) it is interesting how much current research on the writing process occasionally touches on the cathartic value especially of expressive writing:

> We give him the opportunity to write above all because this encourages him to cope with something that is an immediate concern, an immediate problem.
>
> (James Britton, 'Talking and writing', in E. L. Evertts (ed.), *Explorations in Children's Writing*, NCTE, 1970)

> What keeps the writing process going is the writer's recognition that there is something in it for him or her. . . . This can be . . . establishing a discourse with one's self and/or another or solving a problem by writing it out.
>
> (Roslyn Arnold, 'Writers, learners and self-esteem', in *English in Australia*, 62, AATE, 1982)

CENTRE AROUND/ROUND *See* USAGE.

CHATMAN, SEYMOUR – Narratologist who has presented a theory of literary discourse that formalizes the relationships between implied readers, implied authors, narrators, narratees, real authors and real readers. In *Story and Discourse: Narrative Structure in Fiction and Film* (Cornell University Press, 1978), Chatman makes basic distinctions between 'story' (narrative's content) and 'discourse' (narrative's linguistic form), discussing the elements of each of these. As with other narratologists like Genette (q.v.), Chatman's work is now being used in the analysis of children's literature and children's own stories. *See also* NARRATOLOGY.

CHILDREN'S BOOK COUNCIL OF AUSTRALIA – A national association, with branches in all states of Australia and the ACT, working to encourage the reading and enjoyment of children's books. The Council's journal is *Reading Time*.

CHILDREN'S BOOKS OF THE YEAR – An annual guide to children's books, formerly edited by Elaine Moss and now selected and annotated by Barbara Sherrard-Smith. Published by Julia MacRae Books (UK) for the National Book League.

CHILDREN'S LITERATURE IN EDUCATION – An important international journal on children's literature published quarterly by APS Publications, 49 Sheridan Avenue, Albany, NY 12210, USA.

CHILDREN'S READING INTERESTS – There have been many surveys of children's reading interests, particularly in the United Kingdom and the United States. The major UK survey is that of Whitehead, which was undertaken in 1971. Until recently, all Australian surveys have been on a small scale. In 1981, however, a national survey, entitled *Children's Choice*, was undertaken by a team led by Rhonda Bunbury of Deakin University.

Reference

F. Whitehead *et al.*, *Children and Their Books*, London: Macmillan, 1977.

CLASS *See* CAMBRIDGE LANGUAGE ARTS SOFTWARE SERVICES LTD.

CLASSROOM MANAGEMENT – We wish to state quite categorically that there is no disjunction between creative, innovative teaching and good classroom management. The stereotypes of exciting, creative but totally undisciplined classes at one extreme, and quiet, downtrodden but well-controlled classes at the other, need to be destroyed. Interesting, worthwhile teaching and good classroom management should facilitate each other. With this in mind, we offer the following principles as being conducive to good management:

(1) Thorough preparation and well-structured lessons. 'Well structured' is not an antonym for 'creative'. It simply means that planning is careful, that it is sequenced and that it has an overview of what the students will achieve. Small-group discussion and drama workshops need to be as structured in this sense as any traditional chalk-and-talk lesson. Even small details need to be planned for: did you remember to book the library, check that the overhead projector is in working order, get the extension cord and screen?
The plan, however, must be *flexible*, even discarded if the lesson shows signs of taking off in another, worthwhile direction.
(2) What is planned for the students must be appropriate to their developing needs, interests and abilities.
(3) Planning should, for 95 per cent of the time, be in *units of work*. Too many 'one hit' lessons, unconnected with what has gone before or what is to come, cause both teacher and pupils to lose a sense of direction and purpose.
(4) *Variety* is essential, both within particular lessons and from one lesson to the next. Changes of activity within the one lesson are essential if interest is to be maintained, and the units themselves should have variety: thematic units, drama workshops, units built around a core text, and so on. Develop a variety of teaching styles and give the students a variety of activities.
(5) Lessons should arouse and sustain interest and curiosity. Plan in terms of what students will be *doing*.
(6) The physical arrangement of the room should be appropriate to the type of activity. Students need to face one another if they are discussing something; in such a situation clustered groupings or a circular arrangement will be more appropriate than rows of desks.
(7) Provision should be made for groups/individuals who finish set tasks ahead of the rest of the class. A wide reading program (q.v.) is invaluable here.
(8) Positive responses to students' classroom contributions and to their written work will go a long way towards encouraging a classroom environment that students feel is supportive.

The discipline side of classroom management is an area fraught with disagreement when it is debated at all. Hence we realize that the following suggestions are purely subjective. We feel, however that our own teaching experiences have shown them to be worthwhile principles:

(1) Be consistent in what you expect of students with respect to both work and behaviour. Pupils should always be polite to you (and you to them!). Have a consistent set of expectations which are consistently applied.
(2) Build up routines of classroom behaviour for such things as entering and

leaving the room, forming small groups, and so on. Stick to these routines.

(3) Learn the students' names quickly and use them.

(4) If possible, arrange the classroom in the desired manner (e.g. for small-group work) before students arrive. In any case, always be on time.

(5) Act on, rather than react to, discipline problems. If discipline problems appear to be arising, deal with them swiftly before they get out of hand.

(6) At all costs, avoid confrontations with particular students. You are likely to lose much more than they in a standup argument. Deal with problems before they get to the confrontation stage and, where possible, deal with bad offenders away from the gaze of the rest of the class. Classrooms are not meant to be battlegrounds.

(7) Be seen to be available, warm, helpful, and in control.

In a real sense, no book can deal with all the potential problems of classroom management and discipline that may arise or even give advice that is always appropriate in any given situation, but we suggest the following as more helpful than many:

M. Marland, *The Craft of the Classroom*, London: Heinemann.
P. Francis, *Beyond Control?* London: Allen & Unwin.

CLASS READERS *See* NOVELS.

CLICHE – A hackneyed or outworn expression, neatly described by George Baker as 'a coin so battered by use as to be defaced'.

Some years ago Frank Sullivan, an American humorist, invented Mr Arbuthnot, a cliché expert, who gave several interviews in the *New Yorker*. Here he is interviewed on love:

Q. Mr Arbuthnot, what is love?
A. Love is blind.
Q. Good. What does love do?
A. Love makes the world go round.
Q. Whom does a young man fall in love with?
A. With the Only Girl in the World.
Q. They are then said to be?
A. Victims of Cupid's darts.
Q. And he?
A. Whispers sweet nothings in her ear.
Q. Describe the Only Girl in the World.
A. Her eyes are like stars. Her teeth are like pearls. Her lips are ruby. Her cheek is damask, and her form divine.

And another interview:

Q. Where were you born, Mr Arbuthnot?
A. In the altogether.
Q. I see. How?
A. On the impulse of the moment.
Q. And when?
A. In the nick of time.

Q. It is agreeable to find a man so frank about himself.
A. Why not? You asked me a question. You know what kind of question it was?
Q. Impertinent?
A. Oh, my dear man, no.
Q. Personal?
A. Civil. You asked me a civil question. I answered you by telling the truth. I gave it to you, if I may be permitted to say so, straight from the shoulder. I revealed myself to you in my . . .
Q. True colours?
A. Someone told you.

Older pupils will be able to construct similar dialogues.

Sydney J. Harris has an amusing article entitled *Let's Have Varnished Truth*. It begins:

> I should like to read, or hear, just once, about a man with a deuce up his sleeve, a man who was alive and not kicking, a man who was not all things to all men, a man who was at death's window, and a man who was not Grand as well as Old.
>
> And just once, about a distance of sixty miles as the buzzard flies, an inauspicious occasion, a battle that is nonroyal, a plot that thins out, a straight and broad path, a tepid congratulation, a dog that is let out of the bag, a heavy fantastic, and an elephant's share.

Let your pupils continue. (The complete text is in *The Language of Man*, No. 3, ed. B. Evans, and published by McDougall Littell.)

CLOZE PROCEDURE – Readers are required to supply appropriate replacements for portions of the text which have been systematically deleted and represented by lines – usually of uniform length. Cloze tasks necessitate reading behaviours which are consistent with psycho-linguistic accounts of the reading process. Of course, readers do not normally sample the visual display by means of predetermined deletions from the text. However, the ability to construct meaning by responding to graphophonic, semantic and syntactic cues through the use of the non-visual information which the reader brings to the passage, and the partial use of the visual information in the text, is basic to the normal reading process.

Various forms of the cloze procedure have been used for four main purposes:

A – Readability measurement.
B – Diagnostic assessment of an individual's reading behaviour.
C – A teaching strategy to enhance reading development.
D – Standardized comprehension testing.

A – Readability measurement

(1) From the material to be evaluated select a representative sample of approximately 200 to 250 words.
(2) Do not delete any words in the first one or two sentences.
(3) Select any word in the next sentence to delete and then delete every fifth word.

(4) At least thirty-five deletions are needed for reliable behaviour sampling. A deletion of fifty words is convenient for subsequent calculation of percentages.
(5) Replace the deleted words with underlined blanks of uniform length.
(6) Ensure there is at least one complete sentence following the final deletion.
(7) Provide a practice passage before administering the test.
(8) Students should read the whole passage first.
(9) Instruct students to try every space, writing in the *one* word which fits best so that the whole story makes sense.
(10) There is no time limit.
(11) Score as correct replacements the original words of the text only.
(12) Incorrect spelling is not penalized.

Interpretation of cloze readability scores

Below 45 per cent correct	**Frustration level** The material is too difficult and alternative simpler material is needed.
45 to 60 per cent correct	**Instructional level** The material can be understood with some assistance. It is suitable for reading instruction.
Above 60 per cent correct	**Independent level** The material can be read and understood without assistance.

To account for possible ranges of difficulty within the one book, two or three sample passages from different parts of the book should be evaluated in this way.

B – Diagnostic assessment of an individual's reading behaviour
Diagnostic use of the procedure is concerned with a qualitative analysis of the non-exact replacements supplied by readers. In a manner similar to miscue analysis, each non-exact replacement is assessed in terms of its syntactic acceptability, semantic acceptability and whether any loss of meaning is implied. For each of these categories the proportion of non-exact replacements which are acceptable, partially acceptable or not acceptable at all, can then be calculated and this gives an indication of individual reader's strengths and weaknesses. For example, a reader with majority of responses which are syntactically acceptable at the sentence level but not the whole story level and involve partial loss of meaning, may be processing each sentence as a discrete text and failing to use the buildup of the story line to predict appropriate replacements.

Cambourne (1977) identified a number of specific reading/language processes which may be used to replace cloze deletions:

(1) Referring back in the text to find a clue to meaning.
(2) Referring ahead in the text to find a clue to meaning.
(3) Using real world knowledge (the reader's network of meanings and relationships already known about the topic/story being read).
(4) Monitoring the story topic line to enable logical prediction.
(5) Use of letter clues, that is replacements which are controlled by remaining orthographic clues.

In diagnosis these have been used as a partial basis for determining which words to delete (Campbell, 1981) resulting in a minor modification to the mechanical fifth-word deletion rate. Assessment can then be made of the reader's control over these reading/language processes. Applications to diagnostic assessment are a relatively recent and underexploited adaptation of cloze procedure.

C – Teaching strategy

A variety of cloze tasks have been devised as learning experiences aimed at enhancing reading development. Formats include:

(1) The substitution of pictures for words.
(2) Selection among stated alternatives for replacement.
(3) The omission of parts of words.
(4) 'Macro cloze' – the omission of selected phrases, clauses or sentences.
(5) Deletion according to grammatical class, for example adjectives or adverbs.

The effectiveness of cloze as a teaching strategy depends on the discussion of responses especially errors. Readers might be asked to mark those parts of the text which provided clues to the missing words and these could be included in discussions. The value of discussion can also be derived through collaborative cloze tasks undertaken by small groups of readers. Deletion patterns must provide practice in using cues which extend beyond immediate context of the sentence; that is, portions of text should be omitted so that their correct replacement requires the reader to follow the flow of information across sentence boundaries:

> One day, a little boy was playing in the field. Then . . . . saw something big and . . . . The little boy saw . . . . was a big golden . . . . He thought he would . . . . this pumpkin home with him.
>
> (Gunn, 1978)

Oral cloze exercises can be useful, especially with young children. Passages are read out aloud by the teacher who pauses at various points when the listeners are to supply the next word. Knowledge in particular context areas can be tested through cloze tasks and indeed critical reading skills can be developed through the deletions of controversial aspects of text and subsequent discussion of the reader's differing responses.

D – Standardized comprehension testing

A small number of standardized tests have been developed using the cloze procedure. The best known are the norm-referenced Gap (McLeod, 1970) and Gapadol (McLeod and Anderson, 1973) tests. The Gap is intended for pupils of primary school age while the Gapadol is appropriate for older children and adolescents. Each consists of a number of short passages on different topics with a random fifth-word deletion pattern. Readers must supply the exact replacement and aim to complete the test within fifteen minutes for the Gap and thirty minutes for the Gapadol. Although the cloze format suggests consistency with psycho-linguistic accounts of the reading process, these tests still suffer from many of the limitations of standardized tests (q.v.). **(MRT)**

References

B. Cambourne, 'Some psycholinguistic dimensions of the silent reading process – a pilot study', in A. Ridsdale, D. Ryan, and J. Horan (eds), *Literacy for Life*, Proceedings of the Third Australian Reading Conference, Sydney: Ashton Scholastic, 1977.

A. Campbell, 'Language background and comprehension', *The Reading Teacher* 35(1), 1981: 10–14.

P. Gunn, '"Blankety Blanks" for Juniors' in G. Page, J. Elkins, and B. O'Connor (eds), *Communication Through Reading*, Vol. 1. Focus on Comprehension, Proceedings of the Fourth Australian Reading Conference, Brisbane 1978.

C. Harrison, *Readability in the Classroom*, Cambridge: Cambridge University Press, 1980.

COGNITION – Knowledge, or the mental processes by which knowledge is acquired.

COGNITIVE DOMAIN *See* BLOOM'S TAXONOMY.

COGNITIVE GROWTH, STAGES OF – The Swiss psychologist Jean Piaget has suggested that there are four stages of cognitive development:

The sensori-motor stage (0–2 years),
during which the child's physical sensations help build up for him or her a picture of the world.

The stage of pre-operational thought (about 2–7 years),
during which the child learns to use language in order to represent the world. She/he:

> uses language to organise and classify the particular instances but cannot carry out the 'operations' of relating instances. Thus in Piaget's famous 'conservation' experiment a child recognises a quantity of liquid in a thin jar. Because [s/he] judges on one dimension only, e.g. height, [s/he] cannot recognise that there is the same amount of liquid when it is poured into a shallow wide jar.
>
> (Wilkinson *et al.*)

The concrete operational stage (about 7–11 years),
during which the child masters conversation and becomes capable of logical thought. S/he handles concepts of time and space, and can classify.

The period of formal operations (about 11–16 years and beyond),
during which the adolescent goes 'beyond classification and seriation based on the "real" to an ability to work from postulates and hypotheses, to entertain a world of possibilities' (Wilkinson *et al.*).

Piaget and his followers hold the view that, at least until the child approaches the stage of formal operations, language reflects rather than determines cognitive development. In the final stage of formal operations, however, the mind is ready to expand on verbal material. Piaget writes: 'At this level reasoning becomes hypothetico-deductive; it is liberated from its concrete associations and comes to rest in the universal and abstract plane for which only verbal thought appears to furnish the necessary abstract conditions.' It can be argued that Piaget and his associates have undervalued the role of language as a regulator of activities, as a classifier, as a major instrument in the acquisition of concepts. Certainly other theorists, notably Vygotsky and Bruner, see language as having a much more directive role in cognitive development.
See also ACCOMMODATION; EGOCENTRISM.

References

J. S. Bruner *et al.*, *Studies in Cognitive Growth*, New York: Wiley, 1966.
Jean Piaget, *Six Psychological Studies*, London: University of London Press, 1968.
L. S. Vygotsky, *Thought and Language*, New York: MIT/Wiley, 1962.
A. Wilkinson, G. Barnsley, P. Hanna, M. Swan, *Assessing Language Development*, Oxford: Oxford University Press, 1980.

COGNITIVE PSYCHOLOGY – In contrast to behaviourism (q.v.), cognitive psychology maintains that learning comes about as the result of the restructuring of perceptions and thoughts within the individual learner. (*See* ACCOMMODATION.) Cognitive learning theory lays stress upon problem-solving and the importance of meaning, and casts doubt on the value of drills and rote learning.

COHESION – The meaning relationships that exist within a language text, enabling it to be recognized as an integrated text rather than as a random collection of unrelated sentences. A language text can be any piece of writing distinct within itself from a short passage to a full-length book, or any speech or conversation. The cohesion in a text enables some elements in the text to be interpreted in terms of other elements which occur elsewhere in the text – usually earlier. Cohesion is expressed by means of various grammatical and lexical devices which establish cohesive ties within a text. These devices include reference, achieved for example by pronouns like *he*, *she*, *it* and *they*; substitution by means of words like *one*, *the same*, *do so*; ellipsis, that is, the omission of items which can be presupposed; conjunction and relationships between lexical items such as repetition, synonymy and antonymy. **(JC)**

References

J. Chapman, *Reading Development and Cohension*, London: Heinemann, 1983.
M. A. K. Halliday and R. Hasan, *Cohesion in English*, London: Longman, 1976.

COLLECTIVE NOUNS *See* USAGE.

COLLOCATION – The habitual occurrence of two or more words with each other, for example 'green grass'.

COLLOQUIAL LANGUAGE – 'A term of some slipperiness of definition', note the authors of *Watch Your Language!* They go on: 'Colloquial language is presumably what most of us employ in day-to-day affairs. Syntactically its manner is more relaxed, it has a wider vocabulary, it is more inclined to experiment.'

See also REGISTER.

COLOPHONS AND TRADEMARKS – Have pupils collect a range of trademarks and colophons. Discuss their 'language' – the image they are intended to project. Then have pupils design colophons for fictitious products, for their favourite authors, for themselves.

COMPLEX SENTENCE – A sentence having both a principal clause and one or more dependent clauses.

COMPOUND SENTENCE – A sentence having two or more co-ordinate principal clauses but no dependent clause.

COMPREHENSION – Comprehension involves what the reader already knows of the language, the topic and the typical organization of texts (q.v. non-visual information). This frames the reader's anticipation of meaning. A conscious application of such knowledge (metacognition) during reading assists the reader to make sense of a text (Bartlett, 1982).

Comprehension is the product of comprehending. It is an internal construct. Teachers cannot see it directly. It can only be inferred from observations of the action or from a report of the comprehender (Bartlett, 1982). This report, in school settings, frequently takes the form of responses to questions, statements of a passage's main idea, details, mood, bias or relevance, and so on. Comprehension in school settings, then, has often been narrowly equated with quality of a reader's performance on a small selection from a range of possible outcomes of comprehending.

A number of writers have discussed comprehension in terms of a presumed hierarchy of categories. A common four-category description includes:

(1) Literal comprehension – understanding information which is explicitly stated in the text.
(2) Inferential comprehension – understanding of ideas and relationships which are implied by actual textual information.
(3) Critical reading – evaluating what is read in a critical way (q.v. critical reading).
(4) Creative reading – providing a creative, original response to reading material.

Lists of discrete comprehension skills have also become well known. These include understanding word meanings, identifying the main idea of a passage, locating supporting details, following directions, drawing accurate conclusions, seeing cause-effect relationships, and so on. These categories and so-called 'skills' no doubt characterize important outcomes in the area of reading comprehension, but there is no clear evidence that they describe a hierarchy of discrete skills which can be directly taught. (Rosenshine, 1980.)

Teachers should ensure that reading tasks facilitate pupils comprehending. Pupils should receive real or vicarious experiences related to the topic. They should be given the opportunity to explore the topic via their own oral language. Through discussion with peers and the teacher pupils will become increasingly aware of the range of vocabulary and language structures through which relevant ideas can be expressed. To the extent that pupils have been familiarized with appropriate purposes for reading, the concepts involved, the essential vocabulary and dominant language structures, they will be able to utilize syntactic and semantic cues in bringing meaning to print in the form of expectations and in constructing meaning in the form of a response to those expectations. **(MRT)**

References

B. J. Bartlett, 'Prose comprehension', in L. Unsworth, (ed.), *Reading to Learn*, Sydney: Milperra CAE, 1982.

Mike Hamlin and David Jackson, *Making Sense of Comprehension*, London: Macmillan, 1984.

E. Lunzer and K. Gardner, *The Effective Use of Reading*, London: Heinemann, 1979.

Bob Moy and Mike Raleigh, 'Comprehension: bringing it back alive', in J. Miller (ed.), *Eccentric Propositions*, London: Routledge & Kegan Paul, 1984.

B. Rosenshine, 'Skill hierarchies in reading comprehension', in R. J. Spiro, B. C. Bruce, and W. F. Brewer, eds), *Theoretical Issues in Reading Comprehension*, New Jersey: Erlbaum, 1980.

COMPREHENSION EXERCISES *See* EXERCISES, ENGLISH THROUGH.

COMPUTER-ASSISTED LEARNING *See* MICROCOMPUTERS IN ENGLISH.

COMPUTER LITERACY – Dr Claire Woods, Research Officer of the AATE, has written:

> I think of computer literacy, in a broad sense, as being comfortable with computers, being able to gain information from them and being able to use the computer for purposes you want. It doesn't necessarily mean that to be a computer literate you can program as a trained programmer would, but it means that you can use the computer to assist your living and learning as you need it.

COMPUTERS IN ENGLISH *See* MICROCOMPUTERS IN ENGLISH.

CONCEIT – The well-known term is defined by Yelland, Jones and Easton (*A Handbook of Literary Terms*) as 'An ingenious and fanciful expression, generally taking the form of an elaborate analogy'. Donne is the most familiar exponent to teachers of senior English.

> they shall find your picture in my breast
> You think a sudden damp of love
> Will through all their senses move,
> And work on them as me
>
> (Donne, 'The Damp')

CONCEPTS ABOUT PRINT – In learning to read children must be helped to understand the purposes and uses of written language, and to develop an understanding of the technical features of the task and the conventions of print. A wide range of research indicates that acquisition of these concepts is an essential factor in success or failure in learning to read (Clay, 1979; Downing, 1979).

Programmes which teach children to read and write using part-to-whole methods in which subskills are taught first with a view to integrating them later, have been found to hinder the development of essential concepts about print in many children, especially those with literacy-deprived backgrounds (Guthrie, 1977).

Instructional programmes which engage the children in listening to, reading and discussing real books; which include the reading and writing of a wide variety of printed material (stories, messages, letters, lists, diaries, labels, notes, signs, recipes, directions, instructions and diagrams) will enable children to learn these concepts within integrated and purposeful reading and writing experiences (Mason, 1985). **(MRT)**

See also READING READINESS; LANGUAGE EXPERIENCE.

References

Marie M. Clay, *A Diagnostic Survey of Early Reading Difficulties*, 2nd edn, Auckland, NZ: Heinemann, 1979.

J. Downing, *Reading and Reasoning*, Bath: W. & R. Chambers, 1979.

J. Guthrie, 'Concept construction', *The Reading Teacher* 31(1), 1977: 110–12.

Joan M. Mason, 'Initial reading', in L. Unsworth (ed.), *Reading: An Australian Perspective*, Melbourne: Nelson, 1985.

CONCRETE POETRY – A development of the shaped poem favoured by Herbert (e.g. *The Altar*, *Easter Wings*). 'The object is to present each poem as a different shape. It is thus a matter of pictorial typography which produces "visual poetry"' (J. A. Cuddon, *A Dictionary of Literary Terms*). A good collection is Emmett Williams's *An Anthology of Concrete Poetry*. Notable experiments in the form have been made by the Australian Alan Riddell and the British poet Ian Hamilton Finlay.

CONFERENCE APPROACH *See* WRITING: PROCESS CONFERENCE APPROACH.

CONJUNCT – A kind of adverbial (q.v.) which is outside the main structure of a clause, and which connects what is being said to what has been said before, as 'then' does in the sentence 'If you ask her, then I'm sure she'll agree'.

CONNOTATION AND DENOTATION – The *denotation* of a word is its literal or neutral meaning, its agreed-upon sense apart from any feelings it may arouse. The *connotation* of a word is its emotive power: the feelings it arouses as a result of our experiences and associations with the word and what it stands for. The word 'school', for example, denotes a building where children are educated, but the word carries positive connotations for some people and negative ones for others.

The importance of connotation was neatly illustrated by Aldous Huxley when he changed one of Tennyson's most famous lines, 'And after many a summer dies the swan', to 'And after many a summer dies the duck.'

Advertising (q.v.) provides a fertile source for the study of connotation, a study which can be introduced quite early in the secondary school. Junior secondary pupils, for example, can discuss the connotations of the brand names given to cars – Valiant, Jaguar, Commodore, Mustang, Statesman.

Discussion of pejorative connotations (with older pupils) can begin with Bertrand Russell's famous 'conjugation of an irregular verb': 'I am firm. You are obstinate. He is a pig-headed fool.' A *New Statesman* competition yielded the following:

> I am sparkling. You are unusually talkative. He is drunk.
> I day-dream. You are an escapist. He ought to see a psychiatrist.
> I am beautiful. You have quite good features. She isn't bad-looking, if you like that type.

Senior pupils can develop their own conjugations, starting with statements such as 'I am slender'.

CONTEXT – *Context* is one of the key concepts in modern theories of language acquisition (q.v.) and hence in English, and a whole book could be written on this topic alone. If we consider the three areas of language development – learning language, learning through language, learning about language – we can see its overwhelming importance.

Learning language involves the development of the four central skills of speaking, listening, reading and writing, and this development depends crucially on learning to discriminate appropriate usages depending on context. A central line of language development is developing awareness of *social* context, a growing awareness that the language one speaks varies with the situation. As with speaking, so with writing; the language one chooses will depend very much on elements of the social context: the degree of formality of the situation, the physical setting, the speaker/writer's status in relation to that of the person addressed, and so on. It should always be borne in mind that different contexts make different demands on language.

Learning through language in the English classroom is related to the provision of a relevant variety of *learning contexts*. Opportunities for small-group work, whole-class discussion, role play, improvization and the like are vitally important if the students are to make fullest use of the most important tool of learning at their disposal.

Learning about language leads us to distinguish between using language and evaluating uses of it. And evaluating uses of language means above all else having an awareness of the contexts in which it is used. Thus any conscious study of language should be done in the contexts in which it is used: a study of how register (q.v.) varies with audience, of how meaning varies with tone (q.v.), of how tone can be influenced by style. Similarly, particular points of structure or punctuation should be studied in the context of particular children's needs.

In a narrower sense, the term *context* will refer to the way in which the language surrounding a particular unit of written or spoken language acts to constrain the meaning. The semantic and syntactic context facilitates the use of prediction in meaning. If one encounters unknown words, the context frequently allows one to infer the meaning. Context is also important in distinguishing among a number of possible meanings for certain words; for example, 'He proceeded towards the range' will be interpreted in different ways depending on whether the immediate context relates to a mountain range or a rifle range. An appropriate strategy for training readers in the use of context clues is cloze (q.v.).

CONTROLLED VOCABULARY – Many basal readers are developed on the basis of limiting the number of new words introduced at each level of a series or in a book.

This is based on the assumption that each word must be frequently rehearsed and become part of the child's sight vocabulary before it will be recognized in a sentence.

The use of controlled vocabulary in texts usually results in a distortion of the normal development of the story. Sentence structures are often stilted and may be far removed from the child's own language usage (e.g. 'Ben is at play').

(MRT)

COPULA – A verb that connects a subject and a complement so that the complement describes the subject (e.g. John is the captain).

CORRECTIVE READING – *Corrective Reading* is one of the reading programmes developed by SRA based on the principles of Direct Instruction (q.v.). Corrective Reading is designed for poor readers from the upper primary years to secondary school, who lack adequate decoding skills. It consists of highly structured and sequenced lessons which are scripted for the teacher and which focus on getting students to discriminate between words and word families, and on the improvement of oral reading performance and comprehension.

Besides the general limitations identified in the entry on *Direct Instruction*, Corrective Reading has been criticized because of its emphasis on decoding for sound and because many of the children for whom it is designed have failed to learn to read despite intensive instruction in decoding skills.

In addition, it has been pointed out that much of the textual material contained in the programme is inherently meaningless, and that there is a strong American influence which is apparent in content, vocabulary and pronunciation. **(MRT)**

Reference

F. Gollasch, 'A Review of DISTAR Reading I from a psycholinguistic viewpoint', *Reading Education* 5(1), 1980: 77–86.

CREATIVE WRITING – There is a sense, of course, in which all writing which is more than mere copying is 'creative', and thus an entry on creative writing could fill a book on its own. But the term has become a double-edged one in English curriculum. Under the impact of books like Margaret Langdon's *Let the Children Write* and Alec Clegg's *The Excitement of Writing* and the 'new English' generally, 'creative writing' in the 1960s and early 1970s heralded a healthy development towards more spontaneous, personal and 'poetic' writing. Unfortunately, the term came to be synonymous with terms like 'free writing', and was set up as being opposed to writing which was more formal, objective, logical or argumentative. 'Loose' and 'undisciplined' came to be the derogatory terms for creative writing.

The influence of models of writing development such as those of Britton (q.v.) and Moffett (q.v.), and works such as Moffett's *Active Voice* has given a theoretical basis to the importance of variety in developing writing – variety of task, of purpose and of audience. The popularizing of the process-conference approach (q.v.) has also given teachers a way of aiding writing development over a variety of tasks. All this important and continuing research has helped restore the real meaning of 'creative' to creative writing.

See also WRITING, ASSESSMENT OF; WRITING: PROCESS-CONFERENCE APPROACH.

CREDITON PROJECT *See* WRITING, ASSESSMENT OF.

CRITERIA *See* USAGE.

CRITERION-REFERENCED ASSESSMENT – In this approach, students are told the standards their work must reach to receive a certain result. In mechanical tasks like typing this is relatively easily done. The speed for a pass may be forty words per minute of accurate copying.

It is the nature of English that it is more difficult to specify what is to be required of the student. It is not satisfactory to say such things as, in every 100 words there should not be more than two spelling errors, because this would discourage experimentation with new words.

Criterion-referenced assessment can be applied to English by specifying the rhetorical demands of a required task and classifying the work accordingly. Bill Corcoran provides an example:

Assignment: Recall or imagine a location which creates *one* predominant mood in you. Try to recapture, through the use of specific images, the essence of that mood for someone who was there at the time.

Primary Trait: Demonstrates ability in writing to establish a mood using imagery.

Scoring Guide:
(1) No attempt to establish a mood with images.
(2) Some attempt. Include here statements of mood with a few images, and images which do not create a mood.
(3) There are specific images and mood established. Lack of unified tone or impact.
(4) Unified and precise response. Specific details and images build an effective mood.

Many students will not need the rhetorical demands of tasks spelt out. They will achieve them more or less intuitively. But those students who fail to achieve definable rhetorical demands and are in danger of failing should have the demands explained to them. They should also be shown models to clarify these demands. Although this removes some of the mystery of good writing, we should be prepared to not only tolerate, but even encourage, mechanical attempts at writing, as a step in learning. The obligation to 'come clean' about the demands of tasks applies whenever some students are in danger of being labelled as not being successful. **(BJ)**

References

Bill Corcoran, 'Evaluating writing: some schema and their assumptions', *Words' Worth* 15(2), June 1982.

R. Lloyd-Jones, 'Primary trait scoring', in C. R. Cooper and L. Odell, (eds). *Evaluating Writing: Describing, Measuring, Judging*, Champaign, Illinois: NCTE, 1977.

CRITICAL READING – Most texts on the teaching of reading include lists of critical reading skills, which are concerned with evaluating the validity, relevance, effectiveness or worth of what is read according to a set of criteria. Skills such as detecting fallacies in logical reasoning and recognizing propaganda techniques, involve criteria based on internal properties of the text. Skills such as distinguishing fact from opinion, detecting authors' biases, and evaluating authors' qualifications are based on external criteria such as the reader's knowledge of the subject matter, and the individual's biases and purposes in reading the text.

There is some evidence that appropriate teaching strategies are effective in developing the capacity for critical reading. There is even greater evidence that critical reading depends on a more generalized capacity for critical thinking associated with the understanding that such a capacity must be applied in the practice of reading. **(MRT)**

References

I. Lehr, 'Developing critical reading and thinking skills', *Journal of Reading* 25(8), 1982: 804–7.

A. Whimbey, J. Carmichael, L. Jones, J. Hunter and H. Vincent, 'Teaching critical reading and analytic reasoning in Project SOAR', *Journal of Reading* 24(1), 1980: 5–10.

CULTURAL HERITAGE MODEL OF ENGLISH – That model of English studies which sees the aim of English as the passing on of a given culture, that culture consisting of the 'great literature' of English. John Dixon, in his *Growth Through English* (London: Oxford University Press, 1975), outlines the limitations of the cultural heritage model:

> There was a constant temptation to ignore culture as the pupil knows it, a network of attitudes to experience and personal evaluations that he develops. . . . But this personal culture is what he brings to literature. . . . What is vital is the interplay between his personal world and the world of the writer . . . by re-emphasizing the text, the heritage model confirmed the average teacher in his attention to the written word . . . as against the spoken word . . . It confirmed him too in presenting experience to his pupils, rather than drawing from their experience. (p. 3)

See also DIXON, JOHN; GROWTH THROUGH ENGLISH.

'We ignore the child's urge to show what [s/he] knows. We underestimate the urge because of a lack of understanding of the writing process and what children do in order to control it. Instead, we take the control away from children and place unnecessary roadblocks in the way of their intentions.'

(Donald Graves,
Writing: Teachers and Children at Work)

d

DARTMOUTH SEMINAR – An Anglo-American conference on the teaching of English, reported on in *Growth Through English* (q.v.) by John Dixon (q.v.).

DARTS: Directed Activities Related to Texts – A new approach to reading and comprehension pioneered by Eric Lunzer and Keith Gardner of the University of Nottingham. They recommend that students be encouraged to interrogate texts through such techniques as the following:

(1) Text reconstruction:

(a) Prediction – stopping a text at particular points to encourage students to speculate on what will happen next.

(b) Cloze – deleting some key words (not too many!) from a poem or prose passage and asking students to discuss possible alternatives. Final choices are then compared with the original.

(c) Sequencing – re-ordering a scrambled text. For example, a poem is cut up into stanzas and students, in groups, are asked to determine an appropriate order.

(d) Beginnings and endings – give students the beginning and ending of a text and ask them what they think the missing section might be about.

(2) Text analysis:

(a) Finding boundaries – ask students to divide a text into what they think are its sections.

(b) Underlining and labelling – students mark the text in some way to indicate its most significant features or pattern.

(c) Drawings and diagrams – presenting some of the information in the text in a visual way (e.g. drawing, flow-chart, a network). One variant is the 'idea-web' or 'spider-plan'.

(d) Responding to statements – present students with a range of statements about the text and ask them to discuss which ones they consider the most important or relevant.

(e) Asking questions – have students, in groups, decide on a set of questions *they* want to ask about the text.

References

E. Lunzer and K. Gardner, *Learning from the Written Word*, Edinburgh: Oliver & Boyd, 1984.

M. Hamlin and D. Jackson, *Making Sense of Comprehension*, London: Macmillan, 1984.
B. Moy and M. Raleigh, 'Comprehension: Bringing It Back Alive', in Jane Miller (ed.), *Eccentric Propositions*, London: Routledge & Kegan Paul, 1984.

DATA *See* USAGE.

DEAR, 'DROP EVERYTHING AND READ' – Another name for Sustained Silent Reading (q.v.).

DEBATING: DUTIES OF SPEAKERS – For class debating in the secondary school it is appropriate to choose two teams of four members each. These teams would contain three speaking members and a non-speaking member, called an adviser or co-ordinator. After the subject has been chosen, a coin can be tossed to determine which teams are Affirmative or Negative. Each speaker is given an equal amount of time to speak in the debate. Beginners should probably commence with a three-minute speech that has a warning bell at two minutes. The Affirmative team needs to prove the proposition expressed in the subject while the Negative team has to dispute this proposition. No team can simply afford to argue their own points, no matter how good these points may be. All speakers then, with the exception of the first speaker of the Affirmative team, must make some effort to come into conflict with the ideas expressed by the other team.

Proposer:

(1) Puts the subject in its context.
(2) Defines any difficult or key words in the subject. Key words would include 'only', 'should', 'too much'.
(3) Presents team's line of argument and case.
(4) Explains the subject matter to be discussed by the first and second speaker. Allocates speaking areas to both speakers.
(5) Presents own allocated material.
(6) Concludes with a short summary placing the subject and the team's line of argument in context.

Opposer:

(1) Establishes the conflict of interests in the debate. A good first negative speaker will show:
How the two teams differ.
Where the two teams differ.
Why the two teams differ.
Differences may in the area of:
– context
– definition
– line of argument
– emphasis or degree
– appropriateness of subject matter.
(2) If necessary the first negative will offer a new context in which to explore the subject, an alternative definition of difficult or key words, a new line of argument, change the emphasis given to. . . .

(3) Allocation of speaking areas between first and second negative.
(4) Presentation of allocated material.
(5) Concludes with a short summary placing the subject and the team's line of argument in context.

Second Proposer and Opposer
The second affirmative speaker has a similar role to that of the first negative speaker. This speaker needs to re-establish the affirmative line of argument showing where the two teams are in conflict. New points should only be established after refutation has taken place.

The second negative speaker should be primarily concerned with the development of ideas from the first affirmative speaker to the second affirmative speaker. What aspects of the negative's line of argument have been misunderstood by the affirmative? What aspects have been ignored or fabricated? By attacking through specific arguments and examples raised by the affirmative, the negative case can be firmly re-established. Refutation should then lead to a presentation of material as indicated by the first negative speaker.

Third Proposer and Opposer
The role of both speakers is to compare and contrast the cases and arguments presented by the two teams in the debate, and to show why their own team is superior. Both speakers should begin their respective speeches by seizing on an issue in the debate which best located the conflict of interest between the two teams. A short summary should conclude both speeches. A third negative speaker is not allowed to introduce any new material into the debate. **(RL)**

DEBATING: SETTING UP A CLASSROOM DEBATE –

(1) Floor Design

Affirmative Team | Chairperson and Timekeeper | Negative Team

Audience

(2) Duties of Chairperson
- (a) Introduces the team members to the audience.
- (b) Reads out the subject.
- (c) Introduces the timekeeper and states the bell times. (Warning bell – 1 ring; final bell – 2 rings.)

(3) Adjudication
Those students who are not speaking in the debate should be encouraged to act as adjudicators. Each speaker is marked out of 100.
Mark Scale:
Matter (information) – 40
Manner (speaking style) – 40
Method (construction; ability to perform speaking duties) – 20
A page of an English exercise book can be set out as follows:

1st Affirm. – Tom			1st Neg. – Sandra		
Comments:					Comments:
Matter	–	/ 40	Matter	–	/ 40
Manner	–	/ 40	Manner	–	/ 40
Method	–	/ 20	Method	–	/ 20
TOTAL	–	/ 100	TOTAL	–	/ 100

2nd Affirm – Lucy
Comments:

2nd Neg. – Zoë
Comments:

At the conclusion of the debate choose a panel of adjudicators to present their decisions to the class. **(RL)**

DEBATING: TOPICS

(1) That the voice of reason has laryngitis.
(2) That we should rock the boat.
(3) That the day of the amateur is over.
(4) That we should lower our expectations.
(5) That we should do the right thing.
(6) That more discipline is needed in our schools.
(7) That inspiration is around the/next corner.
(8) That zoos should be banned.
(9) That we were born to run.
(10) That women's fashion has a lot to answer for.
(11) That our politicians are led by example.
(12) That standards are falling.
(13) That teenage sex should be condemned.
(14) That we should bake our own bread.
(15) That the writing is on the wall.
(16) That the right to censor belongs to the individual.
(17) That father knows best.
(18) That clothes make the person.
(19) That public hospitals should provide abortions on demand.
(20) That our grandparents' generation has a lot to recommend it.
(21) That sport and politics do not mix.
(22) That we should stand up and be counted.
(23) That there is too much secrecy in government.
(24) That the tortoise is a fraud.
(25) That the family is underrated.
(26) That status is overrated.
(27) That smoking is a health hazard.
(28) That obeying the rules doesn't work.
(29) That compulsory school sport should be abolished.
(30) That students should be given a democratic say in running their school.
(31) That experts do more harm than good.
(32) That we have things too much our own way.
(33) That we should keep up with the Joneses.

(34) That sport has become too competitive.
(35) That reading a newspaper is better than watching a television set.
(36) That the commonplace is undervalued.
(37) That our leaders need more leadership.
(38) That strikes are only an easy way out.
(39) That the law is on our side.
(40) That the price is too high. **(RL)**

DECODING – This term has two common usages in describing the way in which a reader responds to print.

The first of these is concerned with 'decoding to sound'. Here the focus is on the way in which the reader is able to transform the symbols on the page into the corresponding sounds of the spoken language. Goodman prefers the term 'recoding' for this function, since the reader responds to one representation of the language (print) and recodes it into another representation of the language (speech).

The second usage is concerned with 'decoding to meaning', where the reader responds to the print in order to reconstruct the meaning of the author.

The notion of decoding for sound is basic to many initial reading schemes. However, such a view of reading is superficial, and is not supported by the increasing body of evidence on the nature of the reading process.

Reference

K. Goodman, 'Reading: a psycholinguistic guessing game', *Journal of the Reading Specialist* 6, 1967: 126–35. **(MRT)**

DEIXIS (adj. deictic) – Deictic expressions are those whose interpretation requires a knowledge of who the speaker/writer is, and the time and place of utterance (e.g. I, we, our, here, now, on my right).

DETERMINER – A word, such as an article or a demonstrative adjective, which specifies what is being referred to.

DIALECT – One of the main characteristics of language is its variety. The English spoken in one region or by one social group may differ markedly from that spoken in another region or by another social group. When such variation occurs, we recognize the existence of a *regional dialect* or a *social dialect*. Indeed, Standard English (q.v.) is itself a dialect, with no intrinsic superiority to other dialects. It is, of course, vital for children to have access to the standard dialect when they need it, for it is the variant of the language in which power resides.

The term *dialect* cannot, however, be used simply to refer to variations in *accent*. One person may speak English with a broad Australian accent, another with a general Australian accent, but both may use the standard dialect. For the language of a community, regional or social, to be recognized as a distinct dialect there must be evidence of variation in the three areas of grammar, lexis and phonology.

Some linguists argue that the non-standard English spoken by some socio-economic groups in Australia differs sufficiently from the standard dialect for it to be regarded as a separate dialect. R. D. Eagleson has written that:

In Australian English a non-standard dialect . . . may be characterised by a broad Australian accent and such grammatical features as:

(a) regularisation of past tense and past participle form (i.e. reduction to a single form) . . . e.g. *shake*: shaked – has shaked;
(b) regularisation of number agreement (i.e. reduction to a single form), e.g. I was – we was;
(c) multiple negation, e.g. The copper wouldn't take no notice of him.

Again, it must be stressed that such a non-standard dialect cannot be considered *sub-standard*. To quote Eagleson again:

> The non-standard social dialects are just as effective types of language for their own environments as the standard dialect is for its environment. All dialects have rules and are properly constructed: it is that the rules may be expressed differently. We have *substandard* language when the rules of a particular dialect – non-standard or standard – are not adhered to. It is the unsuccessful or erroneous use of a dialect.

What is said above about Australian English could be applied equally to English in other countries, e.g. American, Canadian, and English English. In England, in particular, some confusion has arisen over the various forms of West Indian English, which is itself a true example of a dialect of English. Thus, often, apparent 'mistakes' in the writing of West Indian pupils can be ascribed not to their mistaken use of standard English but to their correct use of their own dialect. Richmond has shown, in particular, the ways in which young writers can often achieve subtle effects by switching from one dialectical form to another.

The existence in England of what have been described as 'class dialects', where some forms have more prestige than others, raises important questions for the classroom – to what extent should teachers allow, or encourage, the use of dialects other than standard in the classroom? Informed opinion would generally argue that the aim should be to enable students to develop a linguistic repertoire so that they become bidialectal and learn to make informed choices based upon the appropriateness to the situation and context. Certainly respect for all forms of dialect should be encouraged.

The Bullock Report argued that no child should be expected to cast off the language and culture of the home when he crossed the threshold of the school, and respect for the language the pupil brings to school seems to be essential for school progress. This is one of the issues that should be addressed in language awareness courses.

See also IDIOLECT; LANGUAGE, CONSCIOUS STUDY OF.

References

R. D. Eagleson *et al.*, *English and the Aboriginal Child*, Canberra: Curriculum Development Centre, 1982, Ch. 1.

John Richmond, *The Resources of Classroom Language*, London: Edward Arnold, 1982.

Peter Trudgill, *Accent, Dialect and the School*, London: Edward Arnold, 1975.

DIATRIBE – A highly bitter speech directed at some object of criticism. A modern example from David Williamson's *The Club*:

> He went around to the members of the Committee behind my back and told them I was drunk during the '67 Grand Final. . . . He'd had his eye on the job for years. He just waited till I made one little mistake and went in for the kill. He'll keep. He's going to get his. He promised that Committee the world and he hasn't won them one premiership. Not one bloody premiership and I've won four.

Asking students to rewrite such abusive pieces so as to soften their tone (q.v.) (perhaps by the use of euphemism [q.v.] or words of different connotation [q.v.]) is a useful language exercise.

DICTIONARY WORK *See* LANGUAGE, CONSCIOUS STUDY OF; KNOWLEDGE ABOUT LANGUAGE.

DIDACTICISM – Refers to the tendency of a piece of literature to instruct, particularly in an ethical sense. Obvious examples are such works as *Pilgrim's Progress* or Pope's *Essay on Man*. But the 'genre' of didactic art includes enough works with which the student will be familiar to justify the inclusion of the term in their critical vocabulary. Since all propaganda is didactic we should include such works as *1984* and *Brave New World* (indeed, probably the whole genre of utopian and anti-utopian novels). What about children's literature? What about *A Wrinkle in Time?* What others?

DIFFERENT FROM/TO/THAN *See* USAGE.

DIRECT INSTRUCTION – Direct Instruction is an approach to teaching based on the principles of operant conditioning described in behaviourist psychology, and utilizing the procedures of task analysis and programed instruction.

Direct Instruction requires teachers to use a variety of external reinforcement, punishment and correction procedures in order to acquire and maintain a specified set of behaviours. The particular behaviours to be acquired are derived from a logical analysis of the content area (e.g. reading, arithmetic, spelling), and are organized in a strictly hierarchical fashion, the assumption being that mastery of the higher level behaviours can be gained only if the learner has previously gained mastery over lower-level behaviours. Teacher behaviours are scripted, and children are rewarded for providing 'correct' responses and punished for failing to remain on task.

The success claimed for Direct Instruction can be attributed to:

(1) increased levels of teacher praise and interaction with children;
(2) the amount of time actually devoted to reading-related tasks; and
(3) the fact that the criteria used for measuring the effectiveness of the various programmes are identical to the highly specific objectives which form the basis of the instructional units.

The serious limitations of Direct Instruction have been clearly identified by Gollasch (1980) and include the following faulty assumptions:

(1) that the so-called 'disadvantaged' child has a language deficiency that is manifest in the inability to communicate in the classroom;

(2) that such an inability to communicate can best be remedied through a highly structured and sequenced programme of instruction;
(3) that there is one right way to teach (presumably Direct Instruction is the right way);
(4) that 'one ought only teach what can be measured', and that 'we cannot have one objective for some children and another objective for others';
(5) that children learn most effectively in a teacher-dominated classroom; and
(6) that behaviourist psychology is the most appropriate model for classroom learning.

See also DISTAR READING; CORRECTIVE READING.

References

S. Englemann, *Preventing Failure in the Primary Grades*, Chicago: SRA, 1969.
F. Gollasch, 'A review of DISTAR reading from a psycholinguistic viewpoint', *Reading Education* 5 (1) 1980: 77–86. **(MRT)**

DIRECTED READING ACTIVITY – This is a lesson plan which initially uses non-textual experiences to stimulate the reader's interest and build background knowledge relevant to the material to be read. Appropriate purposes are then set for reading, and after silent reading pupils engage in a range of response and extension activities based on the passage. The preparation for the reading stage may also involve making tentative predictions about the text and then discussing, verifying or modifying these in the follow-up and extension activities. The following lesson plan indicates the kinds of options which teachers may exercise in implementing this general sequence as a specific learning experience for their pupils.

(1) Introduction: Building the Reader's Interest – Background

(a) Pre-requisite Experiences: setting the stage.
- (i) Review previous chapter and/or related readings or experiences.
- (ii) Show a film, filmstrip or video, or play audio tapes.
- (iii) Show pictures, slides, real objects or models.
- (iv) Have someone who is knowledgeable about the subject – a student, another teacher, a parent, a member of the community, etc. – talk to the class.

(b) Vocabulary: word lists, glossaries, italics, parenthetical definitions, context clues, margin notations, footnotes, illustrations, pronunciation clues.
Word games:
- (i) scrambled words and meanings
- (ii) match words with synonyms
- (iii) crosswords
- (iv) categorizing puzzles.

(2) Preparation for Reading

(a) Clarify purposes of reading:
- (i) Purposes might include the acquisition of literal information, for example getting meanings of specific words from context, getting main ideas, sequence, theme, following directions, and so on, and translation activities.

(ii) Purposes might also include a specific question about interpretation (e.g. what will happen if what the author recommends does occur? etc.).
(iii) Purposes might also include eliciting critical-creative reactions. (Are any fallacies of reasoning used? Is there card stacking? Is there one idea that you find useful? By what standards would you evaluate the ideas included in this chapter? Etc.)
(iv) Purposes might also include affective responses or reactions: How do you feel about . . . ? Would you like to have been there? Which character, or real person, would you most like to be? When would you most like to have been the protagonist? Least? Does the resolution of the problem seem fair to you? Which topic was most interesting to you? Why? Would you like further information about any topic?

(b) Survey Material (SQ3R) (q.v.).
(c) Students determine appropriate rate.

(3) Directed Silent Reading

(4) Students Respond to Reading Through Set Tasks

(a) Questions:
(i) should relate to purposes;
(ii) should preferably range from literal, interpretive, critical to creative.
(b) Diagramming.
(c) Completion tasks.

(5) Comprehension Check – Shared Activity

(a) Teacher-directed discussion or quiz.
(b) Display of pupil answers (result of individual or group effort).
(i) slides
(ii) chart paper
(iii) models, illustrations
(iv) dramatization demonstration.
(c) Making audio/video tape.
(d) Submission of written answers.

(6) Follow-up and Extension Activities

(a) Find relevant newspaper articles, pamphlets, books – fiction and non-fiction.
(b) Data gathering – reinforcement charts, table work.
(c) Reinforcement Activities for required skills.
(i) vocabulary games
(ii) comprehension quiz
(iii) simulation games
(d) Appeal to Community Audience
(i) publicity campaigns
(ii) support various appeals
(iii) set up experiments
(iv) carry out surveys
(v) set up displays.

References

P. Sloan and R. Latham, *Teaching Reading Is . . .*, Melbourne: Thomas Nelson Australia, 1981.

K. G. Stauffer, *Directing the Reading-Thinking Process*, New York: Harper & Row, 1975. **(MRT)**

DISCOURSE ANALYSIS – The study of spoken or written language which goes beyond the limits of single sentences or utterances; the focus of the analysis is on the way language operates in texts of potentially unlimited length. Over the past twenty years a great deal of attention has been given to informal conversation, classroom discussion, interviews and meetings where there are several participants in the total discourse and where one aspect of the analysis is the way people use language to interact with each other for various purposes. However, discourse analysis can be applied to monologue speech and to written text (cf. cohesion). Both the analysis of classroom discourse and the analysis of written text have some relevance to the work of the English teacher. **(JC)**

References

M. Coulthard, *An Introduction to Discourse Analysis*, London: Longman, 1977.

J. Grimes, *The Thread of Discourse*, The Hague: Mouton, 1975.

J. McH. Sinclair and M. Coulthard, *Towards an Analysis of Discourse*, Oxford: Oxford University Press, 1975.

DISINTERESTED, UNINTERESTED *See* USAGE.

DISJUNCT – A kind of adverbial (q.v.) which is not part of a sentence or clause. There is usually some evaluative content in the meaning of disjuncts, e.g. 'unfortunately' in the sentence, 'unfortunately, he wasn't home'.

DISTAR READING – Distar Reading is one of the reading programmes developed by SRA based on the principles of Direct Instruction (q.v.). It consists of highly structured and sequenced lessons which are scripted for the teacher and which emphasize the development of decoding skills.

Besides the general limitation identified in the entry DIRECT INSTRUCTION, Distar Reading has been criticized because of its superficial view of reading and readers, and because much of the textual material presented to children is inherently meaningless. Problems also arise because of the American influence which is apparent in content, vocabulary and pronunciation. 'The reading process is highly complicated. It is not, as the authors of Distar suppose, an accurate process that involves letter by letter or word by word processing' (Gollasch, 1980, p. 82).

See also DIRECT INSTRUCTION and DECODING.

Reference

F. Gollasch, 'A review of DISTAR reading from a psycholinguistic viewpoint', *Reading Education* 5(1), 1980: 77–86. **(MRT)**

DIXON, JOHN – British educationist, particularly associated with the personal growth model of English (q.v.). His *Growth Through English* (q.v.), a report of the Dartmouth Seminar (q.v.), has had a profound influence on English teaching.

He headed the Schools Council English 16–19 Project, reported on in *Education 16–19: The Role of English and Communication* (London: Macmillan, 1979). With Leslie Stratta and Andrew Wilkinson he has written *Patterns of Language* (London: Heinemann, 1973) and, again with Leslie Stratta, he has produced a series of booklets on aspects of writing for the Southern Regional Examinations Board (UK).

DOUBLE NEGATIVE *See* USAGE.

DRAMA *See* IMPROVISATION; PLAYS; ROLE PLAY; SHAKESPEARE.

DRAWING: RELEVANCE TO WRITING – Donald Graves's research into early writing development has found an important place for drawing as part of the beginning writer's strategies. Graves has found that drawing, for young children, provides a setting for their text as well as a rehearsal of what they will eventually write. Graves's researchers quote first-graders as responding to the question, 'What are you going to write about?' with 'How should I know? I haven't drawed it yet.' Revising their drawings will often precede revising their writing for these young writers.

Reference

R. D. Walshe (ed.), *Donald Graves in Australia*, Sydney: PETA, 1981.

DROMKEEN – A 'home for children's literature', manuscripts, original artwork, reference library, situated at Riddell's Creek near Melbourne, Australia.

DROMKEEN MEDAL – An annual Australian award for a contribution to the advancement of children's literature. First awarded in 1982 (to Lou Rees).

DUE TO *See* USAGE.

DUMMY-RUN EXERCISES – A term used by John Dixon (q.v.) in his *Growth Through English* when referring to textbook exercises such as sentence correction, fill-in-the-blank exercises, and so on. 'Language is learnt in operation, not by dummy-runs.'

DYSLEXIA – Dyslexia was originally a medical term for severe reading disability, and was frequently used as a more sophisticated term for 'word blindness'. Dyslexia is so defined in the *Dictionary of Reading and Related Terms*: 'Dyslexia in this sense applies to persons who already have adequate vision, hearing, intelligence, and general language functioning'.

Educators are now generally agreed that labels such as 'dyslexia' are simply not useful. Although the term serves only to identify the individual as one with a serious reading difficulty, it is common for it to be used as an explanation (i.e. it is concluded that a child is failing to learn to read *because* she or he is dyslexic). Such an explanation may rapidly degenerate into an excuse for not providing the child with appropriate assistance. **(MRT)**

'It is only through reading that children learn to read and . . . a teacher's role must therefore be to make reading easy for every child . . . children can learn to read only through materials and activities that make sense to them, that they can relate to what they already know or want to know.'

(Frank Smith,
Reading)

e

EACH *See* USAGE: EVERYONE, ANYONE, EACH.

EACH OTHER/ONE ANOTHER *See* USAGE.

EFFECTIVE READING *See* READING MACHINES.

EFFERENT READING *See* AESTHETIC READING.

EGOCENTRISM – Jean Piaget's theory of child development embodies the notion that the young child is egocentric, that is, unable to take another person's point of view. Recent experiments with young children have, however, thrown some doubt upon this belief. See Margaret Donaldson, *Children's Minds* (London: Fontana, 1978).

EITHER . . . OR; NEITHER . . . NOR *See* USAGE.

ELABORATED AND RESTRICTED CODES – In the 1960s the British sociologist Basil Bernstein hypothesized, and later cited evidence to support, the theory that one reason why children of working-class families do less well at school than the children of middle-class families is that most working-class children are confined to a *restricted code* of language use. Middle-class children, on the other hand, have access to an *elaborated code*, and schools 'are predicated upon' an elaborated code. Lack of space prevents our providing definitions of the two codes, a task which in any case is made extraordinarily difficult both because Bernstein's prose is often obscure and because he appears to have shifted ground somewhat over the years. The interested reader is referred to Bernstein's collected papers and to the detailed discussion in Robinson (see below). Two points, however, do need to be made here. First, attempts to replicate Bernstein's findings in the Australian context have come up with largely negative findings. Second, there is some doubt as to whether secondary schools are in fact predicated upon an elaborated code. In a study of the language of mathematics and science lessons taught to 13 year olds in a secondary school, Cooper found a predominance of restricted code. (Cooper's was a UK study, and it would be interesting if it were to be replicated in Australia.)

References

B. Bernstein, *Class, Codes and Control*, Vols 1, 2, 3, London: Routledge & Kegan Paul.

B. Cooper, *Bernstein's Codes: A Classroom Study*, University of Sussex Education Area, Occasional Paper No. 6, 1976.

D. Lawton, *Social Class, Language and Education*, London: Routledge & Kegan Paul, 1968.

Peter Robinson, *Language Management in Education: The Australian Context*, Sydney: Allen & Unwin, 1978.

ELECTIVE ENGLISH – Offering specialized elective courses in English has a number of advantages: students may follow up special interests; they get the opportunity to work extensively in an area of strength (also a bonus for assessment purposes); teachers' areas of interest and expertise can be capitalized upon, and so on. Electives could be offered within a form (indeed, within a class) or across forms into a vertical system. Possibilities include:

(1) writing books for the local primary school;
(2) producing a newspaper/magazine;
(3) drama workshop;
(4) public speaking;
(5) film study;
(6) reading for pleasure; and so on.

Of course, the activities covered in electives should be extensions of the kind of activities in a normal classroom, which should not forego areas of language development simply because they are available as part of certain electives.

ELISION – The omission of a sound in a word in pronunciation, e.g. *I'd, don't*.

ELLIPSIS – The omission of a word or words which would be necessary for complete grammaticality in a sentence, but which is not needed for understanding the sentence in context.

EMPIRICAL RESEARCH – Research based on a scientific paradigm, that is involving the collection and interpretation of 'objective' data, usually of a numerical kind.
See also ACTION RESEARCH; CASE STUDY; ETHNOGRAPHIC RESEARCH.

ENGLISH IN AUSTRALIA – The journal of the Australian Association for the Teaching of English, founded in 1965. Subscription inquiries: The Publications Secretary, AATE Inc., PO Box 203, Norwood, SA 5067.

ENGLISH IN EDUCATION – Journal of the National Association for the Teaching of English (UK). Subscription inquiries: NATE Office, 49 Broomgrove Road, Sheffield S10 2NA.

ENGLISH JOURNAL – One of several journals published by the National Council of Teachers of English (USA), *English Journal* is intended mainly for secondary teachers. For primary and junior secondary teachers, there is the journal *Language Arts* (q.v.). *English Journal* appears eight times a year. Subscription inquiries: National Council of Teachers of English, 1111 Kenyon Road, Urbana, Illinois 61801.

ENGLISH MAGAZINE, THE – Published three times a year by the Inner London Education Authority English Centre, Sutherland Street, London SW1.

ENQUIRY, INQUIRY *See* USAGE.

EPISODIC – A word which refers to a work's tendency to be broken into a series of more or less independent episodes. Of recent popular children's novels, *February Dragon* is an example while *Huckleberry Finn* (granted its artistic unity as a whole) could well qualify among senior texts.

ERIC – Education Resources Information Centre. The ERIC Clearing House on Reading and Communication Skills indexes material on English teaching from all over the world. Many libraries have ERIC materials on microfilm. If you are researching any aspect of English teaching, the first step should be a search of ERIC holdings in the subject.

ERRORS – For too long English teachers have had a negative attitude towards errors, particularly in writing. Yet an undue emphasis on avoiding errors is likely to lead to 'safe' writing, to an unwillingness to experiment, to take risks. English teachers need to promote the concept of the *virtuous error*, the notion that making mistakes is often a first step in learning something new. Research suggests that semantic and syntactic growth are normally accompanied by errors in language use.

References

M. Shaughnessy, *Errors and Expectations in Student Writing*, New York: Oxford University Press, 1977.

Constance Weaver, 'Welcoming errors as signs of growth', *Language Arts*, 59 (5), May 1982.

ETHNOGRAPHIC RESEARCH – In contrast to educational research based on a scientific paradigm, ethnographic research is based on an anthropological model. Ethnographic techniques rest on fieldwork and participant observation: the researcher investigates educational problems in their social context – the school and the classroom – by interviewing teachers and pupils, observing classes, even participating in the various school activities. While the ethnographic approach certainly involves some loss of objectivity, it is much more open to the many factors in a school which affect learning than research based on the pre-test, post-test model. An example of ethnographic research is the case study (q.v.).

EUPHEMISM – Some words have unpleasant or lowly connotations. Euphemism is the substitution of words which soften the reality (e.g. 'coffins' becomes 'caskets'; 'military retreat' becomes 'strategic withdrawal'); or sound more impressive (e.g. 'garbage collector' becomes 'garbologist').

George Orwell, in his essay *Politics and the English Language*, showed how the use of euphemism can blur the truth:

> Defenceless villages are bombarded from the air, the inhabitants driven out into the countryside, the cattle machine-gunned, the huts set on fire with incendiary bullets: this is called *pacification*. Millions of peasants are robbed of their farms and sent trudging along the road with no more than they can carry: this is called *transfer of population* or *rectification of frontiers*.

Ours is the age of euphemism. *The Sydney Morning Herald* reported that a Sydney lift-driver calls himself a 'vertical passenger transport controller'; the Bankstown Council calls its dog-catcher a 'canine impounder'; the term 'used car' has been replaced by 'pre-owned car' (or even 'pre-loved car'!). Here is a fertile area for research and discussion.

EVALUATION *See* ASSESSMENT.

EVALUATION OF ENGLISH PROGRAMMES – In our entry on assessment (q.v.), we provided a model which has four stages, two of which – the Reflection and Prospect/Retrospect stages – involve the teacher in an evaluation of what has been achieved in particular units and thus place him/her in the position of making informed judgements about what has been achieved and where to go next. We are arguing, in effect, that good teaching involves a continual process of programme evaluation.

Every so often, however, a more thoroughgoing evaluation of English programmes should take place at a faculty level. It is all too easy, for example, for teachers to fail to realize that a changing school population may have different needs, and in the last few years most secondary schools have experienced a dramatic change in the composition of the senior years.

For primary schools and secondary English departments wishing to undertake an extended evaluation of their programmes, it would be worthwhile trying to obtain the booklet *Evaluating English Programs*, written by Robert McGregor and Marion Meiers for the Secondary English Committee of the Education Department of Victoria.

Here are a few suggestions which may help those undertaking evaluation. McGregor and Meiers suggest that the process of evaluation must throw light upon answers to four critical questions:

(1) What is being done? (i.e. description).
(2) Why is it done? (i.e. interpretation).
(3) How well is it being done? (i.e. judgement).
(4) What do we do now? (i.e. action).

The first step, then, ought to be information gathering – finding out what teachers actually do in their classrooms, what resources are available, how the students respond to what is being done. In addition to the normal means of data gathering, consideration ought to be given to encouraging teachers to visit one another's classrooms, and to record on audio tape and analyse some of their lessons. (A scheme for analysing lessons involving whole-class and small-group discussion is to be found in Ken Watson's *English Teaching in Perspective*, Milton Keynes: Open University Press, 1987, pp. 77–8.) The videotaping of some lessons for later discussion and analysis would also be valuable.

The question, 'Why is it being done?', involves a careful consideration of current practices in the light of their underlying aims, both explicit and implicit. Are these aims in accordance with what is known about how children learn language? (*See* LANGUAGE ACQUISITION; PERSONAL GROWTH MODEL; SKILLS MODEL.) Are they in accordance with the students' needs?

The question, 'How well is it being done?', involves asking many subsidiary questions. A few of these are:

(1) Are teaching practices in accordance with what is known about language learning?
(2) Is sufficient attention given to individual needs?
(3) If there are graded classes, has the grading been done on the basis of sound and detailed information? Have the arguments in favour of mixed-ability classes been given proper consideration? (*See* MIXED-ABILITY TEACHING).
(4) Are the programming principles of *balance* and *variety* being kept in mind? (*See* PROGRAMMING IN ENGLISH).
(5) Are courses constructed in terms of what students will be *doing* with language (a range of speaking, listening, reading, writing) rather than learning about language?
(6) Are students being given plenty of opportunity to speak and write for different audiences? (*See* AUDIENCE).
(7) Are students given opportunities to respond personally to what they read?
(8) Are judgements of students' work made as far as possible in terms of the individual students' previous performance?
(9) Is an effort being made to encourage students to make their own assessments of work done? (*See* SELF-ASSESSMENT BY STUDENTS).
(10) Do students understand the aims and purposes of the English programme?
(11) Are parents being given sufficient information?

Teachers will have no difficulty in thinking of other important questions.

The outcome of such an evaluation process could well be not only a new policy statement but also a mechanism for monitoring the implementation of policy and an improved method of sharing teaching ideas.

Reference

D. Allen, *Evaluating the English Department*, Bowdon, Cheshire: 1983.

EVERYONE, ANYONE, EACH, EVERYBODY *See* USAGE.

EXEMPLUM – Literally 'an object lesson' or 'example', this term refers to a short tale illustrating a moral principle. It is a term especially of use to students of Chaucer – for example, in the *Nun's Priest's Tale*.

EXERCISES, ENGLISH THROUGH – Books of English exercises abound, despite clear evidence that the performance of fill-in-the-blank exercises, sentence correction exercises and punctuation exercises does not increase language competence. When Sir Alec Clegg was collecting samples of writing for his book, *The Excitement of Writing*, he found that the best writing came from schools which refused to use such textbooks. W. G. Heath, in a ten-month experiment, found that children following a course of 'library-centred English' involving a great deal of reading and writing did much better than those following a conventional course based on the performance of exercises.

Much the same can be said of the comprehension exercises as traditionally conceived. The comprehension exercise which require pupils to read a passage and then answer the questions below it, is a *testing* device not a means of *teaching* comprehension. 'Ability in comprehending is best developed where students have a real reason for searching out the meaning, where they are given opportunities to share their perceptions, modify their viewpoints, and where they grapple with the print until they understand what it means in a total sense' (*Language and Language Learning*, NSW Department of Education Directorate of Studies, 1982).

The only occasion when the use of exercises would appear to have some value is when a *particular* child *recognizes* that he/she has a weakness in some area (say, the use of the apostrophe). Then the teacher, after explaining the particular point, can give the child a set of exercises to reinforce what has been explained.

The practice of setting dummy-run exercises for the whole class is indefensible. To paraphrase a remark of Garth Boomer, the teacher should be spending his/her time involving the students actively in reading and writing, not in teaching *about* reading and writing.

References

A. Clegg, *The Excitement of Writing*, London: Chatto & Windus, 1964.
W. G. Heath, 'Library-centred English: an experiment', *Educational Review* 14 (2), 1962.

EXPERIENCE-CENTRED ENGLISH *See* PERSONAL GROWTH MODEL OF ENGLISH.

EXPLORATORY TALK *See* TALK.

EXPRESSIVE LANGUAGE *See* LANGUAGE, FUNCTIONS OF.

f

FACTOR ANALYSIS – This is a technique for representing the relationships (usually expressed as correlations) among a set of measures in terms of a smaller number of underlying hypothetical constructs. For example, the correlations among the scores of a group of students on measures of addition, subtraction, multiplication, division, vocabulary and reading comprehension might be completely explainable in terms of two underlying variables such as computational ability and verbal ability. **(DS)**

FEMINIST CRITICISM – Feminist criticism is a form of post-structuralism (q.v.) which operates by deconstructing fiction to assess its acceptability for women. Many writers of the past and present may be analysed from a feminist point of view to expose their attitudes towards women and the role of women in society. It also involves the active promotion of literature by women and works that present women in a positive manner. In the UK especially, Virago Press has done a great deal to revive and to introduce many women writers to a wider readership. The method allows readers a means of systematically foregrounding attitudes to women and the experience of being a woman. In schools, feminism and feminist criticism have raised the more general issue of sexism. Many teachers of English, in consequence, are anxious to include in their reading programmes more works by women and more books likely to raise consciousness about the role and achievements of women.

FEWER *See* USAGE: LESS/FEWER.

FILM STUDY – There are two areas here: film study and film-making. The field is large enough to constitute a separate subject in the curriculum, but in most schools it forms part of the English course, in some Year 7 to Year 11. Aside from its relevance to the 'media' component in English courses, it is also, as Dick Stratford points out, a focus for 'speaking, listening, reading and writing'.

Film Study

To ignore *Citizen Kane*, *La Grande Illusion*, *The Grapes of Wrath*, *The Conformist*, *North by Northwest* and the dozens of other great films, is to ignore some of the most important cultural products of the twentieth century, some of the greatest works of imagination. Certainly the majority of films are rubbish, but so are the majority of novels, poems and plays!

To understand and to be able to discriminate among films is as important as to understand and to be able to discriminate among literary works. And as we understand that the kind of literary study we engage in will vary with the age of our students, and with our purposes, so with film. Relevant activities will range through experiencing, recreation, discussion to, at the senior level, quite sophisticated criticism which looks at such aspects as chronology (flashbacks?), pace, camera and lighting techniques, sound track and particular recurrent images.

Dick Stratford's chapter in *English in Secondary Schools, Today and Tomorrow* is essential reading for both film study and film-making. In considering film study at the senior level, some further reading will be required. One excellent resource for the teacher, not over-theoretical, is Louis D. Gianetti, *Understanding Movies*, 3rd edn,(Englewood Cliffs, NJ: Prentice-Hall, 1982). Somewhat more difficult (and semiotic: see SEMIOLOGY/SEMIOTICS) is James Monaco, *How to Read a Film* (New York: Oxford University Press, 1977). An excellent anthology of essays from a variety of viewpoints is G. Mast and M. Cohen (eds), *Film Theory and Criticism*, 2nd edn, (New York: Oxford University Press, 1979).

English in Australia 39 (Feb, 1977) devoted its 'Resources' section to the screen media and it remains indispensable. It covers particular short films, animation films and longer 'feature' films such as *Owl Creek* and *Storm Boy*.

It also suggests ways of running project studies on particular actors, directors and themes. The whole section was incorporated into *Resources III* (AATE) in 1978.

Dick Stratford's suggestions about film clubs, excursions and other ways to bring film into the school programme remain valid, but since 1977 the advent of the video cassette and video libraries has opened up easy access to a much wider range of choice, making easier the inclusion of film study in the school timetable.

Film-making

Improved VTR and cheap super-8 systems make this easier than it once was. Again, what the class actually does will depend on their age, the facilities available, and whether the film-making is being done for its own sake or as a means of expression related to something else.

What better way to learn the 'language of film' than to actually make a film? The key word is 'simplicity'. Even a short exercise will take a surprising amount of time. Film-making is an ideal small-group activity, involving a variety of talents and all the skills of English.

You will need a good, preferably portable video system, or super-8 cameras (cheap ones which will survive 'hands-on' by Year 8 are easily obtained), film, tripod, projector, editor and splicer, movie light and titler. The last two are essential. See Dick Stratford's article for more information on each of these aspects, as well as lots of good general ideas for how to get started and keep it running.

(NJW)

References

Roy Knight, *Film in English Teaching*, London: Hutchinson, 1972.

Douglas Lowndes, *Film Making in School*, London: Batsford, 1972.

Dick Stratford, 'Film and Filmmaking in English', in K. D. Watson and R. D. Eagleson (eds), *English In Secondary Schools, Today and Tomorrow*, Sydney: ETA, 1977.

See also VIDEO IN THE CLASSROOM.

FLASH CARDS – Teachers using a 'look and say' method of reading instruction build up a sight vocabulary using cards on which each word is printed and drilled in isolation until children are able to immediately recognize them. The words are then put together into a sentence for the children to read.

There are two serious and related deficiencies in using this method of building up a sight vocabulary:

(1) In flashcard 'drill' children are reduced to using only visual memory and pattern discrimination techniques which break down because of memory limitations (Tulving and Gold, 1963; Miller, 1956).

(2) Children are prevented from using their knowledge of the flow of language (syntax) and context meaning (semantics) to assist in identifying the word. Without these extra clues the child is unable to engage in organized memory retrieval strategies. **(MRT)**

See also LOOK-SAY; LANGUAGE EXPERIENCE.

Further Reading

D. L. Holmes, 'The independence of letter, word and meaning identification in reading', in Frank Smith (ed.) *Psycholinguistics and Reading*, London: Holt, Rinehart & Winston, 1973.

G. Marchbanks and H. Levin, 'Cues by which children recognise words', *Journal of Educational Psychology*, 56, 1965: 57–61.

References

G. A. Miller, 'The magical number seven, plus or minus two: some limits on our capacity for processing information', *Psychological Review*, 63, 1956, 81–97.

E. Tulving and C. Gold, 'Stimulus information and contextual information as determinants of tachistoscopic recognition of words, *Journal of Experimental Psychology*, 66, 1963, 319–27.

FORMALISM – A difficult term, because the strong pejorative connotations it has attracted often mask out what the original Russian formalists (Victor Shklovsky and others in the 1920s) were trying to do. In the words of one of them:

> Our discussions have been, and can only be, about certain theoretical principles drawn from the study of the concrete material with its specific characteristics, not about one or another ready-made methodological or aesthetic system.
>
> (Matejka and Pomorska, p. 3)

The Russian formalists rejected 'art for art's sake', and also those streams of criticism (some of which became the orthodoxy in Soviet Russia) which stressed the moral or political content of the work.

There is obviously common ground with the American 'New Critics', with such English critics as Empson, and with later developments, particularly following Jakobson, in stylistics.

Formalists have made a valuable contribution to our understanding of how language in literature works: the idea of 'foregrounding', for example. On the other hand, some formalists have exaggerated the difference between 'ordinary language and poetic language', a distinction found also in Britton. Later writers have argued persuasively against such a distinction – R. D. Eagleson and L. Kramer, *Language and Literature: A Synthesis* (Sydney: Nelson, 1976) and Roger Fowler, *Literature as Social Discourse* (Indiana University Press, 1981).

The formalist belief that one important function of literature is 'defamiliarization', or 'making strange', has sufficient connections with the practice of some modern writers (e.g. Beckett, Joyce) to explain the current interest in formalist criticism. **(NJW)**

References

J. Culler, *Structuralist Poetics*, London: Routledge & Kegan Paul, 1975.

Roger Fowler (ed.), *A Dictionary of Modern Critical Terms*, London: Routledge & Kegan Paul, 1973.

L. Matejka and K. Pomorska (eds), *Readings in Russian Poetics*, Michigan: University of Michigan, 1978.

T. Sebeok (ed.), *Style in Language*, Cambridge, Mass.: MIT, 1960.

Raymond Williams, *Keywords*, Fontana, London, 1976.

FREE MORPHEME – A morpheme (q.v.) that can stand alone, for example *some* and *times* in *sometimes*.

FREE VERSE – Verse with no regular metre or line length. The line length is generally dictated by the sense. Walt Whitman was its greatest nineteenth-century exponent; in the twentieth century it has been used by many poets, notably D. H. Lawrence and T. S. Eliot.

FUNCTIONAL GRAMMAR – An approach to grammar which derives from the European tradition of grammatical studies and has also been influenced by socio-linguistics and by the needs of ESL teaching where it has been applied increasingly in the past ten years. Its starting point is the functions for which we use language or the meanings or notions which are expressed; it then sets out the grammatical structures available to express these functions and meanings. Functions such as directing people's actions, giving information, greeting, making judgements, or notions such as time, direction, permission, quantity, and so on, might form part of the basis of a functional grammar. The terms *communicative grammar* and *functional/notional grammar* are also used to refer to grammars following this approach. Moreover, the idea of starting with meaning and working towards forms and structures lends itself to a systemic presentation and a systemic grammar (q.v.) can be seen as a more formal version of a functional grammar. This approach, whose principal exponent is M. A. K. Halliday, may be referred to as functional-systemic grammar. **(JC)**

References

M. A. K. Halliday, *An Introduction to Functional Grammar*, London: Edward Arnold, 1985.

G. Leech and J. Svartvik, *A Communicative Grammar of English*, London: Longman, 1975.

D. A. Wilkins, *Notional Syllabuses*, London: Oxford University Press, 1976.

FUNCTIONAL LITERACY – Functional literacy may be described as the level of competence in reading and writing essential for a person to cope with the particular demands of his or her circumstances. It may relate to 'survival reading skills' involved in day-to-day living within a culture (such as the ability to read signs, fill in forms, etc.), or to those skills in reading and writing which enable a person to engage in those activities required in his or her vocation. **(MRT)**

FUNCTIONAL/NOTIONAL APPROACH TO ESL TEACHING – A reaction against the structural approach (q.v.), the functional/notional approach stresses language as communication. A function is a language act: something that one does *through* language, like accepting, apologizing, refusing. A function operates through a general or a specific notion. A general notion is abstract (e.g. quality, necessity); a specific notion relates to a topic (e.g. food). Functional organization leads to some structural disorganization, but language learning is never linear. *Waterloo Street: A Resource Book for Teachers*, published by the Australian Broadcasting Corporation to support the TV series of the same name, is based on the functional/notional approach. A typical functional/notional text is Peter Watcyn-Jones, *Impact* (Harmondsworth: Penguin, 1979). **(MG-S)**

'Words are chameleons, they change the colours of their skins to fit snugly into the settings in which they find themselves. The importance of context in all language teaching is supreme. We can never neglect either the immediate verbal context or the wider situation in which speech or writing is taking place. This principle is capable of elevation into a major axiom of English teaching.'

(F. D. Flower,
Language and Education)

g

GAP READING COMPREHENSION TEST – This is a fifteen-minute timed silent reading test used with children in Years 4 to 6. It consists of seven short passages dealing with different topics. Words have been systematically deleted from the texts, and pupils' responses are scored as correct only when the original word is restored. Forms R and B are alternative forms of the test. Age norms are provided and scores are expressed as reading ages. For limitations *see* READING AGE; STANDARDIZED TESTS; CLOZE PROCEDURE.

(MRT)

References

J. McLeod, *GAP Reading Comprehension Test*, London: Heinemann, 1976.

P. D. Pumfrey, *Reading: Tests and Assessment Techniques*, London: Hodder & Stoughton, 1976.

GAPADOL READING COMPREHENSION TEST – This is a thirty-minute silent reading test used with pupils in the upper primary and secondary schools. It consists of six passages dealing with different topics. Words have been systematically deleted from each passage and, as in the GAP test, pupil responses are correct only if they restore the original word. Alternative forms G and Y of the test are available. Age norms are provided and scores are expressed as reading ages. For limitations *see* READING AGE; STANDARDIZED TESTS; CLOZE PROCEDURE. **(MRT)**

References

J. McLeod and J. Anderson, *GAPADOL Reading Comprehension Test*, London: Heinemann, 1973.

P. D. Pumfrey, *Reading: Tests and Assessment Techniques*, London: Hodder & Stoughton, 1976.

GENETTE, GERARD – French narratologist who has made important distinctions in the study of narratives between 'story', 'narrative' and 'narrating', which he defines respectively as narrative's content, the discourse of narrative text itself, the producing of narrative action. In Genette's universe, analysis of narrative discourse becomes a study of the relationship between these aspects. In his most famous work, *Narrative Discourse: An Essay in Method* (New York: Cornell University Press, 1980), he analyses these relationships in terms of

what he calls 'tense', 'mood' and 'voice'. His basic assumption is that any narrative is an extension of a simple sentence. (Proust's *Remembrance of Things Past* is an extension of the sentence, 'Marcel becomes a writer'). Narratives can thus be analysed in such terms equivalent to the grammar of a sentence. On the negative side, Genette's work is difficult to penetrate, obsessed as it is with terminology and the labelling of parts. Like many narratologists, his work is reductionist and tells us little about the distinctiveness of particular narratives or why particular narrative strategies should be chosen above others or affect the reader differently from others. More positively, however, narratologists such as Genette or Chatman (q.v.) provide us with tools for narrative analysis that go beyond the single-plot structure analysis provided especially by cognitive psychologists and story grammarians. These analyses of the narratologists are now beginning to be applied not only to literary classics of mainstream culture, but to children's literature and to children's own narrative productions.
See also NARRATOLOGY; STORY GRAMMARS.

GENRES, WRITING IN – At the time of writing there is a developing trend, especially in Australia, towards the systematic training of students to write in the forms of various identifiable genres, such as narrative, report and so on. This trend is being led by linguists with an interest in the improvement of writing in schools. Their main arguments seem to be that:

(1) Genres of writing are identifiable and fixed and delineated.
(2) Genres ought to be consciously followed by writers and their writing conform to the particular genre's structure.
(3) Genres ought to be taught as models of form.
(4) There is too much emphasis on narrative forms in primary school and that this is poor preparation for working in expository modes in secondary school, especially since such modes are characterized by an impersonal, neutral tone not provided for in most primary school narrative.

We believe that all of these arguments need at least to be questioned. Where is the evidence that genres are fixed, immutable and (especially) clearly delineated? What about fluidity between forms of writing as suggested by a model of writing such as Britton's (q.v.) transactional-expressive-poetic? Do writers necessarily make conscious decisions about genre form or does form change in response to the demands of tasks? Do writers write to create a generic form or to make a point or tell a story? What is the evidence that would cause us to abandon the belief that learning is facilitated when children are allowed to see their own language rather than be forced to conform to the conventional forms of a particular discipline? Why should direct teaching of genre be more productive than past attempts at direct teaching of other structures? Might there not be good reasons for preferring narrative in early schooling?

References
Children Writing: Reader, Geelong: Deakin University Press, 1984.
Children Writing: Study Guide, Geelong: Deakin University Press, 1984.
Gunther Kress, *Learning to Write*, London: Routledge & Kegan Paul, 1982.
Wayne Sawyer and Ken Watson, 'Questions of genre', in Ian Reid (ed.), *The Place of Genre in Learning: Current Debates*, Geelong: Deakin University Press, 1987.

GERUND – A gerund is a verb-noun, for example *running* in the sentence 'Running is a beneficial exercise.' Grammar texts insist that a possessive form of noun or pronoun must be used before the gerund in such sentences as 'What are the chances of *his* winning the race?' and 'What are the chances of *Jack's* winning the race?' and a survey of secondary and tertiary English teachers in 1976–7 found that a majority would insist on this in formal writing, though respondents were less certain about requiring the form in speech. Since then the trend has been away from use of the possessive and a majority of our sample of university graduates accepted the sentence 'What are the chances of *them* being found out?' even in formal writing.

Reference

Ken Watson, 'Teachers' attitudes to usage', *Language in the Classroom*, Applied Linguistics Association of Australia, Occasional Papers No. 2, 1978.

GLASS ANALYSIS – This method of word attack has been developed by Gerald Glass of Adelphi University, New York, and explained in his booklet, *Teaching Decoding as Separate from Reading.*

It is based on research into the behaviour of effective readers which indicates that they do *not* use phonic or syllabification 'rules'. The research shows that these effective readers cluster letters into 'chunks' from their sight vocabulary and always break up unknown words the same way. The more experienced the reader, the larger or more useful are the units she or he chooses.

Glass has developed a technique which fosters the visual clustering of letters within a whole word in relationship to the sound normally associated with that cluster.

Method (abbreviated and simplified)

(1) Select the letter cluster the group is to focus on (e.g. *ight*).
(2) Choose three to five appropriate words containing the cluster (fight, night, bright, light).
(3) Identify the whole word, then the letters by *name*, and then the sound of the actual cluster.
(4) Repeat the sound and ask the children to make the letters which represent it.
(5) Name the letters in the cluster and ask for the sound they represent in the word.

This analysis has four features:

(1) It is a decoding aid only.
(2) The learner should be able to see the whole word.
(3) The whole word should be frequently repeated during the session.
(4) Sessions are short and brisk. Games and activities using rhymes and songs can give opportunities to practise word analysis. **(MRT)**

References

G. Glass, *Teaching Decoding as Separate from Reading*, New York: Adelphi University, 1977.

A. Pulvertaft, *Carry on Reading*, Sydney: Ashton Scholastic, 1978.

P. Sloan and R. Latham, *Teaching Reading Is . . .*, Melbourne: Nelson, 1981.

GOAL-BASED ASSESSMENT – Promoted by the Victorians, Bill Hannan and David McRae, this approach sees assessment as a recognition of what the student has done in a course. For example, a goal might be, 'Keep a written, illustrated journal of activities throughout the unit'. It is the student's responsibility to do the activity, with the teacher's help. The teacher has the responsibility to be able to justify the activity educationally, and to ensure that it is an attainable goal.

If the students do the required activities and do not learn, that is seen as the responsibility of the school or teacher, not the students. The course activities would need to be evaluated and improved.

At the end of the course, all students who have engaged in the required processes receive a report outlining what they have done. Goal-based assessment is also known as 'Work Required Assessment'. **(BJ)**

See also ASSESSMENT; CRITERION-REFERENCED ASSESSMENT; NORM-REFERENCED ASSESSMENT; PEER ASSESSMENT; SELF-ASSESSMENT BY STUDENTS.

Reference

Bill Hannan, 'Après assessment', *The Victorian Teacher*, June 3, 1983.
Brian Johnston, *Assessing English*, Milton Keynes: Open University Press, 1987.

GOODMAN, KENNETH – Professor of Elementary Education at the University of Arizona. His special concern is with the reading process (q.v.), which he has described as a 'psycholinguistic guessing game'. His theory of miscue analysis (q.v.), developed in association with his wife, Yetta Goodman, has proved very influential in the teaching of reading.

Reference

F. V. Gollasch (ed.), *Language and Literacy: Selected Writings of Kenneth S. Goodman*, Vol. 1, Boston: Routledge & Kegan Paul, 1982.

GOT *See* USAGE.

GRAMMAR – The organization of meaningful elements in a language, or a description of that organization. Essentially grammar is the internal organization of a language, the ways in which the elements of the language (such as words and components of words – prefixes, endings, etc.) are arranged, modified and related to one another in order to express meaning. However, it is not necessary to know about grammar in this sense in order to be able to use the language. When we speak or write we inevitably use grammar because it is an integral part of language. A child of 3 or 4 does not usually know anything about grammar but none the less may use language with remarkable competence.

However, the term *grammar* also refers to a description of a language's organization, which may be expressed as a set of principles, rules or conventions. The part of grammar dealing with the forms of words and other elements is known as morphology while their arrangement in larger structures is known as syntax. There are several different approaches to grammatical description but by far the most widely known is traditional grammar (q.v.). In this century various modern grammars with different bases for their descriptions have offered us further insight into organization of language. These have included structural grammar (q.v.) which was superseded by transformational/generative grammar (q.v.); more recent developments include functional grammar (q.v.) and systemic grammar (q.v.). Nevertheless, despite some important differences amongst these approaches there are some common features of grammar likely to be found in any description of English grammar. These include word classes such as nouns and verbs, structures such as phrases and clauses, and other features such as number (in nouns) and tense (in verbs).

In the past, grammar has occupied a significant place in the content of English teaching, and while it still has a role to play, its place is no longer so obviously assured. This is partly because the role of content of any kind in English teaching has changed. Much of what was traditionally taught under the heading of grammar was simply a description (classification of words and clauses and relationships between them). But there was also some prescriptive teaching: certain forms, usages and stylistic choices were endorsed while others were condemned. It is not true to say that grammar as traditionally taught in English was all prescriptive, but there was a prescriptive tendency in the teaching because part of the justification for teaching grammar was to influence children's use of the language. This involved getting children to conform to the conventions of educated usage; this was generally promoted as 'correct English' as if it were the only kind of English to be used in any circumstances. Today, our teaching can take account of far more richness and subtlety in the English language than this popular view of language allowed.

Any dialect or register of any language has its grammar and that grammar can be studied and described. The grammar of non-standard (q.v.) varieties of English may be just as complex as that of standard English (q.v.). Yet in any language it is usually the grammar of the standard dialect that is described and codified and that in turn contributes to its prestige in the community. **(JC)**

References

H. A. Gleason, *Linguistics and English Grammar*, New York: Holt, Rinehart & Winston, 1965.

G. Leech and J. Svartvik, *A Communicative Grammar of English*, London: Longman, 1975.

F. Palmer, *Grammar*, Harmondsworth: Penguin, 1971.

R. Quirk, S. Greenbaum, G. Leech and J. Svartvik, *A Grammar of Contemporary English*, London: Longman, 1972.

GRAMMAR AND WRITING – The evidence of the lack of transfer between formal study of a grammatical system and improvement in writing ability is overwhelming. The most important studies in this area include:

R. J. Harris, 'The only disturbing feature', *The Use of English* 16(3), 1965: 197–202. Harris studied two parallel English classes in five schools (in four of which the paired classes were taught by the same teacher) over two years, one class having one lesson each week in formal grammar, while the other had no grammar at all and had an extra writing period. At the end of the two-year period, the non-grammar classes had made such gains that Harris concluded that 'the study of grammatical terminology had a negligible or even a relatively harmful effect upon the correctness of children's writing'.

W. B. Elley, I. H. Bantam, H. Lamb and M. Wyllie, 'The role of grammar in a secondary school English curriculum', *Research in the Teaching of English* 10(1), Spring 1976: 5–21. In this experiment three carefully matched groups of pupils studied three different English programmes for three years: one group's programme included a transformational grammar strand, another group's included a traditional grammar strand and the third group studied no grammar for three years. After three years, the researchers concluded that the non-grammar group 'demonstrated competence in writing and related language skills fully equal to that shown by the two grammar groups. . . . It is difficult to escape the conclusion that English grammar, whether traditional or transformational, has virtually no influence on the language growth of typical secondary school students'.

One area in which grammatical study of a sort seemed to have produced results in improved writing was in the area of sentence-combining. The best-known studies in this area are those of Frank O'Hare (*Sentence Combining: Improving Student Writing without Formal Grammar Instruction*, NCTE, 1974) and John Mellon (*Transformational Sentence-Combining: A Method of Enhancing the Development of Syntactic Fluency in English Composition*, Urbana, Illinois, 1971). James Moffett's (q.v.) comments on the sentence-combining school are relevant here: what such studies show, he argues, is that embedding exercises will improve syntactic versatility, but that it is the experience of embedding kernel sentences, not the learning of nomenclature that achieves the aim. Further, more complex sentences are not necessarily higher-quality sentences. The point is that students should be able, not obliged, to complicate their sentences and that this is best practised in the context of natural writing tasks where complex sentences may be judged on their appropriateness, rather than in a series of sequential exercises. And finally, syntax is only one area of linguistic development and any curriculum which ignores the complexity of language activity and the interplay of audience and purpose contexts cannot be said to be working towards full language development (*Teaching the Universe of Discourse*, Boston: Houghton Mifflin, 1968). Moffett's reservations have been confirmed by recent studies showing that students who have undertaken sentence-combining courses soon revert to their original manner of writing.

The most that can be claimed for grammar study in relation to writing development is that particular points of grammar may be usefully taught to particular students who have a particular weakness, but only within the context of their own writing.

GRAMMAR POEMS – Even the strongest opponents of the teaching of grammar feel that the names of the main parts of speech ought to be known by pupils. One way to keep such terminology in front of pupils is to ask them to write 'grammar poems' to prescribed patterns. For example:

One noun	Tree
Two adjectives	white, tragic
A phrase	with uplifted arms
Verb and adverb	asks mutely
Interrogative	why?

GRAPHEME – The basic unit in the English spelling system. A grapheme is any letter or combination of letters capable of representing a distinct speech sound (or phoneme). Although we spell words in terms of letters of the alphabet, the spelling system is organized in terms of graphemes, which comprise single letters and combinations of letters such as *ch*, *sh*, *ng*, *ea*, *ee*, *oi*, *ay*, *ow*, *air* and *ere*. In the spelling of any particular word, some letters may function in relation to the speech sounds as single-letter graphemes but other letters may form graphemes of two or more letters. Any letter of the alphabet can function as a single letter grapheme but many letters also enter into combinations. Just as some of the single-letter graphemes may in different contexts represent different phonemes, so the two- and three-letter graphemes can on occasion represent different phonemes. **(JC)**

GRAPHO-PHONIC INFORMATION – Grapho-phonic is one of the three major types of non-visual information (q.v.) used by a reader in the process of comprehending print.

> Grapho-phonic information refers to the individual's familiarity with the symbols used in written language, the sounds of spoken language, and the relationships which exist between them. In addition, it is concerned with the individual's familiarity with those sequences of sounds and letters which occur frequently in the language (g at the beginning of a word, *d* may be followed by *a* or *r*, but not by *t* or *n*).
>
> (Parker, 1983)

It is important for teachers to recognize that grapho-phonic information is only one of the forms of non-visual information, and that it should not receive undue emphasis in reading programmes, particularly those designed for beginning readers. An overemphasis on the use of grapho-phonic information can readily lead developing readers to mistakenly concentrate on accurate word identification rather than the most efficient means of making meaning. **(MRT)**

See also VISUAL INFORMATION; NON-VISUAL INFORMATION; SEMANTIC INFORMATION; SYNTACTIC INFORMATION.

References

R. Parker, 'Towards a model of the reading process', in D. E. Burnes and G. M. Page (eds), *Reading: Insights and Strategies For Teaching*, Sydney: Harcourt Brace Jovanovich, 1983.

F. Smith, *Reading*, Cambridge: Cambridge University Press, 1978.

GROUP WORK *See* SMALL-GROUP WORK.

GROWTH MODEL OF ENGLISH *See* PERSONAL GROWTH MODEL.

GROWTH THROUGH ENGLISH – One of the most influential books on English teaching published in the last twenty-five years, *Growth Through English* (London: Oxford University Press, 1975), is a report of the Dartmouth Seminar (q.v.), written by John Dixon (q.v.). It established the personal growth model of English (q.v.).

GUARDIAN AWARD – The *Guardian* newspaper in Britain gives annual awards for adult and children's fiction. Recent winners in the children's books section include Michèlle Magorian's *Goodnight Mr Tom* and Peter Carter's *The Sentinels*.

h

HAIKU – The Japanese haiku is receiving a great deal of attention in English classrooms, with pupils frequently being encouraged to write their own. J. A. Cuddon, in *A Dictionary of Literary Terms* (Harmondsworth: Penguin) says: 'Such a poem expresses a single idea, image or feeling; in fact it is a kind of miniature "snap" in words.' He is wrong, however, in suggesting that it *must* consist of seventeen syllables in three lines of five, seven and five syllables respectively; while such an arrangement is an attempt to come as close as possible to the Japanese 'units of duration', the Japanese themselves seem to feel that it is possible, in English, to break the 5-7-5 pattern and still produce an acceptable haiku, as is evidenced by the fact that one of the prizewinners in a Japan Air Lines competition was the following:

Lily:
out of the water . . .
out of itself.
(N. Virgilio)

From the same competition comes a haiku in the strict pattern which could well serve as a model for students:

A bitter morning:
Sparrows sitting together
Without any necks.
(J. W. Hackett)

See also POETRY, SUGGESTIONS FOR TEACHING.

References

H. G. Henderson, *Haiku in English*, Rutland, Vermont: Tuttle, 1967.
C. van den Heuvel, *The Haiku Anthology*, New York: Anchor, 1974.

HALLIDAY, M. A. K. – Professor of Linguistics at the University of Sydney, associated particularly with the interactional theory of language acquisition (*see* LANGUAGE ACQUISITION) and with systemic grammar (q.v.). He was also responsible for establishing the Schools Council Program in Linguistics and English Teaching, which produced *Breakthrough to Literacy* (q.v.) and

Language in Use (q.v.). His publications include *Explorations in the Functions of Language* (London: Arnold, 1973). *Learning How to Mean* (London: Arnold, 1975) and *Language as Social Semiotic* (London: Arnold, 1978). With Ruqaiya Hasan, he has written a major work on cohesion (q.v.).

HANS CHRISTIAN ANDERSEN AWARD – A biennial international award, established by IBBY (q.v.) in 1956, honouring a distinguished writer and an illustrator in the field of children's literature. Recent winners have been:

1976 – Cecil Bodker (author, Denmark); Tatiana Mawrina (illustrator, Soviet Union)
1978 – Paula Fox (author, United States); Svend Otto (illustrator, Denmark)
1980 – Bohumil Riha (author, Czechoslovakia); Suekichi Akaba (illustrator, Japan)
1982 – Lygia Bojunga Nunes (author, Brazil); Zbigniew Rychlicki (illustrator, Poland)
1984 – Christine Nostlinger (author, Austria); Mitsumasa Anno (illustrator, Japan)
1986 – Patricia Wrightson (author, Australia); Robert Ingpen (illustrator, Australia).

HEATHCOTE, DOROTHY – Dorothy Heathcote has had a considerable influence on notions of drama teaching in schools in the past ten years or so. Her work has been the subject of a number of films of which *Three Looms Waiting* (BBC Omnibus documentary) is perhaps the most widely known in Australia. Dorothy Heathcote's reputation and her ideas received substantial support when in 1976, Betty Jane Wagner published *Dorothy Heathcote: Drama as a Learning Medium.* In the opening chapter, 'What Drama Can Do', Wagner observes of Heathcote's role with children:

> She does not use children to produce plays. Instead, she uses drama to expand their awareness, to enable them to look at reality through fantasy, to see below the surface of actions to their meaning. She is interested, not in making plays with children, but in, as she terms it, burnishing children through play. She does this not by heaping more information on them but by enabling them to use what they already know. (p. 15)

The book has a useful bibliography and a listing of available films about Heathcote's work. **(PR)**

References

Dorothy Heathcote, *Collected Writings on Education and Drama*, London: Hutchinson, 1984.
Betty Jane Wagner, *Dorothy Heathcote: Drama as a Learning Medium*, Washington: HEA, 1976.

HOMONYM/HOMOPHONE/HOMOGRAPH – Strictly speaking, the distinction between these terms is according to the following definitions:

Homonym – words of the same sound and spelling, but of different meanings,

for example 'class' (stylish sophistication), 'class' (a group of schoolchildren), 'class' (a socio-economic division).
Homophone – words of the same sound but of different spelling amd meaning, for example 'for' and 'four', 'by' and 'buy', and so on.
Homograph – words of the same spelling but of different sound and meaning, for example 'tear' (in crying) and 'tear' (to rend).
But in practice 'homonym' tends to be used as a blanket term for all three. The *Concise Oxford Dictionary* defines this term as 'Word of same form as another but different sense', a definition which covers all three terms. The study of the three, in any case, should best be done as part of a unit of conscious language study rather than as fruitless and decontextualized spelling exercises.

'If a teacher stresses the assessment function at the expense of the reply function, this will urge [his/her] pupils towards externally acceptable performances, rather than towards trying to relate new knowledge to old. . . . A classroom dialogue in which sharing predominates over presenting, in which the teacher replies rather than assesses, encourages pupils when they talk and write to bring out existing knowledge to be reshaped by new points of view being presented to them.'

(Douglas Barnes, *From Communication to Curriculum*)

i

IBBY *See* INTERNATIONAL BOARD ON BOOKS FOR YOUNG PEOPLE.

IDEAS BOOKS – The following 'ideas books' will be found useful by English teachers at all grade levels:

Exciting Ideas for Frazzled Teachers, Christine Syme (Holmes McDougall)
Idea Exchange for English Teachers (NCTE)
Kids' Stuff by I. Forte, M. Frank and J. MacKenzie (Incentive)
100+ Ideas for Drama by B. Scher and C. Verrall (Heinemann)
Reading is Response, ed. Ken Watson (St Clair)
Reading is Response: First Supplement, ed. Ken Watson (St Clair)
Reading is Response: Second Supplement, ed. Rob McGregor (St Clair)
Reading is Response: Third Supplement, ed. Wayne Sawyer (St Clair)
Resources I, II, III (AATE)
This Works for Me, ed. E. Furniss and M. Holliday (PETA)
The Whole Word Catalog I, II (Teachers and Writers Collaborative/McGraw-Hill)

An international publication which gives short accounts of work in English teachers' classrooms is *English Teachers at Work*, ed. S. Tchudi (Montclair: Boynton Cook, 1986).

IDIOLECT – The variety of speech used by a particular individual; those aspects of an individual's speech patterns which differ from the speech patterns of his/her group. For example, Professor Harry Messel habitually says, 'the students *which* we teach'.

IDIOM – A familiar enough term which refers to those peculiarities of language characteristic of native speakers of a language. Yet it is common for some of our older, though still widely used, language texts to define 'idiom' in a very narrow way, usually by reference to its lack of correct grammatical construction – for example, Bentley (*English for the Higher School Certificate*) defines idiom as 'A combination of words which is not strictly in accordance with grammatical rules' and Allsopp and Hunt (*Using Better English 5*) define it as 'accepted expressions whose grammatical construction is hard to explain'. (Interestingly, both cite examples which do not accord with their own definitions – Bentley with 'to lead a dog's life' and Allsopp and Hunt in *UBE3* with 'to turn the tables', 'to bury the hatchet', and so on. Idioms yes! Figurative yes! But ungrammatical?) Idiom is an interesting study in the classroom and can lead to an exploration of the difference in idiomatic usage in different English-speaking countries. (Cf. Australian 'to shout', meaning to stand a round of drinks, as in the following exchange, and break down in communication, from *They're a Weird Mob*:

> 'Your turn to shout.'
> 'Why should I shout?'
> 'Because I shouted you.'
> 'I did not hear you shout at me.')

Classes can also collect examples of varieties of idiom from their experience or reading and produce 'translations' to form a class anthology.

IEA *See* INTERNATIONAL ASSOCIATION FOR THE EVALUATION OF EDUCATIONAL ACHIEVEMENT

IFTE *See* INTERNATIONAL FEDERATION FOR THE TEACHING OF ENGLISH.

IMAGINARY ISLAND – A popular unit from Year 5 to Year 10 involves drawing a map of an imaginary island on a blackboard or on sugar paper (every member of the class adds a feature) and then brainstorming possible follow-up activities (e.g. history of the island, tourist brochure for the island, the island's newspaper, election campaign for the island's legislature, reference book on the island's wildlife, etc.). Then each group in the class selects an activity to work on. This one never fails!

Reference

M. Hayhoe and S. Parker have recently produced a computer-based simulation entitled ISLANDS, which takes the form of an adventure game based on the creation of an imaginary island and its exploration. Activities lead out into a wealth of 'island' literature. The program is published by Cambridge Language Arts Software Services Ltd. (q.v.).

IMAGINATIVE RE-CREATION OF LITERATURE – The central problem for teachers of literature is how to extend students' responses beyond their initial unsophisticated reactions without losing touch with these felt responses. How do we extend students' understanding without killing simple pleasure or turning literature teaching into a catalogue of detailed minutiae on plot, character, setting and something called 'theme'? One way is the teaching of literature by re-creation exercises. Through such exercises, students are encouraged to 'get inside' the text, consider it from different angles and extend their understanding of it without resorting to parcels of organized adult information about the text. Exercises can include:

Oral

- Role-play a scene from the novel/play/poem.

- Improvise a scene with a similar setting or similar characters or similar themes.
- Interview a character from the work.
- Improvise being the author and explain the title or significant scenes.
- Put a character on trial.
- Make the work into a radio play and tape it (or a movie and film it).

Written

- Write a diary for a character in the work.
- Change the point of view of particular incidents.
- Write newspaper reports of incidents from the work.
- Change the ending or add another chapter.
- Letters: from one character to another, to the author, to a friend discussing the work.
- Make a film script for incidents from the work.

Other

- Cast the film of the work and justify your choices.
- Make a map/draw the setting of the work.
- Design a cover for a new edition of the work.
- Draw a poster advertising the work.
- Do a comic strip of incidents from the work.
- Make a game of the plot.

References

Michael Benton and Geoff Fox, *Teaching Literature 9–14*, Oxford: Oxford University Press, 1985.

Leslie Stratta, John Dixon and Andrew Wilkinson, *Patterns of Language*, London: Heinemann, 1973.

Ken Watson, Wayne Sawyer and Sandra Bernhardt, 'Imaginative re-creation', *English Curriculum Paper*, NSW Department of Education, 1985.

IMPLIED READER – A notion particularly associated with the work of Wolfgang Iser (*The Implied Reader*, Baltimore: Johns Hopkins, 1974) but present earlier in Wayne Booth's *The Rhetoric of Fiction*, (Chicago: University of Chicago Press, 1961, p. 138) when he writes: '[The author creates] an image of himself and another image of his reader; he makes his reader, as he makes his second self' F. H. Langman stresses the importance for the literary critic of recognizing 'the idea of the reader implied by the work. Not only correct understanding but also evaluation often depends principally upon correct recognition of the implied reader.' Aidan Chambers, in an essay entitled 'The Reader in the Book', has demonstrated the value of the idea of the implied reader when discussing books for children.

See also READER – RESPONSE CRITICISM.

References

Aidan Chambers, 'The Reader in the Book', in N. Chambers (ed.), *The Signal Approach to Children's Books*, Harmondsworth: Kestrel, 1980.

F. H. Langman, 'The idea of the reader in literary criticism', *British Journal of Aesthetics*, January 1967.

Jack Thomson, 'Wolfgang Iser's "The Act of Reading" and the teaching of literature', *English in Australia* 70, December 1984, AATE.

IMPLY/INFER *See* USAGE.

IMPROVISATION – Improvisation usually refers to unscripted drama activity having a concern for coherent structure, development of characterization and emerging from an idea, a theme, movement, plot outline or perhaps snippets of dialogue. Improvisation is prepared through a process of talk and rehearsal with the potential for performance or presentation in some form, even if it is within the class group. Students often start with very little and are asked to work in groups to develop a short play. A theme like 'Today and Yesterday' may lead in a number of directions with the necessity for the students research carefully the topic area they choose to work on. Without doubt students at whatever level of the school will need assistance with the development of who?, what?, where?, when?, how? and why?

John Seely's *Dramakit* provides invaluable suggestions for beginning and continuing the work, particularly with junior students, while Anna Scher and Charles Verrall in their *100+ Ideas for Drama* offer practical suggestions for the inexperienced drama teacher.

The opportunities for drama work in the English classroom are extensive; however, many teachers find it difficult to make the shift from the idea for drama to the preparation of an actual lesson. With this in mind the following theoretical models might be of some use in the planning and development of a sequence in a lesson or in a series of lessons:

Movement ⟶ Mime ⟶ Improvisation

A single lesson might look something like:

(1) Introduction by teacher.
↓
(2) Class broken into smaller groups (individuals, pairs or small groups).
↓
(3) Teacher provides a direction for the lesson in the form of focus materials which leads to student discussion.
↓
(4) Initial practical work – student activity and teacher observation.
↓
(5) Refinement, extension and clarification of activity through teacher/student discussion.
↓
(6) Presentation/Performance. Further whole-class discussion in preparation for next lesson where either a new activity is devised or refinement of current activity is pursued.

This outline is a suggestion only and not something to be taken as a rigid design for all lessons. Performance of student work has a twofold purpose: to allow an opportunity for polished pieces to be seen and to encourage students not involved in the practical work to comment in an informed way upon the work of others.

Parallel Improvisation

A most useful approach to a literary text can often be made through the

improvisation of a parallel scene from a text being studied. By taking an incident from the play or novel a teacher can develop an improvisation with students in their own language as a way into the roles and tease out elements of characterization not immediately obvious from a reading of the surface of the text (*see also* SUB-TEXT). A scene from *Hamlet* or *Macbeth* can be improvised at any stage in the study of the play before returning to the richness of the language of the bard. The result is always a greater appreciation of the quality of the work and a sense of familiarity with what was previously a mystifying experience. **(PR)**
See also SHAKESPEARE; SUB-TEXTING.

References
D. F. Adland, *The Group Approach to Drama*, London: Longman, 1964 (Bks I–V).
Geraldine Brain Siks, *Drama with Children*, New York: Harper & Row, 1977.
Peter Chilver, *Teacher Improvised Drama: A Handbook for Secondary Schools*, London: Bateford, 1978.
Richard Courtney, *The Dramatic Curriculum*, London: Heinemann, 1980.
Kay Hamblin, *Mime: A Playbook of Silent Fantasy*, New York: Dolphin Books, 1978.
Anna Scher and Charles Verrall, *100+ Ideas for Drama*, London: Heinemann Educational, 1975.
John Seely, *In Context*, London: Oxford University Press, 1976; and *Dramakit*, London: Oxford University Press, 1977 (reprinted 1978).
Susan M. Stanley, *Drama without Script*, London: Hodder & Stoughton, 1980.

INDIVIDUALIZED READING PROGRAMMES – These constitute an approach to reading instruction which involves student self-selection and sustained reading of materials, often from a core collection of paperback books. Students work at their own pace, and after completing a book may be requested to choose from a variety of activities which explore the book's themes through writing or some form of artistic or dramatic representation.

Periodically teacher and student engage in a conference which may involve retelling of an extract, discussion and assistance with reading strategies. The teacher maintains records of each student's reading, and students are encouraged to share their responses to books with other children to motivate further reading. **(MRT)**

INFER *See* USAGE: IMPLY/INFER.

INFINITIVE, SPLIT *See* USAGE: SPLIT INFINITIVE.

INFLECTION – A process by which an element is added to the basic form of a word to signal a change in grammatical function, for example tense (walk*ed*), number (boy*s*).

INNER SPEECH – Inner speech is the verbalized thought or speech for one's self which goes on in our heads as we monitor our behaviour, reactions, thoughts, wishes and fantasies. Vygotsky (q.v.) characterizes inner speech as 'a dynamic, shifting, unstable thing fluttering between word and thought' (1962, p. 149). He speaks of the movement from inner speech to outer speech, 'from the motive which engenders a thought to the shaping of the thought, first in inner speech, then in meanings of words, and finally in words' (1962, p. 152).

James Moffett defines authentic writing as 'the focusing and editing of inner speech' and argues that writing must be acknowledged 'as nothing less than thinking, manifested a certain way' (1981a, p. 90). The teaching issues Moffett sees evolving from this definition include setting writing contexts for tapping and focusing inner speech, especially those which involve concentration and meditation. For authentic writing to occur the writer must be aware of his/her own thought processes and feel free to symbolize those processes as they are shaped in inner speech. Through the process of revision and the internalization of various forms of discourse, the writer gradually develops a writing repertoire which both shapes his/her own inner speech and reflects it. The opposite to authentic writing is that which involves the writer meeting some externally imposed form of discourse for purposes at odds with his/her own learning and thinking processes.

Moffett provides a writing programme based on the concept of authentic writing through focused and edited inner speech in *Active Voice* (Moffett, 1981b). For the theoretical outline of the relationship between writing, inner speech and meditation see Moffett's *Coming On Center* (Moffett, 1981a).

The most famous literary example of writing as focused and edited inner speech is James Joyce's *Ulysses*. Joyce's highly complex stream of consciousness technique captures the essence of focused and edited inner speech yet creates a poetic, integrated art form in the process. Even less artistic 'stream of consciousness' writing such as spontaneous monologue writing allows the writer to articulate the flux of his/her mind in order to give form to thought and feeling. All authentic writing involves some selection or abstraction at the point of utterance. It is the focusing of attention which occurs then and in later revision which is central to Moffett's concept of writing as composing the mind. **(RA)**

References

James Moffett, *Coming on Center*, Montclair: Boynton-Cook, 1981a.
James Moffett, *Active Voice*, Montclair: Boynton-Cook, 1981b.
L. S. Vygotsky, *Thought and Language*, Cambridge, Mass.: MIT, 1962.

INQUIRE *See* USAGE: ENQUIRY, INQUIRY.

INTEGRATED DAY – In their book, *The Integrated Day in the Primary School*, Brown and Precious write:

> The integrated day could be described as a school day which is combined into a whole and has a minimum of timetabling. . . . Within this day there is time and opportunity in a planned educative environment for the social, intellectual, emotional, physical and aesthetic growth of the child at [his/her] own rate of development . . . the natural flow of activity, imagination, language, thought and learning which is in itself a continuous process is not interrupted by artificial breaks such as the conventional playtime or subject barriers. The child is encouraged to commit [himself/herself] completely to the work in hand which [he/she] has chosen.

References

M. Brown and N. Precious, *The Integrated Day in the Primary School*, London: Ward Lock, 1968.
Jack Walton (ed.), *The Integrated Day in Theory and Practice*, London: Ward Lock, 1971.

INTEGRATION –

(1) The breaking down of traditional subject barriers, as in integrated Humanities courses.

(2) The combining of the various aspects of English in some way instead of offering pupils a weekly timetable in which English is treated in five or six separate strands (e.g. Poetry on Monday, Novel on Tuesday, etc.).

The fragmented timetable has two clear disadvantages: teachers commonly spend about one-seventh of their time revising what has gone on the week before, and it is often very difficult to make connections between Monday's poetry lesson and Tuesday's novel lesson. (Indeed, research indicates that very few teachers make such connections; that in the pupils' eyes English is often seen as five or six separate subjects.)

The two commonest means of achieving integration of the various facets of English are the thematic unit and the unit built around a core text (usually a novel), but there are many other possibilities: a unit based on a current event (e.g. a flood), a unit based on an excursion, the preparation of a radio documentary programme, and so on. As Leslie Stratta has pointed out:

> a theme is only one way of offering continuity from lesson to lesson. A class working, let's say, on an informal production of *Julius Caesar* has many opportunities for a variety of drama, discussion, reading and writing – provided the teacher is not working within a compartmentalised framework.

Reference

L. Stratta, J. Dixon and A. Wilkinson, *Patterns of Language*, London: Heinemann, 1973.

INTENTIONAL FALLACY – This is the label given to that fallacy of artistic criticism which occurs when we judge a work by measuring it against some supposed (or even known) intention of the author. The problem, if not its label, is one that appears at some time in most senior classrooms, especially when one or two students have been reading a bit of background on a writer being studied.

Apart from being often inapplicable simply because we cannot know the writer's intention (as in the case of Shakespeare), appeal to intention has limited use as a critical tool. Failure of intention, for example, may occasionally produce a better work (Albert S. Gerard has written a famous and very persuasive essay on Wordsworth's 'The Thorn' which depends on the point that if 'The Thorn' is a great lyric, it is precisely because it is not the poem Wordsworth claimed it to be in his 1800 note on the poem). In any case, the whole question of whether writers have failed in their intention is a subjective one depending on the audience – presumably Huxley's brave new world did not look as horrifying to an unemployed Jarrow worker in the 1930s as it did to its middle-class liberal author.

And of course the aesthetic critic would make the logical objection that we ought to be concerned with the qualities of the work as it stands, rather than to some relationship it has to the author's intention.

Having said all that, however, appeal to the author's intention may nevertheless be a useful aid to our senior students floundering in unfamiliar waters. Satire (q.v.) and allegory (q.v.) are particular areas where students might find background reading on intention useful, provided they realize that such reading is not a substitute for study of the text itself and provided that they do judge the writer's intention against the finished product.

INTERNATIONAL ASSOCIATION FOR THE EVALUATION OF EDUCATIONAL ACHIEVEMENT (IEA) – Founded in 1959, the IEA undertook, in the period 1966–73 an empirical study of education in twenty-one countries in six subject areas: Science, Literature, Reading Comprehension, English and French as Foreign Languages, Civic Education. The results are summarized in David Walker, *The IEA Six Subject Survey: An Empirical Study of Education in Twenty-one Countries*, New York: Wiley, 1976. Of particular interest to English teachers is Alan Purves, *Literature Education in Ten Countries*, New York: Wiley, 1973.

INTERNATIONAL BOARD ON BOOKS FOR YOUNG PEOPLE – An organization aiming to encourage high literary and artistic standards in books for young people and to promote international understanding through books for the young. Its headquarters is in Basel, Switzerland. It is responsible for the Hans Christian Andersen Awards (q.v.).

INTERNATIONAL FEDERATION FOR THE TEACHING OF ENGLISH – Formerly the International Steering Committee, the Federation comprises five member countries: United Kingdom, United States, Canada, New Zealand and Australia. Established in the wake of the Dartmouth Seminar (q.v.), it has been responsible for a series of international conferences including the International Conference in Sydney in 1980 and that in Ottawa in 1986.

INTERNATIONAL PHONETIC ALPHABET – A set of graphic symbols designed to allow speech sounds to be labelled unambiguously.

INTERNATIONAL READING ASSOCIATION – An association for the improvement of reading, with headquarters in the United States. The IRA publishes *The Reading Teacher* (elementary level), *Journal of Reading* (secondary and adult levels) and *Reading Research Quarterly* (all levels). Inquiries: IRA, PO Box 8139, Newark, Delaware 19711, USA.

INTERNATIONAL STANDARD BOOK NUMBER / INTERNATIONAL STANDARD SERIALS NUMBER – An international system of book and serial numbering so that each individual publication can be identified.

INTERNATIONAL STEERING COMMITTEE *See* INTERNATIONAL FEDERATION FOR THE TEACHING OF ENGLISH

INTERVIEWING – Interviewing provides practice in a number of different oracy skills and hence is a most useful activity in English. Moreover, when done well, it is a technique difficult to master and students will need to devote time and discussion to planning the most worthwhile questions. This interview preparation also has a number of spin-offs that are most worthwhile in the areas of discussion, writing and group work. Preparation for the interview involves arranging and coding ideas and phrasing questions in precisely the right ways to avoid the short (even monosyllabic) answers.

Subjects for interviewing are limitless: the principal and subject-heads can be interviewed about school policy; the local primary and infants students can be interviewed about a huge range of topics from their expectations of high school to their reading habits; local identities can be interviewed on their area of achievement. Even national sporting, political, musical (etc.) identities can be interviewed – a most useful exercise, especially for older students as it involves an amount of written lead-up through letters and the use of varied social skills in the general arrangement and follow up. A. D. Matthews reports on just such a unit of work with 16-year-old girls in a Day-Continuation College in London ('The Interviewers', in G. Owens and M. Marland, *The Practice of English Teaching*, Blackie: London, 1970). Of course, imaginary interviews can also be among the re-creation exercises used when teaching literature: interviewing characters, the author and so on.

Interviews also have a number of useful follow-up activities:

(1) Class discussion on the effectiveness of the interview and the use of communication.
(2) Transcribing sections of a taped interview and answering questions related to developing listening (q.v.) skills.
(3) Written reports of interviews involve work in note-taking and synthesizing, paraphrasing, adjustment of tone to audience and the mechanics of mixing direct with indirect speech.

INTONATION – The way in which intonation affects meaning can be shown by asking students to say 'I said that' to mean: (a) Yes, it was I who said that; (b) Did I really say that? (c) I told you before. You've not been listening; (d) I mean that one, not the other one. Other sentences can be used in similar ways.

INVENTED SPELLING – Donald Graves argues strongly for the need to start writers into real writing as early as possible. Basic to this is the strategy of invented spelling in which young writers are encouraged to spell words any way they wish with any letters which they know. Graves contends that children need only six consonants (any six) to begin writing. Over-concern with correct spelling will hold up the beginning writer while the sooner he/she begins writing, the sooner he/she will master such mechanics as spelling, because it is writing itself that generates the concern to 'get it right'. *Donald Graves in Australia*, R. D. Walshe (ed.) (PETA, 1981) and *No Better Way to Teach Writing*, ed. by Jan Turbill (PETA, 1982), contain case studies on invented spelling which show the gradual development of young writers' ability to master conventional spelling as they write stories.

IQ TESTING – This term is usually, though with limited accuracy, applied to group tests of verbal intelligence which were used in periods of selective schooling in an attempt to predict those pupils who would succeed in terms of an academic curriculum. (In England and Wales they were a major constituent of the 11+ examination.) Even in a comprehensive educational system they have been used to determine class placement in secondary school. Their use for such purposes is highly suspect and now largely discredited.

The arguments against such tests, once popular as a means of determining class placement, are strong: they discriminate against children whose first language is not English; the validity of the tests themselves can be questioned; they discriminate against the 'late developer'; they enshrine the notion of fixed intellectual capacity. IQ test scores often vary quite markedly over a period of time; in one case known to the editors two parallel versions of one test yielded 98 and 118 IQ respectively when administered a month apart. It seems that the development of intellectual powers occurs at different rates in different children, and that it is affected both by early experiences and by the quality of schooling. Thus it is dangerous to attempt to predict the ultimate level of an individual's intellectual attainment, and unjust to chart a child's course through secondary school on the basis of such a prediction.

This is not to deny that used more subtly as a diagnostic instrument such tests can provide valuable evidence about individual children whose educational achievement may be below their full potential. Such IQ testing will normally employ a battery of tests rather than rely upon Verbal Intelligence Tests (VIQs) alone.

See also MIXED-ABILITY TEACHING; STREAMING.

IRONY – Irony is often a difficult concept for students to grasp in context. Often the literary terms entries in this book have argued that a blanket term (e.g. 'allegory') is probably of sufficient use in most classrooms when describing a literary 'tactic' rather than complicating matters by dealing pedantically with all the sub-categories which such a term includes (in the case of 'allegory', this might include 'fable', 'parable', 'exemplum', 'apologue', etc.). This is not the case with irony. Its basic problem is that it is already used as a blanket term for so many diverse things that students may have problems deciding what it is you mean this time when you say that such-and-such a statement is ironic. In this case, distinctions do need to be made, defined and pointed out to students.

First, there is that sense of 'irony' which refers to saying one thing and meaning its opposite – that use of 'irony' as a synonym for 'sarcasm' (e.g. Antony's 'And Brutus is an honourable man').

Further, there is that sense of 'irony' which we mean when we refer to outcomes or situations as being 'ironic'. Lady Catherine de Burgh in *Pride and Prejudice* visits Elizabeth in order to warn her off Darcy, but the outcome of her visit is that Elizabeth and Darcy are drawn closer together. Such an outcome we would describe as 'ironic'. There is an irony in the whole situation of Tiresias in *Oedipus Rex* – Tiresias being blind and yet 'seeing' more than anyone else in the play.

There is, moreover, the dramatic irony that occurs because we have more knowledge than the characters in a work, and this leads us to see their words in a different light from them. Othello's words to Iago:

> for I know thou'rt full of love and honesty,
> And weigh'st thy words before thou giv'st them breath

are doubly ironic in this sense – the first of the lines we see as simply wrong, yet the second is correct, but in a way that Othello does not suspect.

Students need to be made aware that the term is used for all these situations (and more) and need to be aware of which meaning is intended when. Picking up the irony at all is the central problem for students as it depends so often on tone (q.v.).

-ISE/-IZE *See* USAGE.

ITS/IT'S *See* USAGE.

'It is through the enormous variety of dialogue with others that we gather together the linguistic resources to dialogue in our heads . . . Restrict the nature and quality of that dialogue and ultimately you restrict thinking capacity.'

(Harold Rosen,
Language, the Learner and the School)

j

JARGON – The technical language developed and used by those who participate in some kind of specialized field. Some ideas for a unit of work on jargon could include:

(1) Have the students collect lists of jargon from newspaper and magazine articles: legal, political, sporting, and so on.
(2) Have them make a list of jargon of their parents' (brothers', sisters', own) occupations.
(3) Make lists of the jargon of various fields: sporting, hobbies, various subcultures as well as the more 'visible' fields of politics, law and academia.
(4) Take well-known stories and rewrite them, or interpret them, in the jargon of particular groups (this has been done for 'Miss Muffet' – interpreted from the viewpoint of literary critics, psychologists, sociologists and so on. Frederick C. Crews' *The Pooh Perplex* is an excellent resource for this activity. He parodies (q.v.) various schools of literary criticism by having 'them' interpret *Winnie the Pooh.* The book is a rich source of literary critics' jargon).
(5) In discussing the problems of jargon, don't forget its advantages. Could the class give a radio broadcast of a cricket match and not use any of the game's jargon? What are the disadvantages of trying to do so?

JOURNAL WRITING – One aspect of writing development that has caught on in recent years is the student's keeping of a personal journal. The Writing Commission of the Third International Conference in 1980 began the session on journal writing by defining it as (among other things) 'unassessed, extended, personal writing'. This is a useful starting point for discussing the various ways in which the journal can be approached.

Generally, the journal is a book kept separately from other class books and written in regularly during a time set aside in class for that purpose – each week, each day, whatever is decided. Topics and content are free choice, though many teachers supply topics for those students unable to become inspired on any particular day. Many teachers also set a minimum quantity of writing for each journal session – the basic principle of the journal being that students learn to write by writing and that it is quantity that leads to quality.

The question of audience is important. Ideally, journals are pieces of private writing, with the teacher only doing a close reading if invited to do so. However, a number of factors may preclude attainment of this ideal – the teacher's desire to check minimum requirements, desire to preclude unacceptable language or other offensive material, or even assessment policy (more on this later). Arrangements can therefore range between: totally private journals; generally private journals but with the teacher telling the class in advance that he or she will read a particular entry; two journals – one private, one for general reading; using the journal for two-way written correspondence between teacher and student.

As the journal is meant to be extended personal-choice writing, ideally it should not be assessed. But if schools do insist on assessing this kind of expressive writing (in Britton's sense of this word), a number of possible alternatives exist: assessing only on work done (i.e. if every entry is there, full marks!); telling kids in advance that a particular entry will be marked (but even then, written responses please, not corrections); asking kids to choose the two or three journals *they* would like marked and providing the opportunity for these to be polished before presentation.

Finally, it is worthwhile noting that the journal has two aspects and consideration of these should lead teachers to develop their own strategies for the use of journals:

(1) The journal is an end in itself, a 'self-discovery' mechanism in which students can keep a significant record, an objectively embodied personal experience available for reflection; that is, it is a learning process.
(2) The journal is a means to an end – better writing. If quantity does lead to quality and if expressive writing is, as Nancy Martin says, the 'seed-bed' from which all else grows, then extended free writing will lead to more and better writing.

For important writing on the journal, see William Green, 'Writing and learning – the idea of the journal', *Language Development – Writing*, Paper of the WA Working Party on Writing, Commission B, Strand B, for the Third International Conference, 1980 (January); John Payne, 'More and better writing – through journals', in K. D. Watson and R. D. Eagleson (eds), *English in Secondary Schools: Today and Tomorrow* (Sydney: ETA of NSW, 1977).

See also Marjorie Frank, *If you're trying to teach kids how to write, you've gotta have this book!* (Nashville, Tennessee: Incentive, 1979).

k

KATE GREENAWAY MEDAL – Named after the distinguished nineteenth-century illustrator and writer of verse for children, this British Library Association Award honours the most distinguished work in the illustration of children's books:

1978 – Janet Ahlberg for *Each Peach Pear Plum*
1979 – Jan Pienkowski for *The Haunted House*
1980 – Quentin Blake for *Mister Magnolia*
1981 – Charles Keeping for *The Highwayman*
1982 – Michael Foreman for *Long Neck and Thunderfoot*
1983 – Michael Foreman for *The Sleeping Beauty and other favourite fairy tales.*
1984 – Anthony Browne for *Gorilla*
1985 – E. Le Cain for *Hiawatha's Childhood*
1986 – Fiona French for *Snow White in New York*

KINGMAN COMMITTEE *See* KINGMAN REPORT

KINGMAN REPORT – The Committee of Inquiry into the Teaching of English Language, appointed by the Secretary of State for Education and Science in England and Wales, and chaired by Sir John Kingman, Vice Chancellor of the University of Bristol, reported in April 1988. In response to its terms of reference it recommended a model of the English language with which all teachers should become familiar. The model was divided into four parts:

Part I dealt with the forms of the English language (sounds, letters, words, sentences) and how these relate to meaning.

Part II explored how communication and understanding is established between speakers and listener, writers and readers.

Part III dealt with how children acquire and develop language.

Part IV concerned itself with variation in language and how English has changed over time.

The Report goes into some detail over the implications for the classroom and for teacher education of the adoption of such a model. In Part I of the model especially, a number of technical linguistic terms are used and the more important ones of these are included in this book in their appropriate alphabetical listing.

The Report explicitly rejects any idea that children should be returned to traditional grammar teaching but does argue that they should understand 'the rules and conventions' of English. They 'should learn the structure of language just as they learn about the structure of the atom'. They should also learn to write clearly and accurately in Standard English (q.v.) though their own language should in no sense be devalued in the process. On this, the Report explicitly states that 'it is indefensible to make a pupil feel at any time and in any way ashamed of his or her accent'.

One of its most far-reaching proposals affects the setting of attainment targets for children at the ages of 7, 11, and 16, and these are spelt out in some detail in the body of the Report. Testing is seen as a means towards identifying what help a child needs and, for this purpose, testing at age 7 is seen as being essential.

Other important proposals concern teacher education especially in the light of the continuing situation that more than one in four of those teaching English in secondary schools have no qualifications in the subject beyond O level. They call for all English specialists entering teaching to have a first degree in English by the end of the century and for a linguistic component by that time in all university first degree courses in English. All primary and secondary English specialists are to have a course in language in which much of the time should be spent on 'direct tuition of knowledge about language as proposed in this report' (that is the 'model' described above). Furthermore all trainee teachers, not just English specialists, should have a 'short coherent course in language study'. Such work on language should continue into the probationary year and form a major element of in-service education. This should be supported by the setting up of a National Language Project along the lines of the National Oracy Project (q.v.) and the National Writing Project (q.v.).

The Kingman Report should be compared with its immediate predecessor, the Bullock Report (q.v.). Immediately after Kingman had reported, the Secretary of State announced the setting up of a new working group on the English curriculum to be chaired by Brian Cox, Professor of English Literature at the University of Manchester. Professor Cox was a member of the Kingman Committee and his new group will be considering literature as well as language and making recommendations for the place and content of English within the new proposed national curriculum for England and Wales.

Reference

Report of the Committee of Inquiry into English Language Teaching, London: HMSO, 1988.

KNOWLEDGE ABOUT LANGUAGE (KAL) – A term becoming widely used (1987) to denote the actual teaching about language as a human activity that might take place in classrooms. The issue remains a contentious one although many teachers would agree that there ought to be an element of such teaching in English courses, though not if it implies a return to an approach based on traditional grammar teaching. (*See* GRAMMAR).

Planned courses in Knowledge about Language may also include work in Language Awareness, often bringing together study of other languages, including Latin and Greek, to illuminate a pupil's awareness and understanding of his or her mother tongue.
See also GRAMMAR; LANGUAGE, CONSCIOUS STUDY OF.

'Most children, by the time they are ready to begin school, know the full contents of an introductory text in transformational grammar.'

(Roger Brown, Introduction to 1968 edition of Moffett's *Teaching the Universe of Discourse*)

L

LANGUAGE ACQUISITION – Of the various theories put forward to explain how children learn language, three have had considerable influence:

(1) The behaviourist view, associated particularly with B. F. Skinner, sees language acquisition as a pattern of stimulus–response–reinforcement. (*See* BEHAVIOURISM.)
(2) The nativist view, put forward by Noam Chomsky, which suggests that the child has a highly specific predisposition – 'a language acquisition device (LAD)' – which enables him/her to process the language heard and extract the rules from it.
(3) The interactional view, presented by M. A. K. Halliday (q.v.) in his *Learning How to Mean*. Halliday argues that what the child is born with is not an LAD but a sense of communicating, and an ability to communicate with others. In all other respects language learning is a social process: the child learns language through interaction with those around him or her.

Of the three, it is the interactional model that best fits the evidence.

There is insufficient space here to give more than the briefest outline of language development. For a more detailed picture, the reader is referred to the references below.

Halliday's intensive observation of one child suggests that children begin with a proto-language of two levels only: meaning and sound. There is no lexicogrammar (i.e. vocabulary and syntax) intermediate between the meaning and the sound. Under the pressure of interaction with those around them, children gradually abandon this proto-language in favour of the mother tongue, initially by means of one-word and two-word utterances.

From this stage until the age of 5 progress is very rapid. Commonly children first learn a correct form – 'I ran' – and later, having internalized the rules governing the past tense of most English verbs, overgeneralize and begin to say 'I runned'. The rate of children's progress is associated with the quality of the conversation they experience with adults, but by the age of 5 normal children have internalized almost all the structures of the language. By the age of 8, they have achieved almost complete mastery of the phonological and morphological features of the language. Semantic development, of course, continues throughout childhood and adolescence, the main direction of growth being from the concrete to the abstract.

What aspects of mother-tongue development are susceptible to the planned intervention of the teacher? It would seem that syntactic, phonological and morphological development occur with least deliberate attention; direct intervention by the teacher, such as the teaching of explicit knowledge of sentence structure, is likely to be a waste of time. On the other hand, semantic development, and a sense of the ways in which the written language differs from the spoken, will be encouraged if children are read to by the teacher (at both primary and secondary levels) and if they are encouraged to read widely themselves. Further, an aspect of language growth that has not so far been mentioned is the growth of awareness of the ways in which language is affected by the demands of the social context (*see* CONTEXT; REGISTER); in this area the teacher can do much – particularly through activities like role-play – to make pupils more sensitive to the demands of the situation. In a more general sense, language development (particularly growth in the ability to handle abstractions) will be aided by so structuring the learning situation that pressure is put on students to expand their linguistic horizons. For example, a Year 6 or Year 7 class might be involved in speaking, listening, reading and writing about a relatively concrete topic like 'Bushrangers'; a Year 10, on the other hand, might be asked to explore a more abstract theme like 'Violence'.

The fundamental point that has to be made about teaching the mother tongue in school is that teachers should utilize those processes of learning that have served children so well up to the time they enter school. Five-year-olds have an astonishing proficiency in spoken English, and that proficiency has come about by using language *for real purposes in real situations*. Teachers, then, should avoid the kind of language teaching that deals with fragments of language divorced from purpose and context, and should place children in situations where they are using language for real purposes. For most of the time, then, the focus is not on the language itself but on *meaning*.

In addition to the references listed below, teachers of primary and junior secondary classes are urged to read Connie and Harold Rosen's illuminating *The Language of Primary School Children*, Harmondsworth: Penguin, 1973.
See also CONTEXT; LANGUAGE, CONSCIOUS STUDY OF; PERSONAL GROWTH MODEL; SKILLS MODEL.

References

Courtney Cazden, *Child Language and Education*, New York: Holt Rinehart, 1972.

M. A. K. Halliday, 'How Children Learn Language', in K. D. Watson and R. D. Eagleson (eds), *English in Secondary Schools: Today and Tomorrow*, Sydney: ETA of NSW, 1977.

M. A. K. Halliday, *Learning How to Mean*, London: Arnold, 1975.

Ken Watson, *English Teaching in Perspective*, Milton Keynes: Open University Press, 1987, esp. Ch. 2 and Appendix A.

LANGUAGE ACROSS THE CURRICULUM – This is a concept reflecting a body of theory which suggests that pupils (and, indeed, all of us) acquire most of their knowledge through the use of one or more of the four language modes

(Reading, Writing, Talking, Listening). Given that the language capability of the individual plays a significant role in the learning process, it follows that teachers of all subjects should be aware of the potential of language as an instrument of learning and seek to maximize the efficiency of its use in all learning situations.

Language across the Curriculum is therefore concerned with, first, the ways in which language can be used to acquire knowledge and, second, the ways in which pupils' facility with language can be increased.

All schools, primary and secondary, have always had language policies. These have generally been informal and unstated. Since the work of James Britton (q.v.), Douglas Barnes (q.v.) and others in the London Association for the Teaching of English, and the official sanction given that research by the Bullock Report (q.v.), many schools and educational authorities, in the United Kingdom and elsewhere, have sought to devise and implement more formal language policies.

The purpose of language policies, whether informal or formal, must be to increase the awareness among teachers of *all* subjects of the English language as a teaching/learning tool, thus encouraging the maximum, efficient use of the potential which language offers. **(PS)**

References

D. Barnes, *From Communication to Curriculum*, London: Penguin, 1976.
D. Barnes, J. Britton and H. Rosen, *Language, the Learner and the School*, London: Penguin, 1971.
J. Britton, *Language and Learning*, London: Penguin, 1970.
Education Department of South Australia, *Language across the Curriculum: An Experiment in Learning*, Adelaide, 1977.
M. Marland, *Language across the Curriculum*, London: Heinemann, 1977.
N. Martin, *Language Policies in Schools: Some Aspects and Approaches*, London: Ward Lock, 1977.
I. Robertson, *Language across the Curriculum: Four Case Studies*, London: Methuen Educational, 1980.
M. Torbe, *Language across the Curriculum: Guidelines for Schools*, London: Ward Lock Educational, 1976.
M. Torbe (ed.), *Language Policies in Action*, London: Ward Lock Educational, 1980.

LANGUAGE ARTS – One of the journals of the National Council of Teachers of English in the United States. The emphasis is on primary teaching, but teachers of secondary classes will find much to interest them. Subscription inquiries: NCTE, 1111 Kenyon Road, Urbana, Illinois 61801, USA.

LANGUAGE AWARENESS *See* KNOWLEDGE ABOUT LANGUAGE.

LANGUAGE, CONSCIOUS STUDY OF – As noted above (*see* LANGUAGE ACQUISITION) language learning in school seems to proceed best when the focus is on meaning and purpose rather than on the language itself. This does not mean, however, that the conscious study of language has no place in the

English classroom. As pupils get older, they should be growing in awareness of the language itself, and particularly of the ways in which the choice of language is often the crucial factor in achieving one's ends.

Language in Use (q.v.) by Doughty *et al.* has many suggestions for profitable language work aiming to develop awareness of and sensitivity to the language. Here are some others:

(1) Playing with language – riddles, word games and so on. For specific suggestions *see* WORD GAMES.
(2) Language investigations – pupils can collect examples of euphemisms (q.v.), tautology (q.v.), ambiguous newspaper headlines (*see* NEWSPAPERS). They can investigate how widespread are certain pronunciations (*see* PRONUNCIATION) and other controversial usages (*see* e.g. DIFFERENT FROM/ TO/ THAN).
(3) Dictionary work:
    (a) Norman Hunter's *Professor Branestawm's Dictionary* (Puffin) contains humorous definitions, for example *raucous*, uncooked swear word; *igloo*, Eskimo lavatory. Have pupils make up humorous definitions for unknown words and then look those words up in the dictionary.
    (b) Have pupils make up dictionaries of football terms, surfing slang and so on.
    (c) Older pupils can become amateur lexicographers, carrying out some of the language investigations suggested above in the manner of the makers of dictionaries.
(4) Many of the activities suggested in the entries on ADVERTISING and NEWSPAPERS involve the conscious study of language.
(5) A unit of work on animal communication (q.v.) can provide useful insights as well as giving plenty of opportunity for purposeful talking, reading and writing. A good text for this and other language work is Ian Forsyth and Kathleen Wood, *Language and Communication I*, London: Longman, 1978.
(6) Senior pupils will find investigations of the language of politics (a good one at election time!), the language of religion, the language of bureaucracy, the language of science, worthwhile. An important area of exploration is the language of propaganda: the attempt to pin unfavourable labels on opponents (*commo*, *fascist*); the constant resort to stereotypes (the *Jew*, the *communist*); the clichés (*Business is business*); the slogans (*Ein Volk, ein Reich, ein Fuhrer!*). A useful source of material for seniors is R. D. Eagleson (ed.), *Wordswork*, Sydney: Methuen, 1977 (though as a class text is too difficult for all but the ablest).

While there is little value in teaching pupils a grammatical system (*see* GRAMMAR AND WRITING), there are two grammatical concepts which seem to be of use to writers at *the revision stage* of writing. These are agreement of verb and subject in number (*see* VERB AGREEMENT) and sequence of tense (*see* TENSE). When the need arises, then, these concepts should be taught.
See also GRAMMAR POEMS.

LANGUAGE EXPERIENCE APPROACH – 'The essence of the language

experience approach is the use of the language and thinking of the learner as a foundation for reading instruction. Each learner's language and personal experiences are used to create reading materials that help show the reader the relationship between written language and [his/her] already familiar oral language' (Hall, 1981, p. 1).

Typically, the teacher of young beginning readers who employs a language experience approach, introduces the whole class, a group or an individual to a real and vivid experience. Such experiences may range in complexity and type (e.g. an excursion to the seaside; making pikelets in the classroom; observing the playground on a windy or rainy day; taking turns while blindfolded to feel objects with different textures; performing a science experiment, etc.). After the experience, the children are encouraged to talk about aspects of the experience, and to respond to it in various ways: through drama and movement, discussion of photographs or examination of objects collected at the time of the experience, listening to evocative music, drawing and painting, and so on. Each individual then considers his or her own personal response to the experience and dictates or writes a caption, sentence or whole 'story' which becomes that child's own instructional reading material. Because the content and language structures are the child's own, the predictability of the text and the motivation to read and use the written words is very high.

The principles on which the language experience approach is based can be extended in a variety of ways, including the following:

(1) Experience-based reading programme. Here, the teacher ensures that children in the programme have a range of experiences of a particular topic, and that they have ample opportunity for oral discussion of their experiences. They are then encouraged to write and read widely in that particular area.
(2) Early reading in unfamiliar content areas. The principles of the language experience approach can be applied most effectively to the situation where competent readers first encounter the written material of an unfamiliar content area. The pupil who has never studied science before, can be provided with the appropriate background experiences through participation in an experiment and can be encouraged to use the conventional language of science to describe the steps in the experiment. In this way, the pupil is better equipped for the reading and writing of scientific reports.
(3) Reading programme for disabled readers. Since the process of becoming a proficient reader is the same regardless of the age or experience of the learner, the advantages and procedures of the language experience approach are just as applicable to the older non-proficient reader as they are to the young beginning reader. **(MRT)**

Reference

Mary Anne Hall, *Teaching Reading as a Language Experience*, 3rd edn, Columbus: Merrill, 1981.

LANGUAGE, FUNCTIONS OF – Probably the best-known models of language functions are those developed by M. A. K. Halliday (q.v.) and James Britton (q.v.). Halliday's 'relevant models of language' are those, he argues, with which the normal child is endowed by the time he/she goes to school. These are:

(1) The *instrumental* model – language used as a means of getting things done ('I want a banana').
(2) The *regulatory* model – language used to regulate the behaviour of others ('That's not allowed').
(3) The *interactional* model – language used in the interaction between the self and others.
(4) The *personal* model – the child's awareness of language as a form of his/her own individuality.
(5) The *heuristic* model – language used as a means of investigating reality, of learning about things.
(6) The *imaginative* model – using language to create an environment, not to learn about how things are but to make them as one feels inclined.
(7) The *representational* model – language as a means of communicating about something, of expressing propositions.

Halliday goes on to argue that the representational model is the only model (but not of course the only function) of language that many adults have, yet for the child it is not one of the earliest to come into prominence and does not become a dominant function until much later stages of development.

An understanding of Britton's function categories requires first a familiarity with his concepts of the participant and spectator roles of language. Language in the participant role is the language we use to get things done in the world (informing, persuading, requesting, urging, planning), while language in the spectator role is the language we use when we are not concerned with events taking place in the here-and-now (day-dreaming aloud, chatting about experiences, telling stories, writing poetry).

Corresponding to these two roles of language, Britton postulates the two function categories of *poetic* (for spectator role language) and *transactional* (for participant role language).

The poetic function is characterized by the utterance being an immediate end in itself, (i.e. a verbal artifact) and with attention to the forms of the language – thus novels, plays and poems are all examples of the poetic function, as is oral storytelling.

The transactional function is characterized by the utterance being a means to an end with its form being dictated primarily by the desire to achieve that end efficiently.

Britton goes on to postulate a third, and most crucial, language function – the *expressive* function. Expressive language is 'language close to the speaker' – our principal means of exchanging opinions, attitudes, beliefs and the language in which we rehearse the growing points of our formulation and analysis of experience. Moreover, argues Britton, it is expressive language which is the centre point of language, a kind of matrix from which language grows towards the other two functions (expressive writing, for example, says Britton's colleague Nancy Martin, 'is the seed bed from which more specialised and differentiated kinds of writing can grow – towards the greater explicitness of the transactional or the more conscious shaping of the poetic'). Britton's model of language functions thus looks like this:

Transactional – Expressive – Poetic

The function categories arose in the classifying of 2,200 written scripts of children of 11 to 18 years in all subjects from schools in England and Wales, under the auspices of the Schools Council Project (q.v.).

References

James Britton, 'What's the use? A schematic account of language functions', *Educational Review*, 23 (3), 1971.

M. A. K. Halliday, 'Relevant models of language', *Educational Review*, 22 (1): November 1969.

LANGUAGE IN USE – As part of the Schools Council (UK) Program in Linguistics and English, a team led by Peter Doughty developed *Language in Use*, consisting of 110 units, each of which provides the teacher with an outline for a sequence of lessons. The units are grouped into three divisions: the internal organization of language; the use of language by the individual to order and interpret his/her experience of the world; the individual's use of language to initiate, maintain and control relationships with others. This is a valuable resource for teachers, but it does require time and effort to turn a unit outline into a unit ready for classroom presentation.

References

Peter Doughty, John Pearce and Geoffrey Thornton, *Language in Use*, London: Arnold, 1971.

Peter and Anne Doughty, *Using Language in Use*, London: Arnold, 1974.

LANGUAGE STUDY *See* LANGUAGE, CONSCIOUS STUDY OF.

LANGUAGE VARIATION *See* DIALECT; IDIOLECT; REGISTER.

LEARNING CENTRES – A learning centre or station within a classroom is a location which provides a compactly arranged, self-contained, set of materials and directions aimed at introducing, developing or reinforcing a skill or concept, providing diagnostic information or developing attitudes and interests. Learning centres provide opportunities for individuals or small groups of pupils to choose from clearly defined objectives and then select from appropriate, specified paths towards their achievement.

This involves further selection among a range of multi-level multi-media materials and activities designed to meet the needs and strengths of every pupil. Provision of opportunities for pupil self-evaluation assists in encouraging students to take initiatives in their own learning experiences in scheduling, beginning and completing learning tasks.

A reading centre may focus on reading for pleasure, the development of research skills, reading to follow directions, read along activities with audio tapes, reading games, and so on. They are often effectively used as part of a systematic approach to teaching through group work activities.

References

L. F. Waynant, *Learning Centers*, New York: McGraw-Hill, 1974.
L. F. Waynant, *Learning Centers II*, New York: McGraw-Hill, 1977.

LEAVIS, FRANK RAYMOND (1895–1978) – English literary, educational and social critic, affecting both the Left (Raymond Williams, Richard Hoggart, Raymond Southall) and the Right ('The Black Papers', the later David Holbrook) in English intellectual life. For a period, during which many of the present English teachers were trained, Leavis had a strong influence, not yet exhausted, on thinking about English.

Thought by some as a 'New Critic' (he wasn't), by others as an 'Establishment' figure (he wasn't), and by others as an élitist (sometimes true), Leavis defies classification. He stood for the disciplined application of intelligence and common sense to the reading of literature. His analyses of particular works, and his persuasive dismissals of the trivial, still stand inspection. More debatable are his almost Messianic belief in the uniquely 'civilizing' effect of English Studies, his moral assumptions, and his vision of an 'organic society'. He remains a critic more worth reading than most, so long as one remembers that other approaches to English need also to be explored. Reading 'post-structuralism' (q.v.) only confirms the merits of Leavis. **(NJW)**

References

F. R. Leavis, *The Living Principle*, London: Chatto & Windus, 1977.
F. R. Leavis, *The Common Pursuit*, London: Peregrine, 1962.
F. R. Leavis (ed.), *A Selection from Scrutiny*, 2 vols, Cambridge: Cambridge University Press, 1968.
Francis Mulhern, *The Moment of 'Scrutiny'*, London: Verso, 1981.
William Walsh, *F. R. Leavis*, London: Chatto & Windus, 1980.

LEGEND *See* MYTH, LEGEND, FOLK TALE.

LEND, LOAN *See* USAGE.

LESS/FEWER *See* USAGE.

LEVELS OF LANGUAGE *See* REGISTER.

LEXICAL MEANING – The denotation or dictionary meaning of a content word.

LIE, LAY *See* USAGE.

LIKE *See* USAGE.

LINGUISTIC CRITICISM/CRITICAL LINGUISTICS – These are terms coined by Roger Fowler and his associates to define the sort of books given in the References section below (see for full information). This is an 'impure' form of linguistics, owing much to the Halliday of *Language as Social Semiotic* (London: Arnold, 1978).

The essential point is that language (literary and 'ordinary') is read in its social and interpersonal context, and the ways in which language does things for us or to us are examined. For example, in *Language and Control*, the power relationships between interviewer and interviewee are shown to be realized in the language.

While Fowler and others kept technical terminology to a minimum, it is not all directly teachable. However, if you are exploring language in use in context, along the lines suggested by Leslie Stratta, a reading of Fowler can alert you to points in the language you might otherwise overlook, or find hard to describe.

To quote Fowler, here are studies which are 'socially responsible and progressive, and educationally useful'. **(NJW)**

References

R. Fowler, *Literature as Social Discourse*, Bloomington Indiana: University Press, 1981.
R. Fowler *et al.*, *Language and Control*, London: Routledge & Kegan Paul, 1979.
G. Kress and R. Hodge, *Language as Ideology*, London: Routledge & Kegan Paul, 1979.
L. Stratta, A. Wilkinson and J. Dixon, *Patterns of Language*, London: Heinemann, 1973.

LISTENING – There is not nearly the volume of research into listening that there is into the other areas of language development (reading, writing, speaking). What research we do have (such as that carried out by the Oracy Research Unit in England) suggests that we work best if we adopt similar principles to those that appear to work well in those other areas, namely, we should aim to create real language situations that force students to listen well and also to make them aware of the listening process, rather than to train and then test decontextualized listening 'skills'. The Oracy Research Unit (*see* Wilkinson *et al.*, below) has pointed out the elements that we should be aware of when considering a child's development as a listener:

(1) Intonation – can the child deduce meanings from the intonation of a question or statement?
(2) Register (q.v.) – can the child discriminate between registers?
(3) Relationship – can the child judge the deep structure of a spoken statement and the intentions and motivations of the speakers?
(4) Prediction and probability – can the child predict what is to come?
(5) Content – does the child understand exactly the concepts presented?

Small-group work (q.v.) is one means of training students to listen carefully to one another; it is vital, too, that the teacher shows himself/herself to be a good listener. The teacher should endeavour to build up a mutually supportive classroom atmosphere. An awareness of the listening process can be created by encouraging students to look at speech situations from various points of view, such as tone, relationship between speaker and audience, purpose, pitch, stress, intonation. Speech situations for study could include:

- sermons (from TV and radio);
- phone-in advice on radio (e.g. gardening, 'pet vet', child medicine, suburban wildlife, building and maintenance problems are all currently topics of phone-in programmes);
- sports commentaries (racing, football, cricket); a radio commentary could be compared with the television (q.v.) commentary of the same match;
- disc jockeys from various radio stations could be compared;
- 'great speeches' (a number of these are available on record and tape);
- newscasts (again, radio and TV coverage of the same incident could be compared).

Other activities:

- Have pupils give directions around the school or instructions to make something. Can others follow the directions?
- Can a pupil draw an object from a description spoken by another pupil?
- Have class listen to factual and slanted reports of something and have them discuss the differences, e.g. read a report from the journal *Choice* and an advertisement for the same product.
- Prepare a radio play with sound effects.

See also PERSONAL GROWTH MODEL OF ENGLISH.

References

A. Adams and E. Jones, *Now Hear This*, Edinburgh: Oliver & Boyd, 1987.

L. Stratta and A. Wilkinson, 'Listening and the teaching of English', in K. D. Watson and R. D. Eagleson (eds), *English in Secondary Schools: Today and Tomorrow*, Sydney: ETA of NSW, 1977.

A. Wilkinson, L. Stratta and P. Dudley, *The Quality of Listening*, London: Macmillan, 1974.

LISTENING TO CHILDREN READ –

(1) As a teaching strategy

This activity has serious limitations as a teaching strategy. It tends to develop ineffective reading habits and to limit the amount of reading a child may do during a reading instruction period. Research indicates that ineffective reading habits may be learnt if the teacher interrupts to correct inaccuracies in word identification or omission when the overall meaning of the text is not violated because the child may become overly concerned with the correct identification of every word. Teacher interruptions have been found to be negatively correlated both with young children's comprehension of orally read text, and with their willingness to attempt to read unfamiliar words in the text.

(2) As a performance skill

The teaching of oral reading is most appropriately regarded as a secondary or performance skill, and unless they are reading text well within their ability, children should be encouraged to read and rehearse the text first, and confer with the teacher or a peer about pronunciation, interpretation, expressiveness and presentation, before sharing it with an audience.

(3) As an evaluative procedure

Listening to individual children read is a well-established means of diagnosis of the individual strengths and weaknesses of a reader. This may be carried out in considerable diagnostic detail as a miscue analysis (q.v.) or, if that procedure is not familiar to the teacher, a more superficial 'running record' (Clay, 1979) of the child's preferred reading strategies and meaning-maintaining behaviours may be made as the child first reads a text known to her, and then a previously unsighted text. **(MRT)**

See also ORAL READING; READING MISCUE INVENTORY; ROUND ROBIN READING.

References

Marie M. Clay, *A Diagnostic Survey of Early Reading Difficulties*, 2nd edn, Auckland: Heinemann, 1979.

D. Spiegel and C. Rogers, 'Teacher responses to miscues during oral reading by second grade students', *Journal of Educational Research*, 74 (1), 1980: 8–12.

LITERACY, CONDITIONS OF LEARNING – This is a schematic representation of a theory of how learning to control oral and written forms of language comes about. It is a 'model' which attempts to explain the subtle, complex, elegant processes which underlie language learning. In the jargon of educational psychology it is a 'construct' – an artificial creation which serves to make concrete something which does not exist in the real world so that it can be talked about. Like all constructs it runs the risk of being reified. When this happens the words inside the little boxes take on a separate identity of their own. It is only a short step then to turn it into a stage or developmental model, e.g. 'First I concentrate on immersion then I'll develop high expectations'.

'It's ready to move to the approximation stage of learning.'

Please do not do this to it.

Rather, regard it as a metaphor which helps clarify some of the mysteries of why and how learning occurs. **(BC)**

LITERATURE AND LITERACY – Research into reading development and into children's own storytelling is increasingly suggesting that young children are capable of quite sophisticated narrative moves and thus, for their reading, teachers need not necessarily choose 'simple' texts nor controlled-vocabulary basal readers (q.v.). Such readers will not match the expectations of or competences with language that children have. Increasingly it is being found that learning to read is not first a matter of learning the processes but is tied to what is read. Hence we have the advocacy of 'literacy through literature'

The conditions of learning

Condition		Engagement
Learners need to be immersed in a wide range of texts – surrounded by them and attracted to their production and use.	Immersion	
Learners benefit from demonstrations – that is, from explanations and models that enable them to see how texts are conceived, constructed and used.	Demonstration	
Learners are influenced – either stimulated or inhibited – by the expectations of those around them, mainly by adults or peers they respect.	Expectation	
Learners grow in self-reliance if allowed to make their own decisions about the when-how-what of their learning tasks.	Responsibility	
Learners must have time and opportunities, in realistic situations, to practise or use their developing control over what they are learning.	Use	
Learners work confidently when assured that learning is not copied 'correctness' but 'approximation', the process of striving by trial-error-improvement.	Approximation	
Learners are upheld in their efforts – acknowledged and supported – when those around them respond with interest to their words and work.	Response	

Engagement

These conditions contribute to active learning, not mechanically, but as factors in the interaction between students and a teacher who likes the subject, the children and teaching itself.

Engagement occurs when the learner feels:

'These texts, these demonstrations make me want to have a go myself!'

'Doing so, I'm learning and preparing for the life ahead of me.'

'I'm happy learning here, where nobody's condemned when they're not fully correct.'

The Brian Cambourne Model of Literacy Learning

programmes which have children learning to read through reading *real* stories written for their narrative-literary interest. The best of the picture book world – of Sendak, Ahlberg, Burningham and others – is becoming the material for developing literacy. Meek's case studies of adolescent non-readers *(Achieving Literacy)* has also shown that at adolescence the essential problem is still to learn the conventions of written narrative structures.

References

J. Bennett, *Learning to Read with Picture Books*, Stroud: The Thimble Press.

H. Dombey, 'Learning the language of books', in M. Meek (ed.), *Opening Moves*, London: University of London, 1983.

M. Meek *et al.*, *Achieving Literacy*, London: Routledge & Kegan Paul, 1983.

Wayne Sawyer, 'Literature and literacy: a Review of research', *Language Arts*, January 1987.

G. Williams and D. Jack, 'The role of story: learning to read in a special education class', in *Revaluing Troubled Readers*, Occasional Paper No. 15, Program in Language and Literacy, College of Education, University of Arizona, n.d.

LITERATURE-CENTRED ENGLISH – This phrase refers to that school of thought which sees the need for literature to be at the centre of the English curriculum. This 'literature-centred' school is a diverse one. It includes a strand represented by David Holbrook (*English for Maturity*) who would include ballad, folksong and vigorous oral traditions as being part of his central literature. But it also includes a strand which sees the only valuable literature as being the classics of the cultural heritage (q.v.), and which rejects vigorously the widened definition of literature at Dartmouth that included all writing in the spectator role, including that of pupils, as literature (Whitehead, 1976, 1977).

Literature-centred English generally sets itself up in opposition to experienced-centred English or 'the personal growth model of English' (q.v.) and the shrillness of its attack is often embarrassing:

> Yoked with the personal growth model, relevance in English classrooms meant the presentation of local material to stimulate talk. 'What's it like in your house when the truant officer comes? . . .' The urban underprivileged were marked for salvation. . . . English teachers began to trim their load and either cut back on the freight of literature or jettison it altogether. If all pupils cannot cope with literature, then none need have it.
>
> (I. V. Hansen)

The rational arguments of the literature-centred school revolve around:

(1) The value of literature, which has been neglected by the 'growth' school.
(2) The place of literature as the peculiar 'content' of 'subject English', given that the skills model (q.v.) of English is no longer viable. 'Language' (and even 'experience', when it is conceded a place at all) is the responsibility of the whole school, so the argument runs, while only literature is the peculiar province of English.

But the attacks of the literature-centred school on the personal growth model, both rational and otherwise, have created what is in our opinion one of the great non-issues of English curriculum.

No worthwhile English teacher questions the importance of literature in his/her subject – certainly not John Dixon (q.v.), the arch-enemy of the literature-centred school: 'we look to literature to bring order and control to our world . . . the common ground we found lay in the teaching of imaginative literature' (*Growth Through English*).

What happened at Dartmouth was that the definition of literature was widened to redress an imbalance, but certainly not at the cost of rejecting 'the great texts' (Dixon).

As yet, language-across-the-curriculum (q.v.) is *not* the reality it ought to be in schools. English teachers could ill afford to hope that writing, speaking, reading and listening were being 'looked after' by other subject areas and so concentrate on literature. As far as personal experience goes, Britton's case remains a strong one: nobody else across the curriculum has personal experience as their specialist concern; if English teachers do not provide the opportunity for students to bring language to bear on their personal experiences, then nobody will.

In any case, the question of what should be at the 'centre' of English is not an either–or situation. Literature-entails-experience-entails-language-entails-literature, ad infinitum. English has a built-in literature-language-experience centre. Literature offers one way of exploring language and of exploring experience. Mastery of language is the product of experience and an indispensable part of that experience involves literature. Literature, after all, is the use of language to structure experience. The fullest experience of language involves the study of literature. Moreover, literature is not only the product of language structuring experience; it cannot be read except by bringing experience to bear. The notion of the reader as active collaborator with the writer in the making of meaning makes a farce of any conception of English as literature-centred without at the same time being experience-centred.

References

J. Dixon, *Growth Through English*, 3rd edn, Oxford: Oxford University Press, 1975.

E. L. Evertts and J. Britton, 'Potpourri on writing', in E. L. Evertts (ed.), *Explorations in Children's Writing*, London: NCTE, 1970.

I. V. Hansen, 'The case for literature study in secondary schools: some difficulties', *The Teaching of English*, 36, May 1979.

D. Holbrook, *English for Maturity*, Cambridge: Cambridge University Press, 1964.

D. Robinson, 'Literature or experience?', *English in Australia*, 43, March, 1978.

B. Smith, 'Towards a literature-centred English', in K. D. Watson and R. D. Eagleson (eds), *English in Secondary Schools: Today and Tomorrow*, Sydney: ETA of NSW, 1977.

K. Watson, *English Teaching in Perspective*, Milton Keynes: Open University Press, 1987.

F. Whitehead, 'Stunting the growth', *The Use of English*, Autumn, 1976.

F. Whitehead, 'The present state of English teaching', *The Use of English*, Winter, 1977.

LOOK–SAY – Proponents of the 'look–say' approach to the teaching of reading focus their teaching efforts on children's development of an extensive sight vocabulary (i.e. a bank or list of words which the child can recognize on sight). This is attempted through repeated presentation of a basic list of words in flash-card drill, games, work books, and controlled-vocabulary readers. Such an approach places a great emphasis on visual information and reduces reading efficiency through preventing the young reader from using her semantic and syntactic knowledge as extra strategies to assist her to confirm the correctness of the response. It also inhibits the development of independent self-correcting behaviours because, being deprived of any other information, the child is dependent upon the teacher to say whether she is right or wrong. Such practices reduce reading efficiency and direct the reader's focus away from meaning.

(MRT)

See also CONTROLLED VOCABULARY; FLASH CARDS.

Dying words of Dominique Bouhours (French Grammarian, 1628–1702): 'I am about to – or I am going to – die: either expression is used.'

m

MALAPROPISM – Named after Mrs Malaprop, a character in Sheridan's *The Rivals*, who was always using words incorrectly.

A literary competition yielded the following letter from Mrs Malaprop to Lydia Languish announcing Julia's final rupture with Faulkland (abridged version):

> My Dear Niece,
> Oh, Lydia, was there ever such an apostrophe! All the genteelest and most modish persons in Bath invited to grace the nuptial cemetery and at the last moment Madam Julia throws over her lover and all is Charon! I am almost distorted with grief and irrigation. . . .
>
> In fairness, I own, I must excuse Julia for her share in this unhappy denudation. You know that Faulkland's jealous and relaxing temper made his love for Julia a torment both to her and to himself. . . . Indeed, after the date was fixed for the illustration of their nuptials his jealous whims and rackets seemed to increase, and Julia, who had shown an unpalatable patience till now, began to be wearied with the continence of a jealousy so violent and ill-founded. . . . She saw plainly, she told him, that these fancies he entertained would in the end distinguish his love and would also ineffably destroy her affection.
>
> She could not believe, she said, that he loved her truly, and therefore she would never consent to marry him. Faulkland flung out of the house like a manacle, and is now doubtless inuring the pangs of remonstrance; but nothing, I am convinced, will shake Julia's dissolution. The poor girl is doomed, I procrastinate, to a life of celebrity.
>
> You may suppose I was putrified with astonishment when I heard Julia's story. I have not regained my equilibrium as you may see from my writing, which is hardly eligible.
>
> Your affectionate aunt,
> Martha Malaprop

MARXISM AND LITERATURE – The term 'Marxist criticism' has come to be applied to a number of trends in criticism which could in no way be said to constitute a 'school' in any unified sense. These trends include:

(1) A tendency to judge the literature of the past in terms of its social settings and ideology – the trend that rejects Jane Austen for accepting the narrowness of her class and Dickens for not advocating revolution.
(2) A tendency to judge contemporary literature in relation to its ideological soundness and political effects.
(3) A more general sense of the importance of placing history at the centre of judgement and the adoption of an historicist approach to criticism.
(4) More recently, a trend in literary theory to question the whole ideological background of the very notion of 'literature' itself.

Such trends are, in reality, more or less Marxist according to the particular critic displaying them. The historicist approach, for example, describes critics as diverse as Edmund Wilson, Lionel Trilling and Raymond Williams, each of whom would wear the description 'Marxist' with a different degree of comfort.

References

Terry Eagleton, *Marxism and Literary Criticism*, London: Methuen, 1976.
Cliff Slaughter, *Marxism, Ideology and Literature*, London: Macmillan, 1980.
Raymond Williams, *Marxism and Literature*, Oxford: Oxford University Press, 1977.

MASS MEDIA *See* ADVERTISING; FILM STUDY; NEWSPAPER STUDY; RADIO; TELEVISION.

MASTERY LEARNING – In subjects that have a clearly defined content and an arrangement of that content into a logical developmental sequence, the concept of mastery learning, popularized by Benjamin Bloom, can be applied. It assumes that if students are to succeed to their best levels, they should 'master' each piece of knowledge as they go. That is, they should have a clear understanding of all the knowledge and skills that comprise each segment of the sequence before going on to the next segment. In English, there are rarely clear-cut knowledge and skills to acquire, and therefore there is no clear-cut developmental sequence of knowledge and skills. The aim of English teaching is the development of the capacity to use language for many purposes, and the best way to achieve this aim is to provide activities that allow students to read, write, speak and listen in meaningful contexts. **(PJ)**
See also SKILLS MODEL OF ENGLISH.

Reference

B. S. Bloom, *Human Characteristics and School Learning*, New York: McGraw-Hill, 1976.

MEDIA *See* USAGE.

MEETING PROCEDURE – Since almost all adults are at some time members of a union, a club or other association, it seems important that school pupils be introduced to the standard procedures for the conduct of meetings. This is best done by turning the class on occasions into an association (e.g. a drama club) which has a real purpose.

Usual agenda for meetings

(1) Reading and confirmation of minutes of previous meeting.
(2) Business arising from minutes.

(3) Apologies.
(4) Correspondence.
(5) Accounts – Treasurer's Report.
(6) Reports.
(7) Motions of which due notice has been given.
(8) General business.

Quorum
The rules of most organizations provide for a quorum, that is a certain number of people to be present at a meeting. Otherwise the meeting is invalid.

The Chairperson
Duties:
(1) To preside at meetings.
(2) To conduct meetings in accordance with the rules of procedure.
(3) To preserve order.
(4) To conduct voting.
Rights:
(1) May intervene at any time.
(2) May leave the Chair to speak on a matter. If she or he does so, she or he may not return to the Chair until the motion has been resolved. His or her place is taken by the Deputy Chairperson.

Motions and amendments
(1) A person wishing to propose a motion must rise and address the Chairperson.
(2) A motion must be proposed by one speaker and seconded by another.
(3) A person may speak only once on a motion but the mover has the right of reply.
(4) Speakers must be taken in order – for and against. If debate lapses the motion must immediately be put, unless the mover wishes to exercise his or her right of reply.
(5) If debate seems to proceed for an undue length of time, it is possible to move 'That the question be now put'.
(6) Amendments may be proposed to the motion if duly seconded.
(7) Voting on amendments are taken in order *before* the vote on the motion.
(8) A motion – 'That the meeting proceed to the next business' – may be moved if the mover wishes to shelve a matter for the time being.

Voting
(1) Voting may be by voice or show of hands.
(2) If voting is equal, the Chairperson must declare the motion lost.

Points of order
(1) No speaker shall be interrupted unless a point of order be raised. The point of order may concern such matters as:
   (a) Not speaking on the subject.
   (b) Speaking on a matter already decided.
(2) A person dissatisfied with the Chairperson's ruling may move a motion of dissent: 'That the Chairperson's ruling be dissented from'. No seconder is

needed. The motion is put by the Chairperson in the following terms: 'The motion is that the Chairperson's ruling be upheld'.

Suspension of standing orders
A person may move suspension of standing orders to discuss an urgent matter.

METALINGUISTIC AWARENESS – There has recently been put forward the argument that learning to read requires metalinguistic awareness. Herriman and Tunmer define metalinguistic awareness as 'the ability to deliberately reflect upon and manipulate the structural features of spoken language, treating the language system itself as an object of thought', and argue that this awareness is necessary in learning to read. As far as reading is concerned, this is a similar argument to that which says that children need to develop 'concepts about print' (q.v.) in order to read.

'Metalinguistic awareness' as a term could be widened to include areas such as knowledge of the grammatical system or of larger structures when writing. This ought to remind us to be wary of the notion – or, rather, of how it is applied – to some extent. It has long been accepted that a conscious knowledge of grammar does not transfer to improved writing ability. Similarly, it has recently been implied by those concerned with writing in genres (q.v.) that generic structures ought to be consciously modelled for and by children. The pedagogical impact of this is at the very least extremely debatable.

In general, what we are arguing is that accepting the arguments for the necessity of metalinguistic awareness still should leave open to debate questions about the necessary degree of consciousness of this awareness and certainly should leave open questions about the pedagogy by which this awareness is attained.

See also CONCEPTS ABOUT PRINT; GRAMMAR AND WRITING; GENRES, WRITING IN.

References

M. L. Herriman and W. E. Tunmer, 'Metalinguistic skills as predictors of early reading achievement: preliminary findings', *AARE Conference Collected Papers*, November 1983.

W. E. Tunmer, C. Pratt and M. L. Herriman (eds), *Metalinguistic Awareness in Children: Theory, Research and Implications*, Berlin: Springer-Verlag, 1983.

MICE *See* MICROCOMPUTERS IN THE CURRICULUM – ENGLISH.

MICROCOMPUTERS IN ENGLISH – The microcomputer is a small computer designed to process information fed into it and to perform a variety of tasks both useful and entertaining. Most microcomputer programs ('software') used by English teachers fall into the following types:

(1) Skills based, 'drill-and-practice', programs. These are just gap-filling type exercises transferred from textbook to computer screen and just as useless.
(2) Word Processing. These are general utility programs that enable the writing and editing of text. Learning the skills and conventions of screen-reading and writing are essential elements in the development of literacy in the late twentieth century and should form part of every English programme.

(3) Data handling. General utility programs which enable data from a variety of sources to be easily and quickly stored, retrieved and managed in different ways.

(4) Simulations (q.v.). These provide a computer based simulation often used as part of a larger package of materials to encourage group work and talk in the classroom. Many of them are based upon the concept of the 'Adventure Game' in which players have to work their way through a computerized 'maze', solving problems and avoiding hazards. Recently more sophisticated simulations have been developed which may involve literary contexts.

(5) Language programs. Unlike the 'drill and practice' programs mentioned above, these are programs that enable electronic text to be manipulated in a variety of ways leading typically to discussion and linguistic problem-solving by groups of pupils. They can also be used for extension and support work by pupils in mixed ability groupings. Increasingly, programs of this kind are becoming 'content free', providing a template within which teachers can incorporate their own texts, from nursery rhymes to Shakespeare.

Since programs are constantly being developed examples of programs currently in use are not given here though details of many of them will be found in the books listed in the references, especially in Moore and in Chandler and Marcus.

The term Computer-Assisted Instruction (CAI) refers to those programs (as in 1) which replace human interaction in the teaching situation; Computer-Assisted Learning (CAL), on the other hand, refers to the use of computers as an aid to learning as in 4 and 5. Applications such as 2 and 3 provide an example of the use of computers as a tool in the learning process.

See also CAMBRIDGE LANGUAGE ARTS SOFTWARE SERVICES LTD.; MICROCOMPUTERS IN THE CURRICULUM – ENGLISH; SIMULATIONS.

References

Anthony Adams and Esmor Jones, *Teaching Humanities in the Microelectronic Age*, Milton Keynes: Open University Press, 1983.

Daniel Chandler (ed.), *Exploring English with Microcomputers*, London: Council for Educational Technology, 1983.

Daniel Chandler and Stephen Marcus (eds), *Computers and Literacy*, Milton Keynes: Open University Press, 1985.

Phil Moore, *Using Computers in English*, London: Methuen, 1986.

Brent Robinson, *Microcomputers and the Language Arts*, Milton Keynes: Open University Press, 1985.

MICROCOMPUTERS IN THE CURRICULUM – ENGLISH (MICE) – A 'self-help' group of English teachers who want to share together their developing experience of using microcomputers in the English classroom. The group publishes an occasional news-sheet which gives details of classroom practice and reviews new software. For details contact Phil Moore, 5 Forrest Court, Unicorn Lane, Eastern Green, Coventry, England.

See also MICROMPUTERS IN ENGLISH.

MILITATE, MITIGATE *See* USAGE.

MINIMAL COMPETENCY TESTING – As a result of the Accountability movement (q.v.) in the United States, there has been a growing emphasis on minimal competency testing. Various states in the United States have specified the lowest level of attainment for the award of a high school diploma in English and Mathematics. Inevitably, this has often led to a narrowing of English curricula to those aspects that will be tested.

MISCUE ANALYSIS – As a normal aspect of the reading process there are times when there are differences between what readers think is printed on the page and what is actually there. The resulting deviation is called a miscue. All readers make miscues. Good readers make miscues which are consistent with the meaning and language of the text:

Text: Below was the orange of the flames.
Reader: Below was the orange of the fire.

Poor readers make more miscues which do not fit in with the flow of language and result in meaning loss.

Text: The bird flew crazily about the room.
Reader: The bird flew cheerily about the room.

Readers' miscue patterns then reflect the strengths and weaknesses of their reading strategies. Procedures for miscue analysis have been developed as an informal approach to the diagnosis of an individual's reading behaviour. In broad terms the steps in this procedure are as follows:

(1) An initial interview to determine the child's interests and attitudes to reading, the background influences on reading behaviour and a broad insight into general reading competence.
(2) The selection of a range of suitable reading materials on which to sample the child's reading.
(3) Tape-recording the child's oral reading and retelling of the text.
(4) Teacher marking of the child's miscues on a copy of the text.
(5) Teacher classification of the miscues according to their semantic and syntactic acceptability.
(6) An assessment of the accuracy and completeness of the child's retelling.
(7) Interpretation of the miscue pattern in relation to the retelling.
(8) Preparation of a profile of reader strengths and weaknesses.

There are a number of detailed guidelines which must be followed to ensure a meaningful implementation of this procedure. For example, miscues occurring in the first few lines of text are not coded, at least twenty-five miscues are required for analysis to ensure adequate behaviour sampling, and so on. These details have been codified in a number of systematic guides to miscue analysis listed in the references. **(MRT)**

References

Y. M. Goodman and C. Burke, *Reading Miscue Inventory*, Toronto: Macmillan, 1972.

Y. M. Goodman, C. Burke and B. Sherman, *Reading Strategies: Focus on Comprehension*, New York: Holt, Rinehart & Winston, 1980.

B. Johnson, *Reading Appraisal Guide*, Melbourne: ACER, 1979.

M. Kemp, *Reading – Language Processes: Assessment and Teaching*, Adelaide: Australian Reading Association, 1980, esp. Chs 3, 4.

MIXED-ABILITY TEACHING – The arguments in favour of mixed-ability rather than streamed classes are so persuasive that most schools have been moving steadily in this direction for some years. Briefly, the arguments in favour of abandoning streaming in favour of mixed-ability are:

(1) Streaming is destructive both to the achievement and to the self-image of the great majority of school pupils. As Sir Alec Clegg has written, 'To put a child into a *D* stream is to classify him according to his inferiority – and he knows it.'
(2) Streaming cannot be done accurately, particularly in English. Case histories abound of able children wrongly placed in low classes.
(3) Putting slower learners in separate classes holds them back even more. (*See* SLOW LEARNERS, SEPARATE CLASSES FOR.)
(4) The power of the self-fulfilling prophecy is such that children will perform as they and their teachers expect them to perform.
(5) The social benefits of the abandonment of streaming have been well attested by research.
(6) There is increasing evidence that the bright child is not held back in the mixed-ability class, as long as the teaching methods employed are appropriate (see below).

The key to successful mixed-ability teaching appears to lie in flexible grouping. 'There are times when the class will operate as a single unit: for 'focus' sessions at the beginning of a unit; for summarizing what has gone on; for groups reporting back to the class; for the shared experience of novel, poem, play or short story. A great deal of work in a mixed-ability class will, however, be done in small groups: the discussion of ideas, themes, poems, stories; imaginative re-creation (q.v.) . . . discussion prior to the individual work involved in a writing task; improvised drama. Pair work is an appropriate variant of small-group work for many of these activities, and for such tasks as the 'proof-reading' of written work.

Then there will be individual work: writing, silent reading, activities designed to correct specific weaknesses. It is important, however, for the teacher . . . not to fall into the trap of too much individualization . . . a heavy reliance on worksheets and study guides can short-circuit the learning process' (Watson).

References

Richard Mills (ed.), *Teaching English to All*, London: Robert Royce, 1987.

Ken Watson, *English Teaching in Perspective*, Milton Keynes: Open University Press, 1987, Ch. 11.

MODAL – An auxiliary verb indicating judgement and attitude, e.g. 'can', 'could', 'may', 'might' and 'must'.

MOFFETT, JAMES – James Moffett is a major figure behind the 'New English' as it has been propagated since the Dartmouth Seminar (q.v.). Moffett's model of discourse development, as presented in *Teaching The Universe Of Discourse*, provides an important theoretical underpinning for the teaching of English, especially in the areas of programming and sequencing. James Britton's own model of writing development as outlined in 'What's the Use?' (*Educational Review* 23(3), 1971) acknowledges a debt to Moffett.

Richard Koch has argued that Moffett's *Teaching the Universe of Discourse* was the inspiration of 'An entire school of writing teachers [who] believed that not only was it emotionally healthy for students to get in touch with their feelings, but also the best way to unlock each student's natural language ability' ('Imagination and language', *English Education* 10(3), 1979).

Among Moffett's other important writings are *Active Voice*, *Coming on Center* and *Student-Centered Language Arts and Reading, K-13* (with Betty-Jane Wagner).

MONTAGE – A device in which atmosphere (q.v.) is built up by a series of brief, and usually random, impressions. The opening scene of *A Portrait of the Artist as a Young Man*, much of Virginia Woolf, Eliot's 'Preludes' or 'Rhapsody on a Windy Night' or 'Portrait of a Lady' – all of these make an impressionistic montage.

In the junior school the device itself can be a useful one in film-making with a class.

MORPHEME – The smallest meaningful unit in a language. In English a morpheme could be a word or a part of a word such as a prefix, a suffix or a grammatical ending. It is not necessarily a single syllable. Here are some examples of words divided into morphemes:

farm   farm + s   farm + ing   farm + er
rail + way   forget   un + forget + able

In some words an extra morpheme is added by means of internal modification, for example *foot + s = feet, swim + ed = swam.* The study of morphemes and the forms of words is called *morphology*. **(JC)**

MORPHOLOGY *See* MORPHEME.

MOTIF – A more or less collective term for recurring themes, images, actions or ideas. Blood, darkness and disguise all appear in *Macbeth* as images but also as physical presences and may be regarded as part of the complex series of recurrent motifs in that play.

MOUNT GRAVATT DEVELOPMENTAL LANGUAGE READING PROGRAMME – An integrated language reading programme developed in Australia on the basis of an extensive study of children's language development.

The teaching strategies are firmly based on the belief that children learn to read most effectively when the reading materials used are based on children's participation in real experiences and where the language patterns encountered correspond to children's own oral language development.

While the early levels emphasize the process of learning to read, the later levels are designed to encourage the use of a wide range of reading materials, both fiction and non-fiction across the curriculum, to develop children's ability to read efficiently for a variety of purposes. The teacher's manuals are comprehensive and supportive, but still encourage individual and imaginative implementation by the teacher. (Published by Longman-Cheshire in Australia.) **(MRT)**

See also READING SCHEMES.

MS, Ms – Capitalized, *MS* stands for *manuscript* or for *multiple sclerosis*; as *Ms* it is growing in acceptance (particularly in writing, less often in speech) as the non-sexist equivalent of *Mr.*

See also SEXISM.

MULTICULTURAL ENGLISH CLASSROOM – The special needs of the student moving from the ESL class into the ordinary English classroom must not be overlooked by teachers with no specialist ESL training. The ESL child has problems of cultural adjustment that can be helped by creating a climate in which all pupils are made to feel that their life experiences are of value and by attempting to create a climate in which cultural differences are not a source of antagonism.

Literature in the multicultural classroom should be chosen with the aim in mind of displaying other cultures to the native-born and also demonstrating that many experiences are universal (*see* MULTICULTURAL LITERATURE). Using the myths, legends and folk tales of the countries represented in the class widens the literary experience of all students and helps enhance minority group self-image. A cross-cultural comparison of the same folk tale (the Cinderella story, for example, exists in many cultures) itself makes an interesting unit of work.

When using literature in the multicultural classroom, one should operate on the same assumptions as in a first-language classroom, that is using imaginative re-creation (q.v.) through reading, writing and speaking activities, role-plays (q.v.) and so on. Literature should not become a source of grammar-drill exercises, although it could be used as a model for the students' own writing. Also, 'multicultural literature' could be used as a piece of social and historical evidence: what does it tell us of its society? How is it different from other evidence?

In choosing literature for the multicultural classroom, one needs to be aware of its cultural relevance and also of the dangers of minority-group stereotyping. With respect to cultural relevance, a testing instrument has been devised by Kenneth Goodman for children whose first language is not English and which looks at aspects of cultural relevance in six categories. The instrument is reported by Jan Smith in *The Teaching of English*, 41. With respect to stereotyping and so on, a useful set of criteria for assessing books in a multicultural setting is listed in *Primary English Notes 28.* This includes such danger signs as children being portrayed as our 'cousins' or 'regular Australians' or 'foreigners', or foreign characters being all somehow the same.

Language problems for ESL students will also have to be taken account of, and these may manifest themselves in a number of ways. Unusual vocabulary; lengthy, complex or uncommon sentence structures; functional-structural phrases such as 'meanwhile', 'because of this'; changes from normal sequencing patterns such as 'sometime before' in the middle of a passage – these are all things which the teacher must be aware of and alert students to during reading in a class with ESL students. Structural readers are useful here, though the teacher must weigh up the benefits of more manageable language structures against loss of the author's meaning. In any case, in all texts studied, structural readers or otherwise, the teacher must remain alert to whether the student is gaining a clear mental picture of the story. Jan Smith (1981) has useful advice on all these problems.

Storytelling is important in the multicultural classroom – both by the students and by the teacher. There should be a mixture of fantasy with realistic experiences and storytelling can be used to develop other aspects of language, for example directed listening (such as predicting) and writing activities.

Small-group work is important in the multicultural setting also, though groups should be carefully structured so that ESL students with similar problems do not always form whole groups – language modelling by other students is one of the aims. Language modelling by the teacher is also, of course, important.

In general, one should operate on the same broad principles of language development as for native speakers, namely that one learns language by using it. Thus there should be plenty of reading, writing, speaking and listening activities for a variety of purposes and a variety of audiences. These may have to be deliberately structured so as to work on particular problems such as changes of tense and so on, but one should never lose sight of the principle of language in use. Thus in writing, ESL consultant Jan Smith (1980) recommends use of the Britton continuum i.e. writing in the transactional, poetic and expressive modes (especially the last) combined with a frames/models approach with the mechanics of form (punctuation, spelling, etc.), cohesion (sequencing, using conjunctions), starting and ending strategies, and so on. Of course, all of this should be done within the framework of the process-conference approach (*see* WRITING: PROCESS-CONFERENCE APPROACH) and follow-up language lessons should be based on the contexts of the student's own writing, not on dummy-run exercises.

Speaking should operate similarly. Students can best pick up registers through studying conversations (ideally on tape) in detail and using role-plays to 'try on' different registers.

See also FUNCTIONAL-NOTIONAL APPROACH.

References

K. Goodman, *Final Report. The Reading of American Children Whose Language Is a Stable Rural Dialect of English, or a Language Other than English*, US Department of Health, Education And Welfare, August 1978.

Ian Pringle, 'English as a world language' in R. Arnold (ed.), *Timely Voices*, Melbourne: Oxford University Press, 1983.

B. Rasmussen, 'Multicultural reading', *Primary English Notes 28*, PETA, 1981.
J. Smith, 'I'm not an ESL teacher – what can I do to help all these migrant children?', *English in Australia* 51, AATE, March 1980.
J. Smith, 'Selecting literary texts in the multicultural classroom: some-considerations', *The Teaching of English* 41, ETANSW, Sept. 1981.
K. Watson, *English Teaching in Perspective*, Milton Keynes: Open University Press, 1987.

MULTICULTURAL LITERATURE – We recommend the following as a *very* brief cross-section of worthwhile literature for the multicultural classroom:

Years 2–7
Fairy tales and folk tales from other lands (see list below).

Years 5–7
K. Seredy, *Philomena* (Viking) – Czechoslovakia
P. Bonson, *The Orphans of Similta* (Puffin) – Greece
E. Haugaard, *The Little Fishes* (Heinemann/New Windmill) – Italy
D. Blatter, *Cap and Candle* (Westminster) – Turkey
R. Hoban, *The Dancing Tigers* (Cape) – Indian sub-continent

Years 7–8
J. Kerr, *When Hitler Stole Pink Rabbit* (Lions) – Germany
J. Reiss, *The Upstairs Room* (Puffin) – Holland
J. Ziemian, *The Cigarette Sellers of Three Crosses Square* (Lerner) – Poland
P. Dickinson, *Tulku* (Gollancz) – China
P. Thirabutana, *Little Things* (Collins) – Thailand

Year 9
K. Chukovsky, *The Silver Crest* (Oxford University Press) – Russia
N. Griffiths, *The Lost Summer: Spain 1936* (Hutchinson) – Spain
J. Lingard, *Across the Barricades* (Puffin) – Ireland
F. Selarmey, *The Narrow Path* (New Windmill) – Ghana
A. Wendt, *Sons for the Return Home* (Longman) – Pacific Islands

Year 10
E. Spence, *A Candle for St Antony* (Oxford University Press) – Australia
L. R. Banks, *One More River* (Peacock) – Israel
J. Steinbeck, *The Pearl* (New Windmill) – Mexico
E. S. Canaway, *Sammy Going South* (Penguin) – Egypt
A. Garner, *The Owl Service* (Lions) – Wales

Seniors
M. Lewitt, *Come Spring* (Scribe) – Poland
N. Albery, *Balloon Top* (Deutsch) – Japan
C. Achebe, *Things Fall Apart* (New Windmill) – Nigeria
J. Schaefer, *The Canyon* (New Windmill) – United States
Y. Kemal, *Iron Earth, Copper Sky* (Horvill) – Turkey

Folk Tales, etc.
J. Baudis, *Czech Folk Tales* (Kraus)
B. Picard, *French Legends, Tales and Fairy Stories* (Oxford University Press)
B. Picard, *German Hero-Sagas and Folk Tales* (Oxford University Press)

K. Lines, *The Faber Book of Greek Legends* (Faber)
L. Degh, *Folk Tales of Hungary* (University of Chicago Press)
M. Jogendorf, *Priceless Cats and Other Italian Folk Tales* (Vanguard)
Z. Zajdler, *Polish Fairy Tales* (Muller)
C. Downing, *Russian Tales and Legends* (Oxford University Press)
K. C. Holland, *Faber Book of Northern Myths* (Faber)
N. C. Prodanovic, *Yugoslav Folk Tales* (Oxford University Press)
J. Reeves, *English Fables and Fairy Stories* (Oxford University Press)
F. O'Faolain, *Irish Sagas and Folk Tales* (Oxford University Press)
B. K. Wilson, *Scottish Folk Tales and Legends* (Oxford University Press)
G. Jones, *Welsh Legends and Folk Tales* (Oxford University Press)
R. Erdoes, *The Sound of Flutes and Other Indian Legends* (Pantheon)
R. Sherlock, *West Indian Folk Tales* (Oxford University Press)
R. L. Green, *Tales of Ancient Egypt* (Puffin)
B. L. Picard, *Tales of Ancient Persia* (Oxford University Press)
J. Kunos, *Turkish Fairy Tales and Folk Tales* (Dover)
C. Birch, *Chinese Myths and Fantasies* (Oxford University Press)
J. E. B. Gray, *Indian Tales and Legends* (Oxford University Press)
H. and W. McAlpine, *Japanese Tales and Legends* (Oxford University Press)
G. Graham, *Wishing Pearl and Other Tales of Vietnam* (Harvey) (Oxford University Press)
C. P. Mountford, *The Dreamtime* (Angus and Robertson)
A. W. Reed, *Maori Fairy Tales* (Reed)
A. Alters, *Legends of the South Sea* (Rigby)

MULTIPLE-CHOICE TESTS – It can be stated quite categorically that there is little place for multiple-choice tests in the English classroom. Multiple-choice items generally reduce themselves to only two possible answers and very little higher-order thinking is involved in the whole exercise. As far as the traditional comprehension test is concerned, most multiple-choice items can be answered without even reading the test-passage completely. English should be about active involvement through reading, writing, listening and speaking, not about passive 'guessing games'.

MYTH, LEGEND, FOLK TALE – While the meanings of these terms depend a great deal upon the contexts in which they occur, generally *myth* refers to stories attempting to explain how something came to exist (e.g. myths explaining the creation of the world, the origin of fire, why the sun comes up in the morning) while *legend* refers to stories with some historical basis, however obscure (e.g. there probably was an historical King Arthur, but he would have been a Celtic prince, not a figure of the late Middle Ages). The *folk tale* embraces many kinds of stories mainly belonging to oral tradition: legends, fables, fairy stories, tall stories. The story of the clever trickster, for example, occurs in the folk tales of many nations.

With the decline of the oral tradition and the even more alarming decline in home storytelling, it seems vital that both primary and junior secondary teachers incorporate myth, legend and folk tale into their English lessons. Further, myth and folk tale can play their part in promoting a genuine multicultural English classroom (q.v.).

A splendid collection of Eastern European folk tales for use in middle and upper primary (and possibly also in Year 7 and 8) is Joan Aiken's *The Kingdom under the Sea* (Puffin). Another Puffin collection is Edith Brill's *The Golden Bird.*

Oxford University Press has produced collections of myths and folk tales from many lands including most European countries, India, China, Japan and the Middle East. Many collections of the stories told by Australian Aborigines are available.

The Greek and Norse myths have had such a strong influence on our culture that they must be given a place in the classroom. Books suitable for oral reading by the teacher or for inclusion in wide reading (q.v.) schemes are:

Greece

Kathleen Lines, *The Faber Book of Greek Legends* (Faber)

Ian Serraillier, *The Clashing Rocks*; *The Way of Danger*; *Heracles the Strong* (Heinemann, New Windmill)

And for abler readers:

Rex Warner, *Greeks and Trojans* (New Windmill)

Leon Garfield and Edward Blishen, *The God Beneath the Sea*; *The Golden Shadow* (Longman)

Norse

Roger Lancelyn Green, *Myths of the Norsemen* (Puffin)

Brian Branston, *Gods and Heroes from Viking Mythology* (Hodder)

Kevin Crossley Holland, *Faber Book of Northern Myths* (Faber).

There are many retellings of the Arthurian cycle that can be used in schools. Roger Lancelyn Green's *King Arthur and the Knights of the Round Table* (Puffin) is one such, and Rosemary Sutcliff has recently produced a three-volume reworking of the cycle: *The Sword and the Circle*; *The Light Beyond the Forest*; *The Road to Camlann.*

Here are some suggestions for using myth, legend and folk tale in the classroom:

(1) Have the class read a number of myths from different cultures on a similar theme (e.g. creation myths, fire myths) and then have them write their own myths to explain natural phenomena (e.g. why there are earthquakes, why the sea is salty).
(2) Make a cross-cultural comparison of a folk tale like the Cinderella story, which exists in several versions: the French version (the most familiar version), the German version by the Brothers Grimm, the English *Tattercoats*, the Italian *Cenerentola*, the Russian *Jack Frost*, the Chinese version.
(3) Have the class investigate the origins of the many words that come from the myths, for example *siren*, *hectoring*, *muse*, *mentor.* A useful reference is Isaac Asimov's *Words from the Myths*, and students can be introduced to Brewer's *Dictionary of Phrase and Fable.*

See also MULTICULTURAL LITERATURE.

WASTED WORDS?

Walter de la Mare once remarked that many essentially beautiful words seemed to have missed their vocation. 'Linoleum', he suggested, ought to have been a charming old Mediterranean seaport. The *New Statesman* invited its readers to compose poems giving new meanings to wasted words. Edward Blishen won with a poem which began:

> Sweet Hernia on the heights of Plasticine
> Sings to the nylon songs of Brassiere:
> The very aspirins listen, as they lean
> Against the vitreous wind, to her sad air.

Senior students could be invited to try a similar poem.

n

NARRATIVE – There has been recently a renewed interest in narrative in fields related to education, linguistics and language development. A brief overview of this interest would need to point out the theorizing of James Moffett (q.v.), who saw narrative as the child's main mode of abstracting in *Teaching the Universe of Discourse* (1968). Barbara Hardy's famous definition of narrative as 'a primary act of mind transferred from art to life' in fact effectively describes narrative as the essential manifestation of Britton's 'spectator role' language ('the remembering, dreaming and planning that is in life imposed on the uncertain, attenuated, interrupted, and unpredictable or meaningless flow of happenings'). Sociolinguists such as Goffman, Halliday and Scollon also argue for the centrality of narrative in the child's development of communicative ability, while Rosen, Eagleton and others have echoed its description as 'primary act of mind'.

The argument has been forwarded by Meek and others that this basic communicative act and essential way of ordering experience could provide a way of making connections between the stories children tell and the stories they hear and read. Hence the study of narrative has been taken up by those interested in children's literature, and criticism based on narratology (q.v.) and structuralism (q.v.) generally is becoming more common.

See also CHATMAN, SEYMOUR.

References

Terry Eagleton, *Walter Benjamin or Towards a Revolutionary Criticism*, London: Verso, 1981.

E. Goffman, *Frame Analysis*, New York: Harper & Row, 1974.

M. A. K. Halliday, 'Meaning and the construction of reality in early childhood', in H. L. Pick and E. Saltzman (eds), *Modes of Perceiving and Processing Information*, Hillsdale, NJ: Lawrence Erlbaum, 1976.

Barbara Hardy, 'Towards a poetics of fiction: an approach through narrative', in M. Meek *et al.*, *The Cool Web*, London: Bodley Head, 1978.

Margaret Meek, 'Speaking of shifters', in M. Meek and J. Miller (eds), *Changing English*, London: Heinemann/University of London, 1984.

James Moffett, *Teaching the Universe of Discourse*, Boston: Houghton Mifflin, 1968.

Harold Rosen, *Stories and Meanings*, Sheffield: NATE, n.d.

R. Scollon, *Conversations with a One-Year Old*, Honolulu: University of Hawaii Press, 1976.

NARRATOLOGY – The study of the nature of narrative, often formalist or semiological, in a line running from the Russian formalists, through Propp, Todorov, and others to Roland Barthes' classic *S/Z*, New York: Hill & Wang, 1974 and 'Introduction to the structural analysis of narratives', in *Image–Music–Text*, London: Fontana, 1977.

There are, in addition, eclectic works in the field, such as Roger Fowler, *Linguistics and the Novel*, London: Methuen, 1977; Roger Fowler, *Literature as Social Discourse*, Bloomington: Indiana University Press, 1981 (which includes linguistic criticism of *S/Z*) and Seymour Chatman, *Story and Discourse: Narrative Structure in Fiction and Film*, New York: Cornell University Press, 1978 – the last one of the best in the field, and interesting because it covers both film and novel. A pioneer work, pre-structuralist, is Wayne Booth, *The Rhetoric of Fiction*, Chicago: University of Chicago Press, 1961, and some related issues are taken up in Elizabeth Traugott and Mary Louise Pratt, *Linguistics for Students of Literature*, New York: Harcourt Brace Jovanovich, 1980. One can also consult with profit Jonathan Culler, *Structuralist Poetics*, London: Routledge & Kegan Paul, 1975 and *The Pursuit of Signs*, London: Routledge & Kegan Paul, 1981. Jane P. Tompkins (ed.), *Reader-Response Criticism*, Baltimore: Johns Hopkins Press, 1980, includes a number of relevant essays. For scope, and brevity, I commend Fowler's *Linguistics and the Novel*, London: Methuen, 1977 as a starting point.

What one gains from such studies is a range of things one may relevantly talk about in discussing how a novel works, or to consider in writing narratives oneself. The problem in some, not all, such studies is reductionism; as the generalizations widen, the individual work vanishes. One may be left unable to distinguish a *Thorn Birds* from a *Tree of Man*, since narratology reveals what they have in common rather than what is distinctive. **(NJW)**

See also FORMALISM; STRUCTURALISM; SEMIOLOGY/SEMIOTICS.

NATIONAL ORACY PROJECT – A programme of work co-ordinated in England and Wales through the School Curriculum Development Council (SCDC) under the direction of John Johnson. It seeks to support and disseminate work on all aspects of oracy carried out in about thirty-five different Local Education Authorities. The project produces a newsletter reporting on work in progress. Details from the Project at SCDC, Newcombe House, 45 Notting Hill Gate, London W11 3JB.

NATIONAL WRITING PROJECT – In the United States a programme which grew out of the work of the Bay Area Writing Project (q.v.) encouraging, supporting and disseminating the work of State based writing projects, organized along similar lines to that of the Bay Area Writing Project, under the general direction of James Gray at Berkeley, California.

The work in the United States stimulated the creation in England and Wales of a similar National Writing Project based upon a wide variety of work undertaken in Local Education Authorities. It consists of a programme of work co-ordinated through the School Curriculum Development Council (SCDC) under the direction of Pam Czerniewska. It seeks to support and disseminate work on all aspects of writing carried out in the different participating Authorities. The project produces a regular newsletter reporting on work in progress. Details from the Project at SCDC, Newcombe House, 45 Notting Hill Gate, London W11 3JB.

NEALE ANALYSIS OF READING – An oral reading test used with children in primary school and occasionally in testing older children experiencing difficulty with reading. There are three forms of the test each consisting of six passages of increasing length and complexity. Four comprehension questions follow the first passage and eight each subsequent passage. Age norms are available providing separate scores expressed as reading ages in reading accuracy comprehension and speed. The test is described as a diagnostic test; however, emphasis is frequently put on quantitative scores and all oral reading inaccuracies are penalized whether or not they result in loss of meaning. Hence in terms of psycho-linguistic accounts of reading, the test does not supply relevant diagnostic data. (*See* MISCUE ANALYSIS.) For a detailed critique, see Goodacre, White and Brennan (1980) – for general limitations *see also* READING AGE and STANDARDIZED TESTS.

References

E. Goodacre, J. White and P. Brennan, 'Whatever happened to the black cat?', *Reading Education*, 5 (2), Spring 1980: 41–9.

M. D. Neale, *Neale Analysis of Reading Ability*, London: Macmillan, 1958.

P. D. Pumfrey, *Reading: Tests and Assessment Techniques*, London: Hodder & Stoughton, 1976.

NEO-CLASSICISM – This is the name given to that period of the early eighteenth century which produced in literature writers such as Pope, Johnson and Fielding. Known also as the Augustan age, the philosophy of the period looked back to the writings of Greek and Roman classicism for its inspiration. The Augustan age was marked by little faith in individual freedom, and trust in the order of civilized society. It was also the 'Age of Reason', which distrusted emotion and imagination and looked to the human capacity for rational thought and behaviour as the way to enlightenment. A by-product of the faith in ordered civilized society was a focus of literary concern on urban subjects or, when nature was considered, with a nature ordered and cultivated by humans. A further by-product of the concern for restraint, order and organized reason was a return to tight, rigid, even closed literary forms, most prominently the couplet in verse and the balanced sentence in prose. It was against all these tenets, both in society and literature, that Romanticism (q.v.) rebelled.

NEUROLOGICAL IMPRESS METHOD *See* NIM.

NEWBERY MEDAL – Awarded annually to the 'author of the most distinguished contribution to American literature for children'. The medal is named after John Newbery, the eighteenth-century English bookseller and publisher, who was the first to conceive the idea of publishing books expressly for children. Hendrik Van Loon's *The Story of Mankind* (1922) was the first book selected; since then award winners have included Esther Forbes for *Johnny Tremain*

(1944), Elizabeth George Speare for *The Witch of Blackbird Pond* (1959), and *The Bronze Bow* (1962), Scott O'Dell for *Island of The Blue Dolphins* (1961), Madeleine L'Engle for *A Wrinkle in Time* (1963) and William Armstrong for *Sounder* (1970). The most recent winners have been:

1976 – Susan Cooper for *The Grey King*
1977 – Mildred Taylor for *Roll of Thunder, Hear My Cry*
1978 – Katherine Paterson for *Bridge to Terabithia*
1979 – Ellen Raskin for *The Westing Game*
1980 – Joan Blos for *The Gathering of Days: A New England's Girl's Journal, 1830–32*
1981 – Katherine Paterson for *Jacob Have I Loved*
1982 – Nancy Willard for *A Visit to William Blake's Inn: Poems For Innocent and Experienced Travellers.*
1983 – Cynthia Voight for *Dicey's Song*
1984 – Beverly Cleary for *Dear Mr Henshaw*
1985 – Robyn McKinley for *Nero and the Crown*
1986 – Sid Fleischman for *The Whipping Boy*

NEW CRITICISM – A term used for the views associated with a group of literary critics in the United States, working mainly in the 1940s and 1950s, whose attention focused exclusively on literary texts as unchanging objects of special value. T. S. Eliot had gone some way in his critical writing towards severing the link between the poem and its author, on the one hand, and between the poem and its individual reader on the other. Among those who developed this line of thought were Cleanth Brooks, R. P. Blackmur, Robert Penn Warren and W. K. Wimsatt. Two titles from the works of these critics, *The Well-Wrought Urn* and *The Verbal Icon*, express clearly their view of the status of literary texts.

Among British critics of roughly the same period, William Empson, together with F. R. Leavis (q.v.) and some of his followers, are often seen as showing a similar concentration on the text. In their case, this arose to some extent by contrast with such of their predecessors as the historically-minded E. M. W. Tillyard and C. S. Lewis, who was more widely concerned with morality and aesthetics. **(WDEE)**

NEWSPAPER STUDY – There are many valuable activities that can be undertaken in a unit on newspapers:

(1) Readership surveys in school and neighbourhood. (The results can be displayed in column graphs and compared with a column graph showing the actual circulation of the newspapers.)
(2) A survey of the amount of space given by the various newspapers to such things as foreign news, national news, sport, finance, and so on. Later judgements about the merits of particular newspapers can thus be made on some factual basis.
(3) Comparison of the placement and treatment of the same news items in different newspapers. This can raise interesting questions about the slanting of news and sensationalizing as well as alerting pupils to the fact that newspaper reports are frequently inaccurate.

(4) Newspaper headlines can be used for:
   (a) the study of metaphor, for example Thatcher Faces Storm; or Bridge Designer Blasted
   (b) the study of ambiguity, for example Revolting Officers Shot; or Giant Waves Down Liner's Funnel; or Slugs on Beer, Cigarettes
   (c) choice of words, for example Job Grab Row.
(5) With older pupils there can be fruitful study of the language of the press:
   (a) Comparison of the language used in the editorials of popular and quality newspapers (e.g. comparison of an editorial from the *Sydney Sun* with one from the *Sydney Morning Herald*).
   (b) Analysis of the language of letters to the editor in popular and quality papers.
(6) Older pupils can investigate the power of the press, its links with television, and discuss the ethics of chequebook journalism (i.e. where someone in the public eye, such as Ronald Biggs and his wife a few years ago, is paid a large sum for his/her memoirs, which are usually 'ghosted' in the newspaper office).
(7) Some useful poems (for older pupils) are:
   'Headline History' by William Plomer
   'Gutter Press' by Paul Dehn
   'The Great Newspaper Editor to the Subordinate' by D. H. Lawrence

Reference

Barry Dwyer and Bob Walshe, *Learning to Read the Media*, Sydney: PETA, 1984.

NIM – An acronym for the Neurological Impress Method, sometimes referred to as the impress method or echo reading. It is a technique for impressing upon poorer readers patterns of accurate, fluent readers. Each reader works intensively with the teacher individually for about fifteen minutes daily over a total instructional period of seven to twelve hours. To encourage confidence, the material used should be slightly below the reader's capability. The teacher reads aloud while the student 'echoes' the teacher's words and uses a finger in a smooth continuous movement under the print to reinforce the flow of the oral reading.

The emphasis upon the modelling of fluent oral reading patterns has been successful with less proficient readers. However, it is important that NIM be supported by other teaching strategies which emphasize silent reading and reading as a meaning-gaining activity. **(MRT)**

See also READ-ALONG.

References

R. Heckelman, 'A neurological-impress method of remedial reading instruction', *Academic Therapy*, 4, 1969: 277–82.

P. Hollingsworth, 'An experimental approach to the impress method of teaching reading', *The Reading Teacher*, 31 (6), 1978: 624–6.

NON-FICTION – For suggestions for suitable non-fiction for class use, *see* AUTOBIOGRAPHY; BIOGRAPHY.

NON-STANDARD ENGLISH – English which is not 'Standard English' (q.v.). Non-standard English should perhaps be regarded as a dialect (q.v.) rather than a register (q.v.) variant. In any case students ought not to be given the impression that non-standard is an inferior language – though, of course, students who habitually speak non-standard English ought to have their language options widened to include Standard English.

NON-VISUAL INFORMATION – The term 'non-visual information' is used widely in psycholinguistic accounts of the reading process to describe the information a reader brings to the page in order to make sense out of what is on the page. The non-visual information which a reader may use includes knowledge of the language and how it functions (syntactic information); knowledge of the broad content area being read about (semantic information); and knowledge of the shapes of letters, the sounds of spoken language and some of the common combinations and relationships between them (grapho-phonic information). Competent readers make optimum use of this existing store of information, while at the same time diminishing their reliance on the visual information. **(MRT)**

See also PSYCHOLINGUISTICS; VISUAL INFORMATION; SYNTACTIC INFORMATION; SEMANTIC INFORMATION; GRAPHO-PHONIC INFORMATION.

Reference

Frank Smith, *Understanding Reading*, 3rd edn, New York: Holt, Rinehart & Winston, 1982.

NORM-REFERENCED ASSESSMENT – In norm-referenced assessment, the student is ranked relative to the average performance of a group. Grades are often used (e.g. A, B, C, D, U). Grades like these are meaningful if defined in terms of specified percentile ranges (e.g. A = top 10 per cent) relative to a defined population and if the tasks from which the grades are taken constitute a sensible sampling of what is important in English.

However, commonly, no percentile ranges are defined; reports do not specify the reference group (which may be class, year level within the school, the teacher's guess as to a statewide standard or an unpredictable mixture of these); and the weighting of different tasks (study of texts, personal writing, oral language, etc.) is achieved by accident.

It is interesting to consider whether students should be legally protected against grading systems which cannot be sensibly defended.

Norm-referenced grades are sometimes requested by parents who are anxious about where their children are coming in the race towards entry into the professions. Because part of the function of secondary schools in our society is to offer some the opportunity to enter tertiary courses to study for a high-status profession, while denying this opportunity to others, parents' anxieties need to be respected and responded to.

Consequently, many schools emphasize approximations to norm-referenced assessment.

One difficulty with this is that in a norm-referenced scheme, the most salient part of the assessment, the mark or grade, tells the parent, the student and other teachers no information that can actually be useful to them. A student may have improved in performance remarkably, but if the rest of the class has improved as well, then the student will stay at the same grading or even fall to a lower grading. No matter how good the teacher, there will always be a set proportion of failures in this assessment scheme. It is in fact a disincentive to teaching for success.

A second difficulty is that the time the teacher spends making norm-referenced assessments is time he/she is not spending in a more helpful educational stance towards the student. If we are to make norm-referenced assessments, we should draw upon a wide range of tasks and situations so that our comparisons are fair. But as our emphasis becomes more on telling the students whether they are doing better or worse than their peers, we actually distract them from observing precisely what it is that they are doing.

Most teachers try to achieve a compromise between the two roles. They write helpful comments on students' work and grade it. Then they feel frustrated when many students feel resentful towards them. Yet we would all feel resentful towards someone who was called a teacher but who made unfavourable judgements of us for other people to use. (What if a golf coach said 'You're only a D, you'll need to try harder'?)

To resolve these problems schools might decide to emphasize their educational role and refuse to rank students. Their assessments might then be descriptive, criterion-referenced (q.v.) or goal-based (q.v.).

Alternatively students could be required to select a very small proportion of their work to go to an external judge for ranking. (This still guarantees failure for many, but at least the class teacher is then an ally of the students, not an obstacle to their development.) **(BJ)**

NOVELS – There does seem to be a good argument for the shared experience of the class novel, particularly at secondary level, but it should always be supplemented with wide reading (q.v.). A large number of suggestions for teaching the novel are to be found in the entry on IMAGINATIVE RE-CREATION OF LITERATURE.

Here is a short list of novels suitable for class study:

Age 10–12

Betsy Byars	– *The Pinballs; The Cybil War; The Eighteenth Emergency*
Aidan Chambers	– *The Present Takers*
Gertie Evenhuis	– *What about Me?*
Clive King	– *Stig of the Dump*
Colin Thiele	– *Storm Boy*
E. B. White	– *Charlotte's Web*

Age 12–14

All the above, and:

Natalie Babbitt	– *Tuck Everlasting*
Antonia Barber	– *The Amazing Mr Blunden*
Betsy Byars	– *The Cartoonist; The Two-Thousand-Pound Goldfish*

Susan Cooper	– *The Dark Is Rising*
Leon Garfield	– *Smith; John Diamond*
Janni Howker	– *The Nature of the Beast*
Gene Kemp	– *The Turbulent Term of Tyke Tiler*
Ursula Le Guin	– *A Wizard of Earthsea*
Ruth Park	– *Playing Beatie Bow*
Hans Peter Richter	– *Friedrich*
Randolph Stow	– *Midnite*
Ivan Southall	– *Let the Balloon Go; Ash Road*
Rosemary Sutcliff	– *Dragonslayer*
Robert Westall	– *The Machine Gunners*
Patricia Wrightson	– *I Own the Racecourse!*

Age 14+

Robert Cormier	– *The Chocolate War* (Year 10)
Leon Garfield	– *Black Jack; The Ghost Downstairs*
S. E. Hinton	– *That Was Then, This Is Now; Rumble Fish*
Felice Holman	– *Slake's Limbo*
Linda Hoy	– *Your Friend, Rebecca*
M. E. Kerr	– *Dinky Hocker Shoots Smack!; The Son Of Someone Famous*
Robert O'Brien	– *Z for Zachariah*
K. M. Peyton	– *The Beethoven Medal*
Hans Peter Richter	– *The Time of the Young Soldiers*
Eleanor Spence	– *A Candle for St Antony*
Robert Swindells	– *Brother in the Land*
Paul Zindel	– *The Pigman*

Age 15+

Robert Cormier	– *I Am the Cheese*
Richard Hughes	– *A High Wind in Jamaica*
John Knowles	– *A Separate Peace*
Fred Uhlman	– *Reunion*

See also YOUNG ADULT LITERATURE.

References

Kenyon Calthrop, *Reading Together*, London: Heinemann, 1971.
Rob McGregor (ed.), *Reading Is Response: 2nd Supplement*, Sydney: St Clair, 1982.
Wayne Sawyer (ed.), *Reading is Response: 3rd Supplement*, Sydney: St Clair, 1985.
Ken Watson (ed.), *Reading Is Response*, Sydney: St Clair, 1980. *Reading Is Response: 1st Supplement*, Sydney: St Clair, 1981.

O

OBITUARIES – Ask pupils to write an obituary for the least admirable character in the novel they are reading. Point out that obituaries generally find things to praise in the deceased.

OBJECTIVE CORRELATIVE – 'The only way of expressing emotion in the form of art is by finding an 'objective correlative'; in other words, a set of objects, a situation, a chain of events which shall be the formula of that *particular* emotion; such that when the external facts, which must terminate in sensory experience, are given, the emotion is immediately evoked.'

Eliot's definition of his device stresses that the only way for the artist to express emotion is to represent events or objects which will call forth from the 'receiver' the same response, awareness and emotion that moved the poet. The device is more comprehensive than what we would conventionally call imagery or symbolism, but includes those concepts. Eliot's 'The Hollow Men' consists of a series of such objective correlatives:

> wind in dry grass
> Or rats' feet over broken glass
> In our dry cellar . . .
>
> Sunlight on a broken column
> There, is a tree swinging
> And voices are
> In the wind's singing

OFF/FROM *See* USAGE.

OPEN CLASSROOM – One of the problems with discussing 'open' classrooms is deciding just what one means by the phrase. On one level the phrase 'open classroom' is used to refer to a spatial arrangement. Classrooms which have a number of 'centres' designated for particular activities are often referred to as 'open' (e.g. a reading area, writing area, theatre, library). Perhaps even more 'open' is when this spatial arrangement is in a state of flux according to the demands/needs of the students. On another level, the 'open classroom' refers to the issue of degree of choice given to students in pursuing activities. Within a classroom that contains 'centres' students may be given a choice of any activities offered, they may rotate activities or they may reject all the offered activities and pursue their own. Each of these options is to some degree 'open', though perhaps only the last would fit Herbert Kohl's 'free, non-authoritarian' definition (H. R. Kohl, *The Open Classroom*). Ernie Tucker, himself the creator of an open space workshop in a Sydney high school, adopts Hall's further important distinction between 'philosophy-centred' and 'method-centred' open-space teaching. If a teacher is committed to the philosophy of learning-through-language activity then

> The content of the lessons becomes more student-centred. Students find poems, make up plays, suggest topics, methods of presenting writing, or at a class meeting vote on which directions the class work will take . . . the students learn how to choose and how to initiate. The teacher responds with guidance and encouragement, widening horizons, deepening perceptions.

However, in 'the method-centred open classrooms (the) production metaphor seems to have taken over . . . the worksheet and the textbook predominate. The teacher is reduced to the role of foreman and tally clerk'.

A whole range of factors, institutional, personal and social, will determine the extent to which any teacher (or any department) will implement 'open-ness' in his/her classroom. It does seem important, however, that in a subject concerned so much with process, with personal experience, 'growth' and social interaction, that students be given some degree of choice over their learning. Moreover, we look forward to the day when all classrooms will be able to establish 'centres' for a range of activities.

References

R. Hall, 'Open schools, open spaces, open classes in Melbourne, 1971', *Modern Teaching*, Winter, 1971.

H. R. Kohl, *The Open Classroom*, London: Methuen, 1970.

E. Tucker, 'What's all this got to do with English?' *The Teaching of English*, 34, May, 1978, and 'English in the open classroom', in K. D. Watson and R. D. Eagleson, *English in Secondary Schools: Today and Tomorrow*, Sydney: ETANSW, 1977.

OPIE, IONA AND PETER – Researchers and collectors of material concerned with the world of childhood. The primary scholars in the field of childhood folklore in the second half of the twentieth century. Their important and pioneering books include *The Language and Lore of Schoolchildren* (Oxford: Oxford University Press, 1959) and *Children's Games in Street and Playground* (Oxford: Oxford University Press, 1969).

ORACY – Term coined by Andrew Wilkinson to cover the skills of speaking and listening, just as the term *literacy* covers both reading and writing.
See also LISTENING; NATIONAL ORACY PROJECT.

ORAL READING – Reading aloud with expression and fluency is an important feature of development for all readers. Proficiency in reading before an audience is a requirement of adult life; from reading a formal report to sharing literature or a newspaper article informally with friends or family.

Oral reading is, however, used much less than silent reading, and the process of both giving an accurate word-by-word rendition of the text, and at the same time using intonation to interpret the author's meaning, often inhibits the use of prediction strategies and text sampling which silent reading employs. Oral reading also decreases the speed at which materials may be meaningfully read, and the emphasis on quality of performance invariably results in a marked loss of meaning and ability to recall. It should be noted that all readers, including those who are proficient, make errors or miscues in oral reading, for example 'found' for 'discovered'. This is not a problem where the meaning of the text is maintained.

In the classroom, oral reading should be a performance for an audience, and therefore a rehearsed activity on materials which the reader has previously read silently for meaning. The traditional practice of round-robin reading (q.v.) has no value as a technique for developing reading competence.

Oral reading is also well established as a technique for the teacher to diagnose the individual strengths and weaknesses of a reader. **(MRT)**

See also LISTENING TO CHILDREN READ; READING MISCUE INVENTORY; SILENT READING.

OTHER AWARD – Established in 1975 by the Children's Rights Workshop in the United Kingdom for children's books of literary merit which are progressive in their treatment of ethnic minorities, sex roles and social differences. It is an annual honorary award, and is non-competitive. Some of the books listed in 1982 were Raymond Briggs's *When the Wind Blows*, Susan Hemmings's *Girls Are Powerful* and Marlene Santa Shyer's *Welcome Home Jellybean.* Gene Kemp's *The Turbulent Term of Tyke Tiler*, Rosemary Sutcliff's *Song for a Dark Queen* and Farrukh Dhondy's *Come to Mecca* were award winners in previous years.

'We habitually use talk to go back over events and interpret them, make sense of them in a way that we were unable to while they were taking place. This is to work upon our representation of the particular experience and our world representation in order to incorporate the one into the other more fully.'

(James Britton,
Language and Learning)

p

PARODY – A form of satire (q.v.) which adopts the style or sentiments of a particular work and consciously exaggerates them for a comic effect. Any mock-heroic work such as Pope's *Rape of the Lock* is a parody. A famous example in novel form is *Joseph Andrews* as a parody of *Pamela.* In modern pop culture, the well-known *Rinse the Blood off My Toga* is a parody of the detective story.

PATHETIC FALLACY – The tendency of some writers to ascribe human emotions to the natural world. Unfortunately, 'pathetic fallacy' has tended to be a derogatory term applied to personification striving for very artificial effects. Perhaps, therefore, it ought to be distinguished from genuine symbolic landscapes that serve as a reflection of human emotion or have a metaphysical relationship with human emotions – for example, Tennyson's:

> The woods decay, the woods decay and fall,
> The vapours weep their burthen to the ground
> ('Tithonus')

or Wordsworth's:

> the distant hills
> Into the tumult sent an alien sound
> Of melancholy not unnoticed . . .
> (*Prelude, I*)

PATHOS – That which stimulates pity in the reader. Attempts at pathos often misfire, leading to bathos (q.v.).

PEER ASSESSMENT – In teaching students to assess the work of their fellows it seems best to start with them *recognizing* the strong parts of their peers' writing or speaking. Later the emphasis can move to a more detailed response, in the role of audience. For example, in responding to a peer's writing, early in the year, a student might be asked to indicate the strong parts; later in the year the student might be asked to respond in terms of the following instructions as well:

(1) Indicate any parts you disagree with or find confusing.

(2) Indicate any parts that seem too drawn-out, that could be shortened;
(3) Indicate any parts where you want more detail or explanation.

In this approach, the student who is to respond is being taught to articulate his or her reading (or listening) process. The emphasis is *descriptive.* Students are not required to make judgements of their peers' work, nor to suggest how it could be different, because both of these tasks discourage the reader or listener from *dwelling on* what was originally expressed. **(BJ)**

Reference

Brian Johnston, *Assessing English*, Milton Keynes: Open University Press, 1987.

PERSONAL GROWTH MODEL OF ENGLISH – That model of English studies which stresses the role of 'subject English' in exploring and extending the personal experience of the students. Also known as 'experience-centred English', this model gives 'primary emphasis to pupils' construction of their personal and social worlds' (Dixon, 1975, p. 122). Criticism of the personal growth model has tended to revolve around the supposed denigration of literature in this model (e.g. David Allen, *English Teaching Since 1965: How Much Growth?* London: Heinemann, 1980). But most of this criticism comes from wilful misreading of Dixon's *Growth Through English* (q.v.) since Dixon recognizes that 'we look to literature to bring order and control to our world, and . . . to offer an encounter with difficult areas of experience' and, further, that 'in reading literature at our highest levels we come closest to the ebb and flow of human activity' (p. 57). These are not the statements of one aiming to denigrate the value of literature.
See also LITERATURE-CENTRED ENGLISH.

Reference

John Dixon, *Growth Through English*, 3rd edn, London: Oxford University Press, 1975.

PETA *See* PRIMARY ENGLISH TEACHING ASSOCIATION.

PHONEME – In non-technical usage a phoneme is a speech sound or, more precisely, a significant speech sound in a particular language which contrasts with other speech sounds in that language. From the wide range of speech sounds that humans are capable of producing, each language has its own select set which are recognized as speech sounds in that language. The set of phonemes in one language will differ somewhat from the set of phonemes in another language. Thus in Japanese there is no distinction made between the *r* and *l* sounds, whereas for English speakers these sounds are quite different. On the other hand, some Eastern European languages recognize more than one kind of *l* sound, which in English are the one phoneme. Australian English has about forty-four distinct speech sounds or phonemes.

Technically a phoneme is not the same as a speech sound but rather a part of the range of speech sounds recognized in a given language as distinct from neighbouring parts of the range. There may be some variation of sound within each phoneme, variation which does not count in the particular language. **(JC)**

PHONICS – Phonics instruction attempts to teach reading by increasing the child's familiarity with common sound–symbol relationships. This is done sometimes through the teaching of rules (e.g. long vowel with silent 'e' as in 'race') and, at other times, through the presentation of lists of words (or 'word families') which share a common phonic element (e.g. *oo* words such as *look*, *cook*, *took*, *brook*).

Most phonic-based programmes restrict vocabulary in order to establish regularity of sound–symbol relationships. Linguistic programmes are similar to phonic programmes teaching the alphabet first as a code, then concentrating on regularly spelt whole words which are to be decoded if not immediately recognized.

The instructional materials for the earlier stages of such programmes are at best contrived, stilted and heavily dependent upon illustrations to provide motivation and some meaning which is not evident in the text itself.

Phonics instruction tends to be ineffective because of the lack of phonic consistency in the English language. Furthermore, where phonics instruction is limited to relationships with a high level of applicability, children may develop an overconcern with accurate word identification, a lack of concern for meaning as the central purpose of reading, and a tendency to use 'sounding out' as the major and sometimes only method of attacking unfamiliar words.

There are over 300 phonic correspondences and about 50 per cent of the words listed by Gates as most frequently used by children between the ages of 5 and 9 cannot be 'unlocked' by phonic techniques. Moreover, many children in the early school grades have not reached the stage of cognitive development to enable them to understand the relation between part and whole, or to focus their attention on more than one aspect of something at a time. This would create considerable difficulty in understanding the relation between a sequence of individual sounds and the word which is constituted by the sounds.

A number of reading schemes are heavily reliant upon a phonics approach, particularly at early levels. Examples are, *Words in Colour*, *Hay Wingo*, *Distar Reading*, *Reading 360*. **(MRT)**

See also LANGUAGE EXPERIENCE; VISUAL AND NON-VISUAL INFORMATION; READING SCHEMES.

Reference

Constance Weaver, *Psycholinguistics of Reading: From Process to Practice*, Cambridge, Mass: Winthrop, 1980.

PIAGETIAN STAGES *See* COGNITIVE GROWTH, STAGES OF.

PICARESQUE – From the Spanish 'picaro' ('rogue') this term was originally applied to works in which the main character was something of a villain. More generally, the term is usually applied to novels which concentrate on the life and adventures of a single character and supply a background to his or her times, for examples *Tom Jones*, *The Adventures of Huckleberry Finn*.

See also BILDUNGSROMAN.

PICTURE BOOKS – Picture books, from the nineteenth-century art of Caldecott, Crane and Greenaway through the extraordinarily powerful painting of Rackham, have been an important part of the culture of children. They have been primarily seen as objects of enjoyment, though sometimes previously as a means of moral instruction.

Recently picture books have been taken more seriously as literature; the change in attitude is starkly marked by critical regard for Sendak's *Where the Wild Things Are*, with its haunting rhythm and sophisticated interaction between text and illustration. In Australia, where picture books have closely reflected international developments, the changed attitude is again starkly marked by critical regard for Ron Brooks's illustrations for Jenny Wagner's *John Brown, Rose and the Midnight Cat*.

In England the recent publication of Anthony Browne's *Hansel and Gretel* breaks new ground through the social comment created by the interaction of text and pictures: the familiar Grimm telling is placed against a contemporary world of a rundown council house, television and expensive cosmetics. The use of recurring motifs is both subtle and effective in this book. Raymond Briggs's *When the Wind Blows*, now produced as a play in the West End, is a further example of powerful social comment on an issue of particular concern to youth.

Wordless picture books, once only the 'reading matter' of very young children, still enjoy that status, as with Mercer Mayer's *A Boy, A Dog and a Frog*, but they have also been developed into highly sophisticated art forms. One thinks especially of the Japanese artist M. Anno's books, *Anno's Journey* and *Anno's Italy*. Raymond Briggs's *The Snowman* is a wordless comic which, like Anno's work, requires the reader to make quite sophisticated interpretations through the use of personal and literary experience.

Whereas until recently illustrations in picture books were the major element, the balance between text and story has been recently reassessed. Jorg Muller and Jorg Steiner's *The Sea People* is an example of a short story which has been magnificently illustrated to make the text both more enjoyable and more accessible to young readers. Chris van Allsburg's *Jumanji* is a further example. Peter Dickinson's *City of Gold*, illustrated by Michael Foreman, must be considered as a picture book because of the quality of the art work and the integral relationship between text and illustration, but here the text is certainly the predominant element.

Accompanying artistic and literary development is a new educational interest in picture books, particularly in the possibility that children might learn to read from picture books rather than basal readers. The issue has been discussed in Margaret Meek's *Learning to Read* (London: Bodley Head, 1982) and an invaluable bibliography has been provided in Jill Bennett's *Learning to Read with Picture Books* (Stroud: Thimble Press, 1982). **(GW)**

PICTURE BOOKS FOR OLDER CHILDREN – Teachers of older children (say 9–15) have been slow to appreciate the possibilities provided by today's magnificent range of picture books. Joyce Kirk has pointed out that picture books can be used both as a stimulus to writing (e.g. writing books for younger children and then reading them to a real audience of children at a preschool or infants school) and as a means of providing an understanding of how literature works (e.g. illustrating the idea of *theme* by using *John Brown, Rose and the Midnight Cat* by Ron Brooks and Jenny Wagner).

Further, many modern picture books, as Elaine Moss has shown, are actually quite demanding, and well worth discussing in the classrooms. A recent example is Raymond Briggs's *When the Wind Blows*; others are listed in Elaine Moss's booklet.

References

Joyce Kirk, 'Meet Max, John Brown, Mr Gumpy, Fungus and others', in R. McGregor (ed.), *Reading Is Response: 2nd Supplement*, Sydney: St Clair, 1982.

Elaine Moss, *Picture Books for Young People, 9–13*, Stroud: Thimble Press, 1981.

PLAYS FOR PERFORMANCE – Finding plays suitable for performance by young people is no easy task. Fortunately, a very useful annotated guide has recently appeared: *Plays for Young People to Read and Perform* by Aidan Chambers, Stroud: Thimble Press, 1982. The list offered here is based on the assumptions that teachers will be looking for plays that are reasonably well written and have large casts (so that the whole class can be involved).

One-Act Plays/Short Plays

(1) Plays for younger actors (9–14)

Ace, King, Queen by Dorothy Carr (in A. M. Sharp, ed., *Modern Plays*, 2nd series, Dent)

The Bushrangers' Christmas Eve by Kylie Tennant

Curious Case of O by Richard Blythe (obtainable from Samuel French)

Ernie's Incredible Illucinations by Alan Ayckbourn – for older children (in A. Durband, ed. *Playbill One*, Hutchinson.)

The Farce of M. Pierre Patelin, a play dating from medieval times (various collections)

The Gods of the Mountains by Lord Dunsany (various collections)

The Little Man by John Galsworthy (various collections)

Scuttleboom's Treasure by Ronald Gow (various collections)

In addition, it is possible to extract scenes from longer plays:

Noah by André Obey (Act I)

1066 and All That by Reginald Arkell (trial of Christopher Columbus and Guy Fawkes), for older children

Toad of Toad Hall by A. A. Milne (trial scene)

Shakespeare's *Henry IV, Part I* (Gadshill scenes), *Midsummer Night's Dream* (Rude Mechanicals), *Merchant of Venice* (trial scene)

(2) Plays for 14–18 year olds

Several of the above, such as *Ernie's Incredible Illucinations*, *The Farce of M. Pierre Patelin*, Act I of *Noah*, excerpts from the musical *1066 and All That*, are suitable for use with students of 14+. Additional short plays include:

Androcles and The Lion by G. B. Shaw (shortened version)

Pygmalion by G. B. Shaw (Act I)

School Play by David Howarth (in Alan Durband, ed., *Playbill One*, Hutchinson)

Skin of Our Teeth by Thornton Wilder (Act I).

Speech Day by Barry Hines (in Alan Durband, ed., *Prompt Two*, Hutchinson)

Tamburlane the Mad Hen by Adrian Mitchell (in *Playspace*, Methuen)

Longer Plays

(1) Plays for younger actors

The Burning Bush by Tom Stanier (Heinemann Educational), musical
Johnny Salter by Aidan Chambers (Heinemann Educational)
The Plotters of Cabbage Patch Corner by David Wood (Samuel French), musical.
The Thwarting of Baron Bolligrew by Robert Bolt (Heinemann).
Toad of Toad Hall, by A. A. Milne.
Tom Sawyer by Derek Lomas (Macmillan Dramascript series).

(2) Plays for older actors

Baker's Boy by R. Speakman and D. Nicholls (Macmillan Dramascripts).
The Beauty of Buttermere or a Maid Betrayed by Alasdair Brown (Heinemann Educational)
Before Your Very Eyes by John Challen (Heinemann Educational)
The Caucasian Chalk Circle by Bertolt Brecht
Noah by André Obey
The Royal Hunt of the Sun by Peter Shaffer
Skin of Our Teeth by Thornton Wilder
1066 and All That by Reginald Arkell, musical

To this list of longer plays could be added several of Shakespeare's and many well-known musicals (e.g. *West Side Story*, *Oliver!*).

POETIC LANGUAGE *See* LANGUAGE, FUNCTIONS OF.

POETRY ANTHOLOGIES – There are many excellent anthologies on the market.
Here is a short list:

Middle and Upper Primary

Junior Voices, ed. Geoffrey Summerfield (Penguin).
Over My Shoulder, ed. Susan Groundwater-Smith *et al.*, (Rigby).
Stuff and Nonsense, ed. Michael Dugan (Collins).
Watchwords I, ed. M. and P. Benton (Hodder and Stoughton).

Junior Secondary

The Climb and the Dream, ed. K. Watson and S. Eagles (Macmillan).
Laugh or Cry or Yawn, ed. L. Hannan and B. Breen (Cheshire).
Poetry Is What, ed. L. Hannan and B. Breen (Cheshire).
Stolen Moments, ed. R. and J. Johnson (Wiley).
Touchstones I, II, ed. M. and P. Benton (Hodder and Stoughton).

Middle and Upper Secondary

Blue Umbrellas, ed. P. Richardson and K. Watson (Cassell).
Improving on the Blank Page, ed. D. Cook and K. Gallasch (Rigby).
Kaleidoscope I, II, ed. D. Mallick and R. Jones (Heinemann).
Mainly Modern, ed. J. and D. Colmer (Rigby).
The Rattle Bag, ed. Seamus Heaney and Ted Hughes (Faber).
Strictly Private, ed. Roger McGough (Puffin).
Touchstones III, IV, ed. M. and P. Benton (Hodder and Stoughton).

NB: *The Rattle Bag* and *Strictly Private* do not fit easily into the last category, as they contain many poems which will be enjoyed by younger children.

POETRY, SUGGESTIONS FOR TEACHING – Poetry should be linked both with other aspects of the students' work in English and with their life outside school. The following suggestions, then, are offered not as discrete poetry lessons but as activities which can be incorporated into integrated English units.

(1) Where students are to discuss poems, it is essential that they be given time to come to terms with the poems before they are asked questions. In general, a good reading by the teacher should be followed by silent reading by students and perhaps another oral reading (by teacher or a student) before discussion begins.
(2) Poems should not be turned into comprehension tests.
(3) If whole-class discussion is to form the bulk of the lesson, the placing of pupils in small groups for ten or fifteen minutes beforehand will lead to much greater involvement and a higher level of discussion.
(4) Pupils do find it easier to compare two or three poems of similar theme or topic than to discuss a single poem. For a list of poems grouped by topic or theme, see *Where's that Poem?*, Helen Morris (Oxford: Blackwell, 1987) and *Find that Poem!* eds. K. Watson and W. Sawyer (Sydney: St Clair Press, 1983).
(5) Suggestions for stimulating discussion in small groups:
    (i) Present a poem with some words deleted (i.e. a modified form of cloze). Pupils in groups argue about appropriate words to put in the blanks, using semantic, metrical and rhyming clues. This is a very valuable activity for encouraging close reading.
    (ii) Give groups a poem with each stanza on a separate piece of paper. Ask them to decide on the correct order. This draws pupils' attention to structure.
    (iii) Where a poem exists in several drafts, like Blake's *The Tyger* or Wilfred Owen's *Anthem for Dead Youth*, have pupils discuss the changes that have been made and whether these changes are improvements. Alternatively, make some changes yourself to a poem and have pupils discuss the effect of the changes, for example 'I met a traveller from an olden land . . .' (alteration of the opening of Shelley's *Ozymandias*).
    (iv) Get pupils in groups to formulate a set of questions about a poem to which they really want to know the answers. Pool the questions for whole-class discussion.
(6) Involve students in writing (and discussing) their own poems. For suggestions for stimulating this activity, see *On Common Ground* by Jill Pirrie (London: Hodder and Stoughton, 1987), *What Rhymes with Secret?* by Sandy Brownjohn (London: Hodder and Stoughton, 1982), *A Book to Write Poems by* by Rory Harris and Peter McFarlane (Adelaide: AATE, 1983), Brian Powell's *English Through Poetry Writing* (Sydney: Novak) and several of the articles in David Mallick and Gill Jenkins (eds), *Poetry in the Classroom* (Sydney: St Clair, 1983).
(7) Primary and junior secondary pupils thoroughly enjoy verse speaking.

(Verse speaking has the added advantage of providing a painless method of memorization, recommended for use by those teachers who see this as having value in itself.) Start with simple unison work, using verses like W. S. Gilbert's *To Sit in Solemn Silence* (*see* ALLITERATION), C. J. Dennis's *The Axe-Man* and *Hist!*, Walter de la Mare's *Five Eyes*.

(8) Where a poem gives an account of an incident, it is sometimes a useful activity to have the pupils rewrite the incident in prose form (e.g. as a letter to a friend) and then, in groups, discuss what is gained or lost in the prose version.

(9) A rich source of ideas is an article by Geoff Fox and Brian Merrick, 'Thirty-six things to do with a poem' in Anthony Adams (ed.), *New Directions in the Teaching of English*, East Sussex: Falmer Press.

POINT OF VIEW – Point of view can be a crucial notion for the understanding of much literature. The *Ancient Mariner*'s 'He prayeth best who loveth best / All things both great and small' raises the problem for students of just whose view this is – the poet's or the Mariner's? This sense of 'point of view' as ideology or attitude raises one set of distinctions for students, but 'point of view' in the more literal sense of 'Whose position are we seeing from?' raises a more subtle set of distinctions. Take the following scene from Dickens' *Little Dorrit*:

> 'It seems to me hard', said Little Dorrit, 'that he should have lost so many years and suffered so much, and at last pay all the debt as well. It seems to me hard that he should pay in life and money both.'
>
> 'My dear child – ' Clenman was beginning. . . . The prison, which could spoil so many things, had tainted Little Dorrit's mind no more than this.

What are we to make of this last sentence? Is this Dickens pointing out Little Dorrit's relative incorruption? Or is it, rather, Clenman's point of view on Little Dorrit and hence, perhaps, Dickens' judgement on Clenman? Whose voice is it?

Recently, the increasing incursion of narratology (q.v.) into English studies have made such phrases as 'Dickens' judgement' obsolete and made important distinctions between 'point of view' and 'voice'.

Chatman (q.v.), for example, distinguishes between the real author, the implied author and the narrator, at least the last two of which have points of view which would be discernible in a novel. After characterizing three common uses of the term 'point of view' ('literal', through someone's eyes; 'figurative', the ideological sense referred to earlier; and 'transferred', from someone's interest-vantage), Chatman draws the crucial distinction between 'point of view' and 'voice'. 'Point of view' is the perspective from which an expression is made, while 'voice' is the expression itself.

These need not be lodged in the same person. The distinction is between 'Who sees?' and 'Who speaks?', with 'point of view' the province of the former. Genette (q.v.) makes an identical distinction between what he calls 'mood' and 'voice'.

When these distinctions become important or when the general issue of 'Whose viewpoint?' becomes important, imaginative recreation (q.v.) activities which ask students to change the point of view may help bring aspects to the fore which help open up discussion of the issue.

References

Seymour Chatman, *Story and Discourse: Narrative Structure in Fiction and Film*, New York: Cornell University Press, 1978.

Gerard Genette, *Narrative Discourse: An Essay in Method*, New York: Cornell University Press, 1980.

POSTERS – Discuss the ways in which posters communicate. First World War posters are excellent for this purpose, for example 'What Did You Do in the War, Daddy?'

POST-STRUCTURALISM – This is an umbrella term covering a range of writers, mostly French and American, reacting against the 'dismal science of semiology' (*Barthes*), using elements of semiological and structuralist thought in radical new ways; for example, the idea of 'signifier' (*see* STRUCTURALISM, SEMIOLOGY) is seen as free-floating, not necessarily tied to a 'signified'. Post-structuralism proclaims the 'end of theory'.

Post-structuralist writers share a concern with ideology, power, the nature of the self or subject – which is seen as shattered –, the nature of meta-language (language about language), the possibility of art/writing in our present 'ideological space', and the nature of relations between author, reader and text.

Such issues are, of course, important and interesting. Post-structuralists seek to dissolve the categories and language in which such things have hitherto been discussed. To some, the results are exhilarating; post-structuralism becomes something of an all-consuming passion. Post-structuralist writing is often difficult, elusive, even incomprehensible, since it is held that nothing short of remaking – continually – forms of discourse can adequately deal with the alleged 'epistemological break' consequent upon Freud, Marx, Saussure and Nietzsche, particularly as refracted through Michel Foucault, Jacques Derrida and Jacques Lacan.

Post-structuralism is primarily a philosophical/artistic movement. Its thinkers have replaced the likes of Sartre, Marcuse, McLuhan and R. D. Laing as marks of the 'in' intelligentsia. To those like me who see language as, in realization, far from arbitrary, as rooted in and guaranteeing the life of social humanity, and who are therefore chary of the intellectual antecedents and political/cultural implications of a movement that is essentially destructive and élitist, other approaches seem more sustaining, and certainly of more use in working to assist students gain power over, and through, language. (*See* LINGUISTIC CRITICISM.)

The Roland Barthes of 'From work to text' (in *Image–Music–Text*, London: Fontana, 1977) is a good entry into post-structuralist writing. Other figures, of varying degrees of difficulty, are Foucault, Derrida, and Julia Kristeva.

A special number of the post-structuralist *Oxford Literary Review* 5 (1–2), 1982, contains introductions to and examples of many of the issues raised here. See also J. V. Harari, *Textual Strategies* (London: Methuen, 1979), an anthology of basic post-structuralist texts; C. Norris, *Deconstruction* (London: Methuen, 1982); G. Hartman, *Criticism in the Wilderness* (New Haven, Conn.: Yale University Press, 1980).

A number of Australian journals carry post-structuralist writing: *Art and Text* (Victoria) and *On the Beach* (Sydney) are two. **(NJW)**
See also STRUCTURALISM; SEMIOLOGY.

PRACTICABLE/PRACTICAL *See* USAGE.

PREPOSITION, PLACEMENT OF *See* USAGE.

PRE-READING – This is the term used to describe the activities and experiences designed to prepare nursery school children and kindergarten children for formal reading instruction. **(MRT)**
See also CONCEPTS ABOUT PRINT; READING READINESS.

PRIMARY ENGLISH TEACHING ASSOCIATION (PETA) – An Australian professional association. Inquiries: PETA, PO Box 167, Rozelle NSW 2039.

PROGRAM, PROGRAMME *See* USAGE.

PROGRAMME EVALUATION *See* EVALUATION OF ENGLISH PROGRAMMES.

PROGRAMME PLANNING IN ENGLISH – Any English programme must be firmly based on what is known about how children learn language. (*See* LANGUAGE ACQUISITION.) We would further suggest that there are six other basic principles:

(1) Balance

There must be adequate opportunity for students to engage in reading, writing, speaking, listening. A sensible way of ensuring balance is for the teacher to draw up, early in the year, a *checklist of activities/experiences to be undertaken by students.* For example, under the heading *writing* the teacher of a Year 8 class might list the following experiences:

(i) writing for a variety of audiences – self (journal); peer group; unknown audience;
(ii) writing for a variety of purposes – letters of invitation (e.g. inviting parents and teachers to see a play put on by the class); instructions (e.g. for student use of video equipment); designing questionnaire (e.g. for school poll of TV viewing habits); short stories and poems to be shared with the rest of the class;
(iii) revising writing before publication – the skills of editing.

(2) Variety

(i) Variety of unit organization: thematic units, units based on novels or plays, writing workshops, drama workshops, excursions (*see* UNIT PLANNING).
(ii) Variety of grouping: whole-class, small group, pair work, individual work.
(iii) Variety of content: novels, plays, poems, magazine articles, newspapers, the world outside the classroom.

(3) Awareness of the interests and level of maturity of the class
It is essential for the teacher to begin where the pupils are; it is vital, too, for the teacher not to disregard the experiential background of the pupils. It is unlikely, for example, that Year 8 pupils will have the emotional maturity to cope with a novel like *Catcher in the Rye.*

(4) The importance of context (q.v.)
All activities must be presented in meaningful contexts. Language cannot exist apart from meaning and purpose; therefore, decontextualized exercises should be avoided. (*See* EXERCISES, ENGLISH THROUGH.)

(5) Sequence and continuity
A lockstep progression is impossible in English; nevertheless, the teacher should be striving to place pupils in situations which 'urge them towards the widest range of language use' (C. and H. Rosen) and which take them slowly up the ladder leading from concrete to abstract uses of language.

(6) Flexibility
The demands of the programme should never be such that they force the teacher to ignore the current event, the bright suggestion of a pupil, the availability of a promising resource. Nor should the teacher feel obliged to continue with a unit that is patiently not involving the pupils.

Suggestions for constructing lesson units are to be found in the entry on UNIT PLANNING.
See also INTEGRATION.

References
D. Jackson, *Continuity in English Teaching*, London: Methuen, 1982.
S. Judy, *The English Teacher's Handbook*, Cambridge, Mass: Winthrop, 1979.
N. McCulla and R. D. Walshe, *Balance in the Classroom, K-7*, Sydney: PETA, 1979.
C. and H. Rosen, *The Language of Primary School Children*, Harmondsworth: Penguin, 1973.
D. Stratford, 'An approach to the teaching of English', *Issues and Ideas* 3(3), Oct., 1981.
K. Watson, *English Teaching in Perspective*, 2nd edn, Milton Keynes: Open University Press, 1987.

PRONOUN AGREEMENT *See* USAGE: EVERYONE, ANYONE, EACH, EVERYBODY.

PRONUNCIATION – Like other aspects of language, pronunciation varies over time and place. It is important for pupils to realize that dictionaries, particularly those coming from other countries, will not provide them with accurate guides to pronunciation.

Students can discover the problems of dictionaries as guides to pronunciation by first investigating the pronunciation in their own community of words like *ate*, *patio*, *medicine*, *migraine* and then consulting the *Oxford Dictionary* (which, at least in our edition, recommends *et*, *partio*, *medcine*, *meegraine*). They can then undertake surveys of words which do not have an agreed-on pronunciation, like *kilometre*, to determine which pronunciation has the greatest following. Other words which could be included in such an investigation include *analagous* (hard *g* or soft?), *controversy* (stress on first or second syllable?),

Antarctic (first *c* pronounced?), *aristocrat* (stress on first or second syllable?), *comparable* (stress on first or second syllable?), *deteriorate* (*-or* pronounced or omitted?), *envelope* (*en* or *on*?), *harass* (stress on first or second syllable?), *preferable* (stress on first or second syllable?), *restaurant* (final *t* silent or sounded?), *temporarily* (stress on first or third syllable?). The results could be compared with the pronunciations given in a standard national dictionary (and the editors of that dictionary notified of any discrepancies!).

PROSODICS – A term used by Donald Graves for the devices very young children use in their writing to point up the speech sounds they consider important, e.g. capitalizing main nouns, using multiple exclamation marks, filling in words. These prosodics gradually disappear as the child gains in control over his/her writing, and begins to realize that sentences can carry their own stress signals.

PSYCHOLINGUISTICS – The study of psycholinguistics has emerged in recent years as an area of research and scholarship concerned with the psychology of language. It has drawn heavily on insights derived from the psychology of learning, memory, perception and attention, and from the study of the nature and function of language and its development.

The term 'psycholinguistic' is frequently used to describe a model of the reading process developed by such people as Ken and Yetta Goodman (q.v.) and Frank Smith. The psycholinguistic model of the reading process sees reading as a meaning-reconstructing process, in which the reader engages actively with the author through the printed page. **(MRT)**

References

K. Goodman, 'Reading: a psycholinguistic guessing game', *Journal of the Reading Specialist*, 6, 1967: 126–35.

M. Kemp, *Reading Language Processes: Assessment and Teaching*, Adelaide: Australian Reading Association Inc, 1980.

F. Smith, *Reading*, Cambridge: Cambridge University Press, 1978.

F. Smith, *Understanding Reading*, 3rd edn, New York: Holt, Rinehart & Winston, 1982.

PUNCTUATION PUZZLES – Punctuation can make all the difference. Challenge the class to change the following prohibition into an invitation:

PRIVATE
NO SWIMMING
ALLOWED

Answer:

PRIVATE?
NO! SWIMMING
ALLOWED

The following riddle is solved by inserting two commas:

Every lady in the land
Has twenty nails on each hand
Five and twenty on hands and feet.
This is true, without deceit.

PUNCTUATION, TEACHING OF – Researcher Lucy McCormick Calkins reports on the following piece of case study research in an article 'When children want to punctuate', reprinted in R. D. Walshe (ed.), *Donald Graves in Australia* (Sydney: PETA).

Two classes of third-grade children were studied in relation to their ability to acquire the 'mechanics' of writing. One class stopped studying punctuation skills by drills and exercises and replaced this by an hour's writing a day, three days a week. The other class continued to study the mechanics of writing by a skills-drill approach: pre-testing and post-testing on their use of various punctuation marks with drill and worksheet exercises in between. This latter class rarely did any writing.

At the end of a year, Calkins showed fourteen punctuation marks to each class and asked what each were used for. The 'writing class' could define and explain an average of 8.66 kinds of punctuation, while the 'skills-drill' class could only define and explain an average of 3.85 kinds of punctuation. The writing class defined punctuation marks operationally – if they couldn't name a punctuation mark, they could say what it was used for; as part of these operational definitions, 47 per cent of the explanations the writing class gave for punctuation referred to the way it affects the pace and inflection of language. Only 9 per cent of the 'skills-drill' class's definitions referred to this.

(Calkins's article includes a list of the punctuation marks tested and a table of the number of children from each of the two third-grades who were able to correctly discribe each type of punctuation. Her table dramatically demonstrates the differences in recognition and usage between the two classes.)

Calkins concludes that it is the urge to accommodate the reader and to provide the inflections so that the reader can imitate the writer's voice that leads children to struggle with language mechanics. 'When children write', she says, 'they reach for the skills they need.' The 'writing class', it should be remembered, had no formal instruction in punctuation and that those punctuation marks they could describe were taught individually to children at the time at which they had the need to learn it. At the beginning of the test year, the 'writing class' only needed an average of 2.22 different kinds of punctuation to correctly punctuate a piece of writing, and they used an average of 1.25 different kinds. They wrote mostly simple sentences, without dialogue, sound effects, supportive information or exclamations. By the middle of the test year, after six months of sustained writing, they needed an average of 5.62 different kinds of punctuation in order for their writing to be correctly punctuated, and they used an average of five different kinds in one piece.

The approach to writing used in the classroom was the 'process-conference' approach.

See also WRITING: PROCESS-CONFERENCE APPROACH.

References

Don Smedley, *Teaching the Basic Skills*, London: Methuen, 1983.

R. D. Walshe (ed.), *Donald Graves in Australia*, Sydney: PETA, 1983.

> 'growth in language does not occur in isolation from the life experiences of boys and girls'
>
> (John Dixon, *Growth Through English*)

q

QUESTIONING – Questioning is regarded as one of the basic skills of teaching. Of the many attempts to categorize the kinds of questions teachers ask – such as that based on Bloom's taxonomy (q.v.) – the most useful for English teachers is a modification of that produced by Douglas Barnes (q.v.):

(1) **Closed** questions (those for which only one answer, usually factual, is possible).
(2) **Open** questions (those which allow a range of responses and in general give more scope for thinking).
(3) **Pseudo**-questions (questions which appear to be open but for which the teacher's reception of answers shows that he or she will accept only one answer).

In English and other humanities one would hope that most of the questions asked would be open ones, but this does not seem to be so. Too often, questions simply require factual recall, or require pupils to slip predictable words for phrases into the slots provided:

Teacher: Where did they put the water . . . John?
John: In a big . . . er . . . pitcher.
Teacher: Good . . . in a pitcher . . . which they carried on their . . . ?
John: Heads.

(Barnes, 1971, p. 33)

Another pitfall of questioning concerns what is done with pupils' replies. It is all too easy for the teacher to distort a pupil's answer to fit in with the teacher's frame of reference:

Teacher: What about if you're the speaker in a discussion? You're the one everyone's listening to. What sort of rules must you follow?
Pupil: Sometimes you've got to be careful what you say about people.
Teacher: All right, you've got to think about what you're going to say.

See also WHOLE-CLASS DISCUSSION.

Reference

D. Barnes *et al.*, *Language, the Learner and the School*, rev. edn, Harmondsworth: Penguin, 1971.

> 'The essential moment which calls forth the development of speech is undoubtedly the creation of an objective necessity for speech communication.'
>
> (A. R. Luria and F. la Yudovich, *Speech and the Development of Mental Processes in the Child*)

r

RADIO – Ideas for studying radio as a medium include:

Listening

(1) Surveying and discussing favourite radio programmes in the family – if no 'favourites', discuss listening *habits*: who listens to what and when? and compare these findings to a similar survey on TV.

(2) Listen to selected radio programmes on current affairs for such listening activities as:
  (i) pinpointing speaker's main idea;
  (ii) assessing bias, use of evidence, etc.

(3) Compare BBC/commercial news presentations.

(4) Discuss styles of disc jockeys on different stations.

Working in the medium

(1) Radio class news magazine – different groups in the class could produce a class news tape, perhaps every month.

(2) Prepare class radio interviews with different people from around the school or district, perhaps for inclusion in the radio news.

(3) Make a class radio serial to be taped.

(4) Make and tape ads for radio – how do these sales pitches differ from television?

(5) Adapt sections of the class novel into a radio play for taping.

(6) Imitate particular radio programmes such as BBC's *Science Now* or *My Word.*

(7) Radio documentaries on topics of interest.

All of the above could be done as activities within a particular class simply using a tape recorder, but a number of schools now run lunchtime radio stations for the whole school's listening pleasure, and any of these could be adapted to this format also. All it takes is preparation and a school microphone with speakers around the school. Also, any of these activities could also be done in such other media as television or newspapers and it would be extremely useful to compare the different handling by the different media.

READABILITY – The intention underlying readability measurement is the appropriate matching of reader ability and text difficulty. This suggests a view of readability which implies a sophisticated conceptualization of the interactive relationship between reader and text. The actual practice of readability measurement using readability formulae, however, is based on an impoverished psychology of reading which does not take into account the structure or content of text nor the information processing capacities and strategies of the reader.

Most formulas determine passage difficulty on the basis of obvious surface features such as average word length and sentence length. Over fifty formulas now exist. The best known are Fry (1977), Dale and Chall (1948), Flesch (1948). Once formulas become popular, new formulas simply use the earlier ones as their criterion. Although formulas based on word and sentence length may have satisfactory predictive validity, long words and sentences are not necessarily the *cause* of difficulty and modifying these factors does not remove text difficulty. The use of the cloze procedure may provide a more adequate assessment of the 'interactive' conceptualization of readability. **(MRT)**

References

E. Dale and J. S. Chall, 'A formula for predicting readability', *Educational Research Bulletin*, 27:11–20, 37–54.

R. Flesch, 'A new readability yardstick', *The Journal of Applied Psychology*, 32, 1948: 221–33.

E. Fry, 'Fry's readability graph: clarification validity and extension to level 17', *Journal of Reading*, 20, Dec. 242–52.

C. Harrison, *Readability in the Classroom*, Cambridge: Cambridge University Press, 1980.

READ-ALONG – Another label for the Neurological Impress Method, Read-along and its various adaptations, for instance 'talking books', involves children in frequent, plentiful exposure to meaningful print. The child hears the material read naturally and with expression by a teacher, parent or peer tutor, or even on tape, while he or she follows the print. The child also tries to 'echo' the voice of the modelling reader. Hearing a fluent reading model often provides children with the confidence to begin predicting and anticipating the text. **(MRT)**

See also NEUROLOGICAL IMPRESS METHOD.

Reference

J. Richardson and G. Craker, 'Helping poor readers in the primary school: new insights', *Australian Journal of Reading*, 3 (3) August 1980, 131–6.

READER-RESPONSE CRITICISM – What do readers do when they read books? What is the product of the relationship which builds up between a novel, a play or a poem and its reader, both *while* and *after* the reading takes place?

For many theorists and critics of literature in recent years these have become seminal questions. They have moved the focus of literary study from the unchanging words of the text (which was the centre of attention for the American 'New Critics' (q.v.), F. R. Leavis (q.v.) and his followers in England, and those who based their approach to literature on I. A. Richards' *Practical Criticism*) to the more unpredictable nature of each particular reader's experience in creating a special world for him- or herself, while following the directions offered by the literary work he or she is reading.

Perhaps the most useful introduction to reader-response criticism is the collection of essays edited by Jane P. Tompkins (see p. 160) which uses the phrase as its title. The eleven essays she brings together show writers with a wide variety of theoretical positions – structuralist, stylistic, phenomenologist, psychoanalytical and post-structuralist – all of whom share an overriding concern with the activity of the reader. Tompkins herself, in the first and last chapters, gives a guide to the history of this interest, and indicates that it is no novelty, since it has its roots in the writings of classical Greek philosophers, and was also important in the sixteenth, seventeenth and eighteenth centuries.

For teachers of English literature, at all levels, the shifting of the focus from the text to the reader is very significant. Since from the infant school to the level of undergraduate studies in colleges and universities, most teachers' main business is to educate their students as readers, rather than to insist on the purity and differential qualities of literary texts, reader-response criticism offers many valuable insights.

Teachers may find that the most directly relevant theorists to the questions they raise are Wolfgang Iser, Louise Rosenblatt, and the later work of Roland Barthes (see suggested reading). None of these are easy writers to read in their original texts, and some mediation of their work has been offered, for example by Corcoran, Evans and Chambers. However, a few of the following points may give an idea of what is to be found in the books and articles listed:

(1) A major interest in what happens *while* a reader is reading a book – how are the dry words of a text converted into living images in the mind?
(2) How do readers *predict* their way through a text, and how do they *modify* these predictions as they read?
(3) What is the difference between reading a literary work and a text of some other kind? (Rosenblatt distinguishes between *aesthetic* reading (q.v.), where the concern is precisely with what happens *during* the reading, and *efferent* reading, where we are concerned with what we take away *afterwards*).
(4) What is the nature of *pleasure* in reading? (Here Barthes sees delight in literature as akin to sensual, even at times to erotic, pleasure.)

So reader-response criticism has arisen in recent years partly as a reaction to the almost exclusive concentration of earlier writers on the words of the text, and partly as an attempt to find literary studies a place in the wide-ranging philosophical systems proposed by phenomenology, structuralism, psychoanalysis and other such schools of thought. Inevitably, it has sometimes pressed its claims to extremes (as many people think they find in the work of Stanley Fish, who calls his best-known volume *Is There a Text in This Class?*), and has provoked equally violent reactions from the defenders of text-oriented criticism. Undoubtedly a mean needs to be found, and of those writers already mentioned, Louise Rosenblatt comes closest to doing this. She presses hard (e.g. in the final chapter of *The Reader, the Text, the Poem*,) for us to break down the élitism that crept into literary criticism in the earlier decades of this century, to restore the ordinary reader to his or her proper place, and to subordinate the activities of critics (and teachers) to trying to help ordinary readers to read better. Hence reader-response's particular value to teachers, whose central concern is with the place of literature in society as a whole, rather than in the world of a few dedicated critics and scholars. **(WDEE)**

See also IMPLIED READER.

Suggested Reading

Roland Barthes, *The Pleasure Of The Text*, New York: Hill & Wang, 1975.
Aidan Chambers, 'The reader in the Book', in N. Chambers, (ed.), *The Signal Approach to Children's Books*, Harmondsworth: Kestrel, 1980.
B. Corcoran and W. D. Emrys Evans, *Readers, Tests, Teachers*, Milton Keynes: Open University Press, 1987.
Wolfgang Iser, *The Act Of Reading*, Baltimore: Johns Hopkins University Press, 1978.
Louise Rosenblatt, *Literature As Exploration*, New York: Appleton-Century-Crofts, 1937; reprinted London: Routledge & Kegan Paul, 1976.
The Reader, The Text, The Poem, Carbondale: Southern Illinois University Press, 1978.
Jane P. Tompkins (ed.), *Reader-Response Criticism*, Baltimore: Johns Hopkins University Press, 1980.
For an application of reader-response theory to children's own writing, see also Brian Johnston, *Assessing English* (Milton Keynes: Open University Press, 1987), especially the section 'Showing how you read'.

READERS' THEATRE – This is a phrase which simply refers to performance of literature as a teaching method. The principle behind readers' theatre is that the more active process of *performance* will bring the reader and text closer together. Readers' theatre may be done through individual readings or a group of individual readings or through group performance. Non-fiction, poetry (both lyric and narrative) and prose can be all performed as equally effectively as scripted drama. In a very useful article on readers' theatre, Robert Post suggests such possible variations as:

(1) Programmes of poems on a particular theme such as death (e.g. Browning's 'Prospice', Eliot's 'Journey of the Magi', Owen's 'Strange Meeting', Donne's 'Death Be Not Proud', etc.).
(2) Multi-media approaches, for example students dancing to a reading of e. e. cummings's 'sweet spring is your'.
(3) Scott's 'Lochinvar' with different voices for each character and one for the narrator.
(4) Having only one character, play Capulet *and* Montague and another Lady Capulet *and* Lady Montague to show the likenesses between the two sets of parents in *Romeo and Juliet*.

References

R. M. Post, 'Readers' Theatre as a Method of Teaching Literature', in R. Arnold, *Approaches to Drama in the School*, ETA: NSW, 1979.
Shirlee Sloyer, *Readers' Theatre: Story Dramatisation in the Classroom*, Illinois: NCTE, 1982.

READING ACROSS THE CURRICULUM – Psycholinguistic accounts of the reading process have emphasized that effective reading development is largely dependent on the reader's ability to make use of non-visual information, or appropriate background knowledge, in deriving meaning from print. Learning to read texts in curriculum areas such as science, maths, social studies and so on, should be an integral part of the normal teaching in those subjects. Because of their unfamiliarity with relevant concepts, teachers of English would find it difficult to assist students to read physics texts efficiently. Those who teach the curriculum context must also teach students how this context is used in reading curriculum area materials.

The teacher should ensure that students have received real or vicarious experiences related to the topic being dealt with. Students should be given the opportunity to explore the topic via their own oral language. Through discussion with the teacher students will become increasingly aware of alternative vocabulary and language structures through which they can articulate their ideas. After thorough preparation in this way students are more likely to be able to utilize such non-visual information as semantic and syntactic cues in their reading of the text. To the extent that they have been familiarized with the concepts, have heard the essential vocabulary and met the dominant language structures, students will then bring meaning to the print in the form of expectation and by responding to the cue systems mentioned above, they will extract meaning in the form of a response to those expectations.

Traditionally textbooks on reading in the content areas have provided checklists of reading and reading related skills (i.e. reading maps and charts, locational skills, etc.) with indications as to the relevance of particular skills to the various subjects. There may be some contention about the possibility of isolating some discrete skills and also their proposed degree of relevance. However, it is clear that subject areas make quite different demands of the reader.

> Whereas a degree of fluency, involving skimming and the ability to take in whole passages is associated with the everyday reading of the proficient reader, this 'chunking' can be dangerous to comprehension in mathematics. Not only must the rate be reduced, but also the sheer concentration or density of ideas packed into a single sentence militates against chunking and normal patterns of fluency.
>
> (Priddle, 1978)

Illustrations of various kinds, rather than being an adjunct to the text as in much basal material, now become integral to the interpretation of the text. Children need to develop a critical response to such elements of content area text. Drawings and diagrams, for example, may oversimplify a continuous process by representing it in stages, thus leaving the viewer with the impression that it is not continuous. Nor is it uncommon for an illustration to depict the exception and not the rule. The expectation that pupils should remember a good deal of what they read in the content areas, especially in text books, forms one of the chief problems of reading in those fields. Problems in remembering may be related to rather superficial levels of understanding achieved.

Some readers find it difficult to remember content area material because their depth of processing is shallow in that they make relatively few, if any, associations with past experiences, either first-hand or vicarious. This underlines the need for the integrated teaching of reading and content.

> Both primary and secondary teachers need to be aware of the specific demands their subject makes upon a student's reading ability and assess the

potential of each student to meet these demands. It is essential to recognise the contribution that reading competence makes to all subjects.

(*Reading K-12*, p. 20)

(MRT)

See also LANGUAGE ACROSS CURRICULUM; SQ3R.

References

A. Priddle, 'Reading in mathematics', in G. Page, J. Elkins and B. O'Connor (eds), *Communication Through Reading*, Proceedings of the Fourth Australian Reading Conference, ARA, Brisbane, 1978.

Reading K-12 – Curriculum Policy Statement, NSW Dept of Education, 1981.

READING AGE – An outmoded form of expressing a reader's score on a norm-referenced test. For each particular age group in the standardized sample the mean raw score is determined and assigned the corresponding reading age. The derivation of reading-age scores is associated with the mythical average reader for each age group. Reading ages are not absolute. Many contaminating influences affect test scores and indeed each test should indicate its standard error which shows how much, on average, a reader's score may vary just because of the crudeness of a test. In addition, reading ages are only relevant within a reasonable period of the time, when the norms are collected. Norms derived in the 1950s are hardly relevant to the children of the 1980s. As a result of the method by which norms are derived, various tests may assign significantly different reading ages to the same individual. A further weakness results from the attempt to use one test to obtain valid reading ages for a wide age range of readers. Since the range of performance of older readers is much greater than that for younger readers, proportionately more of the older readers will be one year behind their chronological age than will younger readers (Pumfrey, 1977). Teachers are thus quite unwise to base educational judgements on data which are so ill-defined.

Despite the limitations noted above, some schools continue to use standardized tests as a screening device identifying pupils who have difficulty in reading on the basis of reading ages scores. A more useful approach would be to use teacher-made cloze tests based on reading materials for current curricula.

(MRT)

Reference

P. D. Pumfrey, *Measuring Reading Abilities: Concepts, Sources and Applications*, London: Hodder & Stoughton, 1977.

READING GAMES – A popular and motivating approach to reinforcing aspects of reading development is to have available in the classroom a number of reading games which children play in small groups.

However, many of these games do little to promote the use of meaning-gaining strategies. Variations of 'Bingo', 'Dominoes' and 'Fish' are used to reinforce knowledge of individual words and sound–symbol relationships isolated from a natural reading context. Most games depend upon pupils' existing reading ability, they do not develop it further. A simple criterion for evaluating games is to consider whether the game is more useful to pupils than engaging in sustained reading of interesting books. **(MRT)**

READING GROUPS – Are usually created by the division of pupils within a regular class into smaller groups on criteria such as reading ability (frequently inferred from a single score on a standardized reading test), reading interests and the allocation of pupils to reading 'skills' groups. Intra-class grouping commonly results in three groups supposedly based on some broad category of reading ability. In some schools inter-class divisions require pupils from all classes to leave their regular class at a particular time and join composite reading classes according to their reading achievement level. The development of reading should be seen as part of the pupils' total language development in the context of meaningful learning across all curriculum areas. The approach to inter-class grouping noted above militates against the practical achievement of this aim.

The research and literature dealing with grouping have recently been summarized (O'Donnell and Moore, 1980, pp. 198–9) as follows:

(1) Homogeneous grouping has not been demonstrated to be an effective method for raising the reading achievement levels of pupils.
(2) Ability grouping tends to result in a hardening of the categories, especially among low achieving pupils.
(3) Interaction among pupils of different attainment levels tends to stimulate less able pupils.
(4) Criteria for composing groups have to be carefully examined.
(5) Grouping plans should include analysis of strengths and weaknesses with groups.

Among teachers who make effective use of reading groups guidelines such as the following seem to be emerging:

(1) Composition of groups
(i) There are no permanently set groups.
(ii) Groups are periodically created, modified or disbanded in order to meet new needs as they arise.
(iii) There are times when there is only one group – consisting of all pupils.
(iv) Group size will vary from two or three to nine or ten to the whole class, depending on the group's purpose.
(v) Group membership is not fixed and varies according to differing needs and purposes.

(2) Management
(i) Pupil commitment is enhanced if they know the group work is related to the overall programme.
(ii) Children should be able to evaluate and recognize the progress they make and the teacher's assessment of it.
(iii) There should be a clear strategy for supervision of task performance.

(3) Nature of group tasks
(i) Task structure is appropriate to the needs and interests of pupils.
(ii) Directions to complete are clear and can be referred to if forgotten.
(iii) Follow-up activities should be available when main assignment is complete. There must be a clear and distinct method of coding or labelling so

that pupils can obtain materials appropriate to them without disturbing others.

(iv) A variety of activities should be included. **(MRT)**

Reference

M. P. O'Donnell and B. Moore, 'Eliminating common stumbling blocks to organisational change', in D. Lapp, (ed.), *Making Reading Possible Through Effective Classroom Management*, Newark, Delaware: IRA, 1980.

READING INTERESTS – Current theories of the reading process which emphasize the importance of pupils using their background knowledge in developing efficient reading have provided further impetus to teachers' efforts to engage pupils' interests and promote positive attitudes through selection of appropriate materials for reading language programmes. Teachers will perhaps most frequently gain insights into pupils' attitudes through informal interaction; however a range of measurement tools dealing with interests and attitudes are available.

Interest inventories are designed to tap students' preferences within and among various reading topics, reading genres and print forms.

Attitude inventories assess general feelings toward reading in a range of contexts. **(MRT)**

Reference

Ken Dulin, 'Assessing reading interests of elementary and middle school students', in D. L. Monson and D. McClenathan (eds), *Developing Active Readers: Ideas for Parents, Teachers and Librarians*, Delaware: IRA, 1979.

READING INVENTORY – Also referred to as Informal Reading Inventory (IRI). A series of passages of increasing difficulty are selected and questions are constructed based on the view that these can be equated with liberal, interpretative, critical and creative aspects of comprehension. The grading of passages is usually achieved by selection from successive levels of basal readers on the application of readability formulas. Pupils are asked to read the sequence of passages and answer the questions until they fail to achieve predetermined criteria of reading accuracy and correct response to comprehension questions. The last level at which criteria are reached is used to indicate the pupil's reading level. Passages are used to assess silent and/or oral reading, and sometimes they are read to pupils in order to test listening comprehension. The original implementation of this testing procedure was not consistent with current psycholinguistic accounts of the reading process because the inventory's criteria overemphasized accurate reading and did not distinguish oral reading errors which resulted in distortion of meaning from those which did not. Informed teachers sometimes adapt the use of the IRI in the light of knowledge about miscue analysis, making qualitative assessments of oral reading 'errors' and using less restricted indication of comprehension such as free and probed recall. **(MRT)**

Reference

D. Holdaway, *Independence in Reading*, Sydney: Ashtons, 1972.

READING LABORATORIES – A boxed set of commercial materials for reading instruction. They are organized on the basis of 'hierarchical skill development' and in format typically comprise several sets of workcards, at each of several levels. They are intended to be self-correcting with answer cards included.

Children must attain certain criterion scores at a level before progressing and are responsible for recording their own progress on charts provided.

The concern to develop materials which can be self-corrected frequently leads to 'comprehension' questions which require only a superficial interaction with the text. The nature and structure of the materials results in competitive task completion rather than engagement in meaningful reading.

Some common examples are RFU, SRA, International Reading Laboratories Series, and WARDS. **(MRT)**

READING MACHINES – Several different types of reading machines have been developed with the purpose of increasing the speed and efficiency of reading. Some expose lines of print at a particular (and variable) rate with the express purpose of eliminating regressions while others have briefly exposed sequences of letters and words in the belief that an individual's visual span could be so increased.

Recent insights into the nature of the reading process (see Smith) indicate that one's capacity for visual processing cannot be greatly improved. This would lead to the conclusion that reading machines are superfluous to an effective reading programme.

Reference

Frank Smith, *Reading*, Cambridge: Cambridge University Press.

READING MISCUE INVENTORY – A commercially published system for implementing miscue analysis procedure.
See also MISCUE ANALYSIS.

Reference

Y. Goodman and C. Burke, *Reading Miscue Inventory*, Toronto: Macmillan, 1972.

READING PROCESS – Building on the insights offered by Kenneth Goodman (q.v.) we can illustrate the reading process in the following way:

What the Reader Brings to the Print	**The Reading Process**
Implicit knowledge of the language and how it works.	(1) Sampling graphic, syntactic, semantic cues.
Experience of the world.	(2) Predicting both structure and meaning on the basis of selected cues.
	(3) Testing the prediction.
	(4) Either confirming the prediction or correcting if necessary.

Reading involves decoding to *meaning*, not decoding to sound.

READING READINESS – Some specific kinds of experiences which prepare a child for reading. Reading readiness is facilitated by opportunities for the child to listen and respond to all kinds of literature; by opportunities to handle books; by experiences with books which will develop a sense of story; by opportunities for the child to see language being written down; and by opportunities to play the role of a reader and writer (Clay, 1979; Downing, 1979).

In former times, perceptual skills training was the basis of a reading readiness programme: measurable minutiae such as auditory discrimination of sounds, visual discrimination of shapes, knowledge of letter names, ability to associate a letter with an appropriate sound, etc. However, it has been found that these are not necessarily pre-requisites to reading, and in fact such skills as are necessary are best learnt through early experiences with reading itself.

Other traditional measures of reading readiness such as social maturity, motor skills, laterality, and manual dexterity are *not* factors involved in a child's ability to read although they may affect the child's response to specific types of formal instruction in a classroom.

A reading readiness programme should involve children in many opportunities to interact with books and print in various ways so that they develop an understanding of what reading is all about and *a desire to learn to read.* There should be no clear division between getting ready to read and beginning to read. **(MRT)**

See also CONCEPTS ABOUT PRINT; LANGUAGE EXPERIENCE; AUDITORY DISCRIMINATION; VISUAL DISCRIMINATION.

References

M. Clay, *Reading: The Patterning of Complex Behaviour*, 2nd edn, Auckland: Heinneman, 1979.

J. Downing, *Reading and Reasoning*, London: Chambers, 1979.

READING SCHEMES – A comprehensive set of materials including teachers' manuals, readers, activity books, supplementary readers and sometimes supporting audio visual material. Schemes are frequently organized into levels which usually correspond to traditional grade level progression in the primary school.

In the least appropriate application reading schemes have been used to form a whole reading programme through which children progressed in a lock-step fashion. Informed publishers and teachers have recognized the need for more selective and flexible usage of such schemes as part of a variety of materials within a total language arts programme. Some teachers, such as Pauline Curmi, make no use of a reading scheme at all: 'This year I have initiated a reading program for K/1/2 class *totally based on children's literature*. We make no use of a reading scheme, but do use our own specially designed support materials' (Curmi, 1983, p. 39). **(MRT)**

Reference

P. Curmi, 'Uses of children's literature in my classroom', in R. D. Walshe, D. Jensen and T. Moore (eds), *Teaching Literature*, Sydney: PETA and ETA, 1983.

READING STAGES – A number of educationists have defined various stages of development through which a reader progresses as she or he gains control over the reading process:

Stage 1: Pre-reading or readiness
The child is developing concepts about language in print.
Stage 2: Initial or emergent reading
The child begins to get meaning from print using a combination of clues – the context, the flow of language, and grapho-phonics – but is heavily dependent upon his or her ability to use context and his or her own language to predict and confirm what is in the text.
Stage 3: Dependent reading
The child is becoming more confident in using various reading strategies to predict and confirm what is in the text. There is an attempt to match linguistic skill to the complexity of the text.
Stage 4: Independent reading
The capacity to handle longer and more varied pieces and to adapt approaches depending upon the demands of the materials and the purposes of reading.

(MRT)

See also READING AGE; CONCEPTS ABOUT PRINT.

READING TESTS – Standardized tests (q.v.) in reading are usually distributed commercially or through educational agencies such as the Australian Council for Educational Research. The tests consist of a fixed set of test materials and specified procedures for administration. Although few test constructors provide an explicit definition of reading on which their materials are based, many standardized tests imply, contrary to current knowledge of the reading process, that reading development necessitates the progressive mastery of a theoretical hierarchy of discrete skills, by focusing separately on tasks such as sound–symbol matching, word identification, vocabulary knowledge, comprehension skills and reading speed.

Silent reading tests frequently require written responses and allow group administration, while tests involving oral reading are usually given individually. The test item format is often some form of selection among alternative responses – mainly of the multiple choice variety. Time limits are imposed on test completion.

Scores may be norm-referenced or criterion-referenced. Norm-referenced tests commonly express scores in terms of reading age. Such scores are only meaningful as an indication of how the reader's performance stands relative to the performance of the reference group on whom the test was standardized. In isolation they are an inadequate basis for making judgements about a reader's relative competence.

Criterion-referenced tests are based on the concept of mastery. Their purpose is to determine whether the student can accomplish a specified behaviour or not. In most published tests the specified behaviour relates to various aspects of phonic analysis and other so-called sub-skills of reading which, according to current psycholinguistic theory, are not basic to the reading process.

There are many severe limitations to the use of standardized tests both in measuring attainment and for diagnostic purposes. While misconceptions about the accuracy and nature of normative scores, such as reading ages, compound the misuse of standardized tests, a more fundamental shortcoming is that such tests do not relate to the context or process objectives of programmes which informed teachers design for their particular classes.

Furthermore, all known standardized tests imply a view of reading which is inconsistent with current theoretical and empirical knowledge of the reading process. Such tests then do not focus on appropriate reading behaviours and it could be argued that they are invalid ways of assessing the meanings readers derive from texts. This understanding has led many teachers to adopt teacher-made test materials and informal assessment procedures, such as miscue analysis, which attempt to examine normal reading behaviour. **(MRT)**
See also CRITERION – REFERENCED ASSESSMENT; NORM REFERENCED ASSESSMENT.

REASON . . . BECAUSE or WHY . . . BECAUSE. *See* USAGE.

REGISTER – The variation that occurs in any individual's use of language as he or she moves from one activity to another in the course of daily life. The main factors which influence this variation are the situation, the purpose for which the language is being used, the subject matter, the speaker's relationships with other people in the situation, the mood of the speaker and the mode of language use (speech or writing). Various aspects of language, especially features of pronunciation, choice of words and structures, are likely to reflect the influence of these factors. Most fields of human activity have their own characteristic styles of language and terminology. Situations can vary in their degree of formality which in turn can be related to how well the participants know each other or what their purpose is. The different registers of a language have also been referred to as *functional varieties* but this term gives emphasis to only one aspect of register variation. **(JC)**

REGISTER: CLASSROOM ACTIVITIES –

- Study the origin of slang words.
- Have the class compile a dictionary of: school slang / sporting slang (e.g. cricket, surfing, / regional slang / the jargons (q.v.) of various groups.
- Drama is a most useful way of working on register: have the class act out scenes in which the register changes, for example recounting an incident to a school friend and the same incident to the headmaster, or have the class act out scenes in which they try to persuade someone to do something for them and then discuss the appropriateness of the register-strategies employed.
- Have the class change passages of prose (their own scripts?) from one register to another and discuss the effects of the changes, especially when tone changes without the essential message changing.
- Have them write for various purposes: to tactfully reject an invitation or make a complaint, to persuade, to express controlled anger, to amuse, to explain, to instruct.
- Identify the context of various 'unseen' passages.
- Discuss the appropriateness of the register to the purpose in various passages, perhaps in terms of Halliday's three contextual factors: field, tenor and mode.

RELIABILITY *See* VALIDITY AND RELIABILITY.

REMEDIAL READING – A separate programme of instruction for pupils whose reading development is not progressing satisfactorily in the regular classroom. Pupils are usually withdrawn from class to work either individually or as part of a small group in a special class, group or clinic, with a specialist trained as a remedial teacher. Criteria for placement of pupils into remedial reading groups frequently include scores on standardized tests indicating performance significantly below the norm. The practical expression of this is often: 'a reading age more than two years below chronological age' (for limitations *see* STANDARDIZED TESTS; READING AGE). In many cases remedial teaching in this mode is not consistent with current psycholinguistic accounts of the reading process but emphasises the strengthening of supposedly component skills such as phonics, word attack vocabulary, growth and so on. This skills-based, 'compartmentalized' view of reading is exacerbated by withdrawal from regular classroom activity.

Traditional approaches to the provision of remedial reading are currently being revised in favour of programmes where specialist resource teachers work with class teachers to provide remedial reading in the context of regular classroom learning experiences.

Remedial reading which occurs in several sessions during a week where pupils are withdrawn from regular classes is essentially backward looking – it is concerned with events after they have happened. There are several additional limitations.

(1) There appears to be little successful carry-over into regular lessons of isolated remedial work.
(2) Class teachers may have welcomed some relief for a few hours but were seldom provided with insights into more effective educational programming in the classroom for students with a range of learning skills.
(3) Some students who require 'extra' assistance in developing reading skills may not be included in the remedial programme because the remedial teacher is already taking the 'maximum' number of students and there are no vacant 'places'.

The resource teacher model is more concerned with preventing learning problems in the classroom than with curing them outside.

> The function of the resource teacher as a change agent as well as the emphasis on interventions within the regular classroom indicates the importance attached to preventative action. Class teachers can work in a situation which encourages the development of competencies necessary for dealing with a wide range of student needs:
>
> (a) They can be introduced to the use of formal and informal techniques of educational diagnosis related to reading and other aspects of classroom life.
> (b) They can be given the opportunity to relate more closely to students in individual or small group learning situations.
> (c) Methods of modifying learning materials (especially in the content

area) to meet the needs of students with reading difficulties can be demonstrated.

(d) Various methods of within-class grouping of students can be implemented.

(e) The use of audio visual materials and multi-level learning materials in organizing instruction for more personalized teaching can be shown.

(f) Teachers can be exposed to alternative teaching methods and a variety of strategies to individualize instruction.

(g) A greater number of students experience broader, more direct, if less intensive support in learning situations.

It is unduly restrictive, however, to view the remedial and resource teaching models as dichotomous. There is no doubt that some students require intensive support which is best accomplished in some form of a withdrawal programme. This should constitute part of a much broader support programme and should encourage transfer of accomplishments with the remedial teacher to the students' wider environment.

(Unsworth, 1978)

(MRT)

Reference

Len Unsworth, 'Working with a resource teacher', in G. Page, J. Elkins and B. O'Connor (eds), *Communication Through Reading*, Vol. 2, *Diverse Needs; Creative Approaches*. Proceedings of Fourth Australian Reading Conference, Brisbane, 1978.

RESTRICTED CODE *See* ELABORATED AND RESTRICTED CODES.

RETELLING – Perhaps most widely known as a measure of comprehension following pupils' oral reading of passages administered for purposes of miscue analysis. Pupils are asked to give an oral recall of the passage in as much detail as they can, immediately after reading. Following free recall the teacher may use probe questions to elicit further response provided these questions do not contain any information which has not been mentioned by the reader. The retelling is scored by comparison with a teacher prepared outline listing character analysis, theme, plot and events, each element of which has a possible point score allocated on an intuitive basis. A modified outline format is used for informational passages. Retelling proficiency is expressed as a percentage score of passage elements listed on the teacher prepared outline.

This approach does not take into account recent research which deals with the effects of text structure on memory. It is now well established that even in adult readers certain story elements such as the 'major setting' and the 'outcome' have a very high probability of recall while other less significant elements have a much lower probability of recall (Mandler and Johnson, 1977; Thorndyke, 1977). Research dealing with expository prose has similarly indicated that top-level information is recalled with much greater probability than low-level detail (Meyer, 1975). It may be that the theoretical retelling outline gives too much emphasis to text elements which one would not normally expect to be remembered. The scoring of retellings should be based on firm theoretical foundations. A number of models of text comprehension are now available (Kintsch and Van Dijk, 1978) which may facilitate wider and more effective use of recall as a measure of comprehension. **(MRT)**

References

W. Kintsch and T. Van Dijk, 'Toward a model of text comprehension and production', *Psychological Review*, 85 (5), 1978: 363–93.

J. M. Mandler and N. S. Johnson, 'Remembrance of things parsed: story structure and recall', *Cognitive Psychology*, 9, 1977: 111–51.

B. J. Meyer, *The Organization of Prose and its Effect on Memory*, Amsterdam: NM Holland Publishing, 1975.

P. W. Thorndyke, 'Cognitive structures in comprehension and memory of narrative discourse', *Cognitive Psychology*, 9, 1970: 77–110.

RHETORIC/RHETORICAL – Like 'irony' (q.v.) 'rhetoric' and 'rhetorical' are terms used in many different contexts to mean many different things and students need to be clear about the particular meanings being used at a particular time.

In its most general sense, 'rhetoric' refers to the arts of speech or prose writing. In a narrower sense, the term once referred to that body of particular skills and devices which made speech and writing particularly impressive. From classical times, such devices included figures of speech (such as 'complexio': the repetition of both the first and last words of a series of phrases) and figures of thought (such as 'epimone': dwelling upon, and returning to, the strongest topic on which one's case rests).

The effects used to persuade and impress have led to the derogatory connotations of the term. 'Mere rhetoric' has come to be a phrase used to describe insincere and pretentious composition or speech-making. Hence a 'rhetorical style' which employs many rhetorical devices such as figures of speech has come to be regarded as ostentatious and artificial. (The 'rhetorical question' – a question which requires and expects no answer – derives its name from the fact that it was one such device used to gain effect.)

Reference

L. A. Sonnino, *A Handbook to Sixteenth Century Rhetoric*, London: Routledge & Kegan Paul 1968.

RIB-IT – A booklet by Jo Goodman published by VATE, 1982, describing RIB-IT (Read-In-Bed), the reading programme in force at Swinburne Technical School. Available from VATE, PO Box 265, Carlton South, Vic. 3053.

ROLE PLAY – In our day-to-day lives we play several well-defined roles and many other less dominant roles when the situation demands it. A 'wife and mother' can also be a business or professional person, a friend, a neighbour, a local councillor or politician, and much more. We expect to react to the demands of a situation and to fulfil the roles as required. There are of course many roles we will never be asked to play in our lifetime and it is often easy to underestimate the demands of any one particular role when we have little or no experience of it. Role play is concerned to allow space and protection for children (and adults) to experience through play the constraints of a particular role in fictitious situations where participants assume attitudes and stances which are not normally their own. In role play there is little or no characterization in the theatrical sense since we are dealing with the influence of situation upon character rather than the opposite. The emphasis is on the assumption of teacher-imposed attitudes which are presented with realism. Role play makes few demands upon the teacher and has been readily adopted in various curriculum areas for use in normal classroom spaces. The focus of role play is clarification of an issue, facts, the exploration of language and status and can be useful in the initial exploration of a text. It is essentially a tool of exploration and does not demand the technical skills of performance or presuppose presentation.

As with all work in drama, in whatever curriculum area, an essential aspect of teacher planning and implementation is the allowance of sufficient time for reflection and discussion (*see* John Seely's *In Context* (Oxford: Oxford University Press, 1976) for an excellent discussion of this point). Clearly the simple adoption of roles does not promote development in itself and if stereotypical, cliché responses are to be avoided in favour of more significant learning, then teacher questioning and discussion will be prominent aspects of the process.

Suggestions for Activity

Interviews: Role play the interview between the following people:

(1) A job applicant at: a factory; a bank; an advertising agency; a school. (You specify the level and status of the job and the applicant.)

(2) Interview with a parent about: leaving school; drinking; smoking; pocket money; going out and staying out late.

(3) A factory manager has to tell an employee with twenty-five years with the company that he or she is being made redundant.

Groups:

(1) Role play the arrival of a group of refugees at Sydney airport. They do not speak English and must be processed by custom agents before being allowed to enter Australia.

(2) Role play the situation where a group of residents from a particular street meet to oppose the demolition of a number of old houses. The residents are angry that the council has allowed a company to purchase the houses so that they can be demolished to make way for high-rise flats. **(PR)**

References

John Hodgson and Ernest Richards, *Improvisation*, rev. edn, London: Eyre Methuen, 1977.

John Seely, *In Role*, London: Edward Arnold, 1978.

Betty Jane Wagner, *Dorothy Heathcote*, Washington, DC: NEA, 1976.

ROMANCE/ROMANTIC/ROMANTICISM – Students need to be aware of the various distinctive meanings of terms like 'romance' and 'romantic'. The literary roots of the term 'romance' explain the various later uses of the term in literary terminology and in everyday parlance.

In early Norman times the term 'romance' referred to a story (usually a long poem) in a Romance language such as French. Such stories usually dealt with chivalric love and adventure and in the later Middle Ages the term came to be applied generally to stories and poems dealing with chivalric love – hence its modern everyday use. The adventures undergone by the chivalric heroes were often strange and supernatural and this aspect led to the more general literary use of 'romance' as referring to a work of fantasy and imagination – the sense of 'romance' which we would use in describing *Morte d'Arthur*, *A Midsummer Night's Dream*, *Pericles* or Keats's *Eve of St Agnes*.

It is this latter use of 'romance' as in a general way akin to fantasy and imagination (and the supernatural) that makes connections with the term 'Romantic' as we would apply it to the late eighteenth and early nineteenth centuries. Generally applied characteristics of the Romantic period include:

(1) Supremacy of the imagination and emotion.
(2) A rejection of the complexities of modern social life that led to:
  (i) belief in the unfettered supremacy of the individual and of individual genius;
  (ii) return to a more natural life and hence the deification of Nature;
  (iii) revival of medievalism and an interest in the supernatural.

ROUND-ROBIN READING – Traditionally a whole-class or group activity in which children take turns to read aloud from their own copy of a teacher-chosen selection (often a basal reader). While one child is reading aloud, the others are expected to follow the text silently and to keep pace with that reader – both getting behind and reading on are frowned upon. The teacher corrects oral reading 'errors' and directs children's use of decoding techniques to 'attack' unfamiliar words. He or she may also ask questions as a gauge of children's 'comprehension' of the text.

The emphasis on the oral production of an accurate word-by-word rendition of the text means that the reader is most likely to focus attention on the decoding to sound and pronunciation of individual words for meaning, and so processing of the meaning is greatly reduced. Some teachers mistakenly believe that a correct oral production of a text indicates comprehension, but this is often not the case. Round-robin reading is likely to reinforce sounding out or 'word-calling' strategies, while discouraging children's processing of syntactic and semantic information (q.v.).

The practice reflects a view of reading inconsistent with a psycholinguistic model of reading.

For positive alternatives to this practice, *see* ORAL READING. **(MRT)**

'Great literature is simply language charged with meaning to the utmost possible degree. . . .'

'If a nation's literature declines, the nation atrophies and decays . . . A people that grows accustomed to sloppy writing is a people in process of losing grip on its empire and itself.'

(Ezra Pound
ABC of Reading)

S

SATIRE – Any attempt to hold something up to ridicule could broadly be described as satirical. Parody (q.v.), irony (q.v.) and sarcasm are only a few of the devices and methods employed by the satirist. Satire is notoriously difficult to teach at a school level and there are probably at least two important reasons for this. At any cognitive level of reading (whether we mean the simple act of following a storyline or the most deeply analytical critical reading), simple experience of the most general kind is necessary for understanding. Often students may not have knowledge of, or experience of, the object under satirical attack, and if this is the case the satirical element is lost. A knowledge of American funeral practices or the widely read eighteenth century London poets is necessary if students are going to simply 'see the jokes' in Waugh's *The Loved One* or Pope's *Dunciad*. But this background knowledge can at least be supplied. A further, more crucial, problem is that of tone (q.v.). A certain sophisticated 'ear' that only comes with wide reading is often necessary to capture the subtle tone of much satire. Even a reasonably 'obvious' satire such as Jane Austen on Elizabeth Bennet's sisters requires such an ear: 'Their eyes were immediately wandering up the street in quest of the officers, and nothing less than a very smart bonnet indeed, or a really new muslin in a shop window, could recall them' (*Pride and Prejudice*). The teaching of, and understanding of, satirical pieces will often require reasonably extensive background work and sensitive, dramatic reading by the teacher. It is often best done as part of a wide reading programme.

SAUSSURE, FERDINAND DE – The founder of modern structural linguistics. His most famous work is a series of lectures published as *Course in General Linguistics* (1916). Saussure viewed language as a system of signs made up of a 'signifier' (a word, letter, sound or image) and a 'signified' (the concept or meaning referred to by the signifier). Relationships between signifiers and signifieds are purely arbitrary – the result of cultural and historical convention. Saussure's other important distinction was between what he called 'langue' and 'parole', the latter referring to actual speech and the former to the objective structure of signs which made their speech possible. Saussure saw the proper study of linguistics as 'langue' and 'signifiers' rather than actual speech or signified concepts. Saussure's ideas have influenced structuralism (q.v.) and semiology (q.v.).

Reference
Ferdinand de Saussure, *Course in General Linguistics*, London: Fontana, 1974.

SCHEMA (pl. schemata) – A pattern of knowledge formed from experience that enables an individual to make sense of what he or she perceives or reads. Schemata form a mental context important for finding meaning. Learning involves building up a repertoire of useful schemata for understanding new information.

References
Tom Nicholson, *The Process of Reading*, Sydney: Martin Education, 1984.
S. L. Smith *et al.*, 'The contexts of reading of reading', in A. Berger and H. A. Robinson (eds), *Secondary School Reading*, Urbana, Ill.: NCTE, 1982.

SCHONELL READING TESTS –

(R1) Graded word reading test

This individual, oral test requires pupils to read single words aloud until a criterion score of errors is reached. Scores are expressed as reading ages. This test has no construct validity whatever because it does not sample normal reading behaviour of connected prose. Similar tests are the ACER Word Identification Test (Australian Council for Educational Research, 1972); and the St Lucia Graded Word Reading Test (R. J. Andrews, St Lucia Graded Word Reading Text, Teaching and Testing Resources, Brisbane, 1969).

(R2) Simple prose reading test

An individual oral reading and comprehension test. Consists of one four paragraph story: 'My Dog' followed by fifteen comprehension questions requiring short responses from the reader. It is intended for children about 6 years to 9 years of age. The norms are dated and should not be used. Teachers would be better advised to discard this test in favour of current informal assessment techniques (*see* MISCUE ANALYSIS).

(R3) Silent reading test A

This is a nine-minute timed test consisting of eighteen very short paragraphs each followed by one question requiring a brief response from the reader. It is intended for children between the ages of 7 and 11 years. Once again the norms are dated and should not be used. Some of the questions are not text dependent, especially for Australian readers. *See* STANDARDIZED TESTS for further limitations.

(R4) Silent reading test B

A fifteen-minute timed test of silent reading to be used with children aged from about 9 years to 13 years. It consists of twenty short passages dealing with different topics. Each paragraph has two words deleted and for each pupils must choose appropriate replacements from five alternatives given below the paragraph. Apart from shortcomings related to the use of reading-age scores and others associated with standardized tests, the content of these tests is 'dated' and unlikely to be relevant to the reading experiences of pupils in today's schools. **(MRT)**

References
P. D. Pumfrey, *Reading: Tests and Assessment Techniques*, London: Hodder & Stoughton, 1976.
F. J. Schonell and F. E. Schonell, *Schonell Reading Tests*, Edinburgh: Oliver & Boyd, 1955.

SCHOOLS COUNCIL PROJECT ON THE WRITTEN LANGUAGE OF 11–18 YEAR OLDS – Under the direction of James Britton (q.v.), this project involved a developmental study of 'the processes by which the written language of young children becomes differentiated . . . into kinds of written discourse appropriate to different purposes'. Aspects of the project are touched on in the entries on AUDIENCE and LANGUAGE, FUNCTIONS OF.

Reference
James Britton *et al.*, *The Development of Writing Abilities (11–18)*, London: Macmillan, 1975.

SELF-ASSESSMENT BY STUDENTS – Self-assessment can refer to three fundamentally different activities: judging one's self, articulately describing one's actions or reacting to one's own work as if one is someone else.

Self-assessment can refer to students forming judgements of themselves, often of their strengths and weaknesses. For example:

'I am good at English'
'I am not good at English'
'I am good at writing essays'
'I never listen'
'I don't concentrate well'.

Report cards sometimes have a space for students' self-assessment and comments like these often appear. This type of self-assessment does not help students develop. On the contrary, if self-assessments like this have any effect on students at all, it is to reinforce them labelling themselves in ways which limit their self-perceptions. Each of the above examples, although more specific than 'I am clever' or 'I am stupid', are too general to be true, let alone useful. For no one never listens, and no one does well on every aspect of essay writing each time they write. If I have a problem in listening, it applies in a specific context, and I'll not handle that problem till I stop labelling myself and work towards articulately specifying when I don't listen well and what I am doing at that time. Similarly, if I want to help someone write a better essay I need to start with a specific problem not a generalized label.

Facing the specific problems can be hard work and students often avoid that challenge by deciding that they are either good or bad in certain areas of the curriculum. They either have got 'it' or they haven't. Now when *we* encourage them to think in terms of being generally good or bad at something, we are actually encouraging them to *avoid* learning. Of course, this is precisely the opposite of educating, but, unfortunately, it is very common in schools and actively promoted by those who encourage teachers to differentiate so-called 'above-average', 'average' and 'below average' students.

In contrast to that emphasis on self-labelling, *self-assessment can refer to students describing their actions and reactions in specific situations.* Now students are sometimes asked to grade a piece of their own work, but a grade is simply a label, not an articulate description; consequently self-grading does more to encourage students to categorise themselves, than it does to help them develop articulateness. If, on the other hand, students learn to describe their actions in more articulate language than grades, numbers or 'good' and 'bad', then their self-assessments can be very useful in encouraging future learning. The aim is that the students leave a course knowing what they have been able to do, rather than that they leave dependent on others' judgements of their work or speaking vaguely about good and bad work.

It is often very difficult to get students to fully engage in self-assessment tasks; they say 'It is the teacher's job'. To be helpful, self-assessment requires that they show the teacher their problems, but traditionally they have been told to always do their best, not to highlight their problems! So teachers who want self-assessment to be more than just an imposed and superficial exercise need to structure their whole programme so that the students feel free to bring up their problems. In particular, the students need to know that what they bring up in self-assessments will not be used against them in determining their grades. Teachers often overlook the fact that the major role they play for many students is that of judge. Until they get out of that role, they should not expect many of their students to explore their problems openly.

A useful starting point is to have students regularly express their reactions to the lessons. For example:

> *Q: How have you felt about how things were run in this English class?*
> I didn't think things were very good when we started but they got better because I like expressing my feelings but I had to adjust because last year I felt really squashed.

It is not particularly articulate, but it is a start.

The second example is a girl's more articulate identification of how she has *reacted* to a teacher. She is not labelling herself (or the teacher) but describing herself in process. It is a powerful statement with obvious implications for action:

> When you set homework on Tuesday night and it is due in on Wednesday, I feel annoyed, because it means I won't spend enough time on it to get satisfaction out of it.

When the students have been having their say about the lessons, they are then more likely to write openly about themselves.

> *Q: How have you felt about yourself as a writer?*
> Well, at first, I thought 'what are they asking of me? I can't do this'. But the further I went along, the more confidence I gained. Sometimes though I have mental blocks and can't seem to write anything and other times I get brainstorms and can't stop writing.

Having students write about how they reacted to comments or grades put on their work also encourages open self-descriptions.

> *Q: What do you think was the grader's main reaction to your work? Express it in your own words How do you feel about that reaction?*

I think he thought it was fairly average. I chose the point of Lady Macbeth's ambition and pressure along with quite a few other members of the class, so it wasn't an unusual line of argument. He did say that it needs more back up from the text because people could argue that it was *his* ambition, not hers. Also he said that my connection with today was 'good work'. I was quite happy with his reaction. I don't set standards for myself and then get cross, angry or disappointed if I don't reach it.
Q: What might you work at to develop your writing in future?
I could develop arguing skills, and finding and using more and better back ups from texts. Also using smaller and more precise quotations and trying to express myself more clearly so that there aren't any question marks!

The teacher can follow up on statements like these by clarifying a goal or an area of experimentation which the student sees as important. At this stage, the teacher will often need to introduce specific criteria quite directively, because students will not usually be familiar with them. Then the student can learn to be articulate in the form of self-assessment which is the most useful of all – describing how one solves problems in one's expression.

Here is a Year 8 boy doing that:

The main idea I want to get across is that we waste a lot of time thinking about what we might do in the future. I wanted to make the beginning a bit different, so I wrote the short sentence 'Time moves quickly and slowly'. I don't like the title. ('Time.') It doesn't sound interesting enough. I thought of 'My Ideas on Time', which is probably better but it still sounds a bit boring.

This self-assessment has obvious implications for action (trying out different titles and checking that the different parts of the essay relate to the title and to the main idea). So the progression is from the students assessing something outside themselves (the curriculum), to them then indicating how they think about themselves, to them describing specific choices they make in their expression.

The third type of self-assessment refers to students commenting on their work as if they were someone else. This is an imaginative exercise and many students find it easier to show very articulate self-assessments this way, than when they are asked to describe their own work.

Students might be asked to play the role of the audience for a piece of writing, or perhaps a very critical teacher, or a very supportive, understanding teacher. This type of self-assessment can often be most useful if the students write a dialogue between themselves and the other person, continuing to write until some resolution is found between the two voices. When that happens the self-assessment will usually have a clear implication for action. The following example comes from a Year 10 class.

Me: As with most of my writing I started off quite well but then it got weaker and weaker as I went. By the time I got to the end it was totally unrealistic. Also, I started off thinking I had lots of room to fill up (two thousand words) and ended up explaining everything only briefly because I didn't have room for any more detail.

Teacher: I think you went wrong because you didn't really think much about

> the actual story. You would have been much better off to write the whole thing while you had it in your mind, but instead you ended up spending two to three hours every night (which would be plenty to do the whole thing for anyone but you). If you did it all at once the whole story would be written in the same mood.

However, some students' dialogues are governed by a judgemental, labelling voice.

> *Teacher*: If you had studied more, you may've done better.
> *Me*: I have other things to do you know! I can never think of things to write.
> *Teacher*: Some people have it and some people don't.

Here the student is thinking of a teacher who ignores his or her problem ('I can never think of things to write') and labels him or her. We need to give students strong experience of teachers who are different from that: teachers who can articulately describe their own reactions to students' work, and who structure the class so that students begin to describe the problems they are experiencing.

(BJ)

Reference

B. Johnston, *Assessing English. Helping Students to Reflect on their Work*, Milton Keynes: Open University Press, 1987.

SEMANTIC INFORMATION –

> *Semantic information* refers to the experience the individual has of what the world is like and how it functions. It includes the vast range of concepts that the individual has built up (e.g. the concept of a family). It includes the words the individual uses to label and organise his or her experiences. Of particular relevance to reading, it includes the individual's experiences of reading and being read to: in particular, the understanding that has been built up of why and how people read.
>
> (Parker, 1982)

Semantic information is one of the three major types of non-visual information (q.v.) that a reader uses in the process of comprehending print. It is through the use of such information that the reader's reliance on the print (or non-visual information) is reduced.

See also VISUAL INFORMATION; NON-VISUAL INFORMATION; SYNTACTIC INFORMATION; GRAPHO-PHONIC INFORMATION.

References

R. Parker, 'Towards a model of the reading process', in D. E. Burnes and G. M. Page (eds), *Reading: Insights and Strategies for Teaching*, Sydney: Harcourt Brace Jovanovich.

F. Smith, *Reading*, Cambridge: Cambridge University Press, 1978.

SEMIOLOGY/SEMIOTICS – Both terms refer to the study of 'signs' in society (*see* STRUCTURALISM), and are attempts to put such study on a 'scientific' basis, with linguistics as the core area from which terminology is derived, often by analogy rather than necessary logic. The terms 'sign', 'signifier', 'signified' and 'code' are freely used, along with other terms taken from various schools of linguistics, syntax and rhetoric. The result is sometimes impenetrable, and matters are not improved in the various post-structural schools of 'semio-analysis' where Freudian, Marxist or other sources of jargon are added to the list. (*See* POST-STRUCTURALISM.)

Semiology primarily refers to the European tradition deriving from Saussure (q.v.) through Barthes (q.v.): *Semiotics* primarily refers to an American tradition deriving from philosophers such as Charles Peirce, but also refers to Italian and Eastern European schools. In fact, the distinction is now quite blurred.

There are six pages in Umberto Eco's *A Theory of Semiotics* (Bloomington: Indiana University Press, 1979), simply naming areas to which the practice might be applied. Naturally, they have not yet all been explored, and many of them probably can't be. I rather like Eco's description of the field: 'Semiotics is concerned with everything that can be *taken* as a sign. A sign is everything which can be taken as significantly substituting for something else. . . . Thus *semiotics is in principle the discipline studying everything which can be used in order to lie*' (p. 7). Positively, semiotics opens up for socially and personally useful criticism (or 'reading') many areas we might not have considered, text-bound as we are, and gives some useful tools for such criticism. Negatively, it can end up being rather like scholasticism, or certain allegorical readings of Scripture, ingenious but of doubtful value. This is to leave aside the way in which much semio*logy* (particularly) has wedded itself to various ideologies to produce readings Orwell could not have foreseen in *1984*.

With the reservations I have suggested in mind, the best approach is to look at semiological/semiotic studies in areas that might interest the English teacher.

There have been many such studies of aspects of literature, some sensitive and revealing, others subject to the same strictures as '*Formalism*' (q.v.). In addition to Hawkes and Culler (*see* STRUCTURALISM), a good non-technical introduction by someone who confesses to glazed eyes when he sees a tree diagram – my heart warmed to him – is Robert Scholes, *Semiotics and Interpretation* (New Haven, Conn.: Yale, 1982).

In film, a key text is James Monaco, *How to Read a Film* (New York: Oxford University Press, 1977), an eclectic work which covers all aspects of film-making and film study. There is also John Fiske and John Hartley, *Reading Television* (London: Methuen, 1978), and, finally, Judith Williamson, *Decoding Advertisements* (London: Marion Boyars, 1978). Also G. Mast and M. Cohen (eds), *Film Theory and Criticism*, 2nd ed., (New York: Oxford University Press). *See also* STRUCTURALISM. **(NJW)**

SENTENCE COMBINING *See* GRAMMAR AND WRITING.

SEXISM IN LANGUAGE AND LITERATURE – The McGraw-Hill Book Company in its 'Guidelines for equal treatment of the sexes', states that 'the word sexism was coined, by analogy to racism, to denote discrimination based on gender.' In its original sense, sexism referred to prejudice against the female sex. In a broader sense, the term now indicates any arbitrary stereotyping of males and females on the basis of their gender.

Considerable attention has been given recently to sex stereotyping in children's books. Bob Dixon, in *Catching Them Young*, writes that in children's books

> girls are more restricted than boys in physical activities. Girls tend to hold mummy's hand, to be more attached to the house, to be standing at the bottom of the tree or looking on. Boys range further. . . . They are shown climbing and indulging in interesting and active games . . . people don't bother so much if they get dirty. As far as attitudes go, girls are usually shown as unimaginative, placid, inward-looking, concerned with trivialities, docile and passive. Girls often just are. Boys do – they invent, plan, think about their future careers. . . . They are confident, outgoing and give instruction (usually to girls).

While this was true of most picture books, basal readers and novels for children until recently, there were honourable exceptions, like Astrid Lindgren's *Pippi Longstocking* and Scott O'Dell's *Island of the Blue Dolphins*. The last few years have seen the publication of many more non-sexist children's books, and even the more conventional books no longer have boys making derogatory remarks like 'Not bad – for a girl!' The Other Award (q.v.) has as one of its objects the encouragement of children's books which avoid sex-role stereotyping.

An attempt is also being made to eliminate sexism in the written language. The McGraw-Hill guidelines suggest that generic terms, such as doctor and nurse, should be assumed to include both men and women, and that work should never be labelled as 'women's work' or 'a man-sized job'. Terms like 'man's achievements' should be replaced by 'human achievements'.

A profitable unit for seniors would be an exploration of sexism in language.

Non-sexist picture books

Betsy Byars, *Go and Hush the Baby*
Michael Foreman, *All the King's Horses*
Russell Hoban, *Best Friends for Frances*
Margaret Mahy, *The Man Whose Mother Was a Pirate*

Non-sexist novels

John Branfield, *Nancekuke*
Vera and Bill Cleaver, *The Whys and Wherefores of Littabelle Lee*
Jean George, *Julie of the Wolves*
Gene Kemp, *The Turbulent Term of Tyke Tiler*
E. L. Konigsburg, *From the Mixed-up Files of Mrs Basil E. Frankweiler*
Katherine Paterson, *Bridge to Terabithia*.

References

Bob Dixon, *Catching Them Young*, London: Pluto Press, 1977.
Jenny Pausacker, *Sugar and Snails: A Countersexist Booklist*, rev. edn, Melbourne: Women's Movement Children's Literature Cooperative, 1977.
Dale Spender, *Man Made Language*, London: Routledge, 1980.

SHAKESPEARE, TEACHING OF – As a general principle, there is no reason why Shakespeare should be taught differently from any other drama texts. This should always involve:

(1) a lot of 'acting out' by students and discussion of how particular lines and scenes should be played. (Would you have a ghost in the ghost scene of *Macbeth*? What would be Macbeth's tone in the 'I go and it is done . . .' speech? What props in different scenes? etc.)
(2) imaginative re-creation exercises (q.v.) – write Banquo's letter home to his wife after meeting the witches; have a royal commission into the events of Lear's kingdom; in a modern setting, how would you rewrite Romeo's and Juliet's death soliloquies?; as a director invite someone to play Iago and explain why you see them as suitable for the role of Iago.

However, because of the unfamiliarity of language and experiences, especially in their first readings of Shakespeare, students may need to concentrate especially on such aspects as:
(3) 'blocking' particular scenes through drawing stick figures and creating ground plans – as a preliminary to detailed discussion of how a particular scene should be presented;
(4) much preliminary discussion to provide a 'picture' of the characters: how they would be dressed; build up a profile of their lifestyle if they were alive today;
(5) language – while remembering that much of Shakespeare's poetry is un-'translate'-able, still a lot of focus needs to be on language simply for understanding quite apart from literary criticism. Groups of students could follow key words through a play; underline key words in speeches; juxtapose speeches from the same character at different stages of the play; close study of important soliloquies; have groups trace particular images through the play.

References
R. Adams and G. Gould, *Into Shakespeare*, London: Ward Lock, 1977.
D. Adland, *The Group Approach to Shakespeare* series, London: Longman.
R. Arnold (ed.), *Approaches to Drama*, Sydney: ETA of NSW, 1979.
D. Mallick, *How Tall Is this Ghost, John?*, Adelaide: AATE.
W. Michaels, *When the Hurly Burly Is Done*, Sydney: St Clair, 1987.
V. O'Brien, *Teaching Shakespeare*, London: Arnold, 1982.

SHALL/SHOULD/WILL/WOULD *See* USAGE.

SHARED BOOK – This is a shared reading procedure (using an enlarged text for a group) using choral and group reading which encourages considerable participation from the child. For beginning readers especially, the chosen material should be memorable, enjoyable and predictable because the story structure is cumulative (e.g. *The Gingerbread Man*), circumlocutive (e.g. *The Three Billy Goats Gruff*), repetitive (e.g. *Brown Bear, Brown Bear*), indicates cause and effect (e.g. *The Little Red Hen*) or has predictable and regular rhyming patterns (e.g. *Green Eggs and Ham*). Outstanding features of this procedure for reading a book, a song, a poem or any other piece of written material, are:

(1) Using a clearly visible text, strategies of reading are modelled, demonstrated, exemplified and taught within context.
(2) The teacher/parent models reading behaviours involving the children in anticipating meanings, vocabulary, outcomes and shared pleasure.
(3) Repeated readings of the material – for pleasure, dramatization, discussion of alternative events and outcomes, choosing alternative rhymes, examination of the conventions used to write the material (e.g. punctuation, print size, direct speech, relationship between illustrations and writing) and so on.
(4) Further independent pupil reading of the material – sometimes supported by a tape recording of the text. **(MRT)**

See also STORY BOX; STORY CHEST.

References

Bill Martin, *Brown Bear, Brown Bear*, New York: Holt, Rinehart & Winston, 1972.
A. S. Geisel (Dr Seuss), *Green Eggs and Ham*, Glasgow: William Collins, 1980.

Further Reading

Don Holdaway, *The Foundations of Literacy*, Sydney: Ashton Scholastic, 1979.
Bill Martin and Peggy Brogan, *Teachers' Guide to the Instant Readers*, New York: Holt Rinehart & Winston, 1972.
Barbara Park, 'The big book trend', *Language Arts*, 59 (8), 1982: 815–21.

SHORT STORY COLLECTIONS – Some useful collections of short stories are:

Ages 11–12
C. Coroneos, *Short Story Discovery*
L. Hannan and G. Tickell, *The Bad Deeds Gang and Other Stories*
R. Mansfield, *Short Stories One and Two*
R. Chambers, *The Ice Warrior and Other Stories*

Ages 13+
R. A. Banks, *Ten Science Fiction Stories*
C. Coroneos, *Short Story Quest*
W. McVitty, *Short Story Favourites*
R. Mansfield, *The Storytellers – One and Two.*

SIGHT VOCABULARY *See* LOOK–SAY APPROACH.

SIGNAL – A critical magazine for people with a strong interest in children's literature. Edited by Nancy Chambers, it has three issues a year. Subscription inquiries: The Thimble Press, Lockwood, Station Road, South Woodchester, Stroud, Glos. GL5 5EQ, UK.

SIGNAL BOOK GUIDES – Published by the Thimble Press (*see* SIGNAL), these include:

Jill Bennett, *Learning to Read with Picture Books*
Jill Bennett, *Reading Out: Stories for Readers of 6 to 8*
Aidan Chambers, *Plays for Young People to Read and Perform*
Peggy Heeks, *Ways of Knowing: Information Books for 7 to 9 Year Olds*
Elaine Moss, *Picture Books for Young People, 9 to 13*.

SIGNAL POETRY AWARD – The journal *Signal* launched this award for poetry written for children in 1979.

1979 – *The Moon Bells* by Ted Hughes
1980 – No award.
1981 – No award.
1982 – *The Rattle Bag*, ed. Seamus Heaney and Ted Hughes.
1983 – *Sky in the Pig* by Roger McGough.
1984 – *What is the Truth? A Farmyard Fable* by Ted Hughes.
1985 – *Early in the Morning* by Charles Causley.
1986 – *Song of the City* by Gareth Owen.

SILENT READING –

> In silent reading, one reads to oneself, not others. . . . Beginning with the second decade of the twentieth century, the emphasis upon the teaching of silent reading soon replaced that upon oral reading. Silent reading is now the most common form of reading emphasised in the teaching of reading.
>
> (Harris and Hodges, pp. 296–7)

This changed emphasis appears to have resulted from several factors:

(1) The recognition that understanding the author's message is more important than giving a fine oral rendition.
(2) The understanding that oral reading makes different cognitive demands of the reader from those made by silent reading.
(3) A decreasing concern with pronunciation as an index of comprehension.
(4) Most of the reading practised by adults is silent.

See also ORAL READING; SUSTAINED SILENT READING.

Reference

T. L. Harris and R. E. Hodges, *A Dictionary of Reading and Related Terms*, Newark, Delaware: IRA, 1981.

SIMULATIONS – One of the most powerful learning experiences in a classroom is some reproduction of an actual situation through a simulation. Simulations such as a courtroom trial as part of a unit of work can be easily created by the teacher. In *Teaching about Television*, for example, Len Masterman discusses a simulation which re-enacts the scene of a newsroom before the nightly TV news broadcast as part of a unit of work on television. An equivalent simulation entitled, *Newscast*, is available from the NSW Department of Education.

Increasingly, commercially produced simulations are proving of great value.

Computer simulation games which involve discussion and pose problems to solve are also extremely useful in the English classroom for promoting group work and discussion. Examples of these would include SPACE PROGRAMME ALPHA, a 'space simulation', and BIG BROTHER, a simulation built around George Orwell's '1984', both published by CLASS (q.v.).

References

Ken Jones, *Simulations: a handbook for Teachers*, London: Kogan Page, 1980.
L. Masterman, *Teaching about Television*, London: Macmillan, 1980.
J. L. Taylor and R. Walford, *Learning and the Simulation Game*, Milton Keynes: Open University Press, 1978.

SKILLS MODEL OF ENGLISH – The skills model is based on the belief that language competence can be broken down into a number of discrete skills and items of information which can then be taught separately, leaving the learner to resynthesize them. Such a view of English is not in accord with what is known about how children learn language (*see* LANGUAGE ACQUISITION).

Reference

Ken Watson, *English Teaching in Perspective*, Milton Keynes: Open University Press, 1987, Ch. 8.

SLANG – Language of a highly colloquial nature; 'the diction', writes Fowler, 'that results from the favourite game among the young and lively of playing with words and renaming things and actions; some invent new words, or mutilate or misapply the old, for the pleasure of novelty, and others catch up such words for the pleasure of being in the fashion.' Many words, such as *mob*, have begun as slang and risen in status; others disappear after enjoying a brief popularity. Two entertaining and useful compilations of Australian slang are G. A. Wilkes's *A Dictionary of Australian Colloquialisms* and Bill Hornadge's *The Australian Slanguage.* British readers will find the many works of Eric Partridge invaluable. See especially his *Dictionary of Historical Slang* (Harmondsworth: Penguin Books, 1972).
See also COLLOQUIAL LANGUAGE; JARGON.

SLOW LEARNERS, SEPARATE CLASSES FOR – The evidence is quite clear that slow learners (i.e. those with IQs in the 65–90 range) are best catered for in normal streams, unless they are also emotionally disturbed. Calberg and Kavale surveyed fifty studies of special-class versus regular-class placement and concluded that 'there is no justification for the placement of low IQ children in special classes'. A recent New Zealand study by Olive Frampton has confirmed this finding.

References

C. Calberg and K. Kavale, 'The efficacy of special versus regular class placement for exceptional children: a meta-analysis', *Journal of Special Education* 3, 1980.
O. Frampton, *Slow Learners, Segregated and Integrated*, research report available from Education Department, University of Canterbury, Christchurch, NZ.

SMALL-GROUP WORK – The value of small-group work in English (and indeed in almost all subjects) is now widely recognized. Small-group work encourages a more active involvement in the learning process; provides a non-threatening atmosphere in which students can try out their ideas and voice their difficulties; encourages hypothetical thinking; develops social skills; allows students to learn from one another. When Douglas Barnes (q.v.) and Frankie Todd carried out their study of 13-year-old boys and girls working in small groups, the teachers of the children expressed surprise and delight when the recordings of group talk were played: 'They were surprised because the quality of the children's contributions typically far exceeded the calibre of their contributions in class; and were pleased to hear the children manifesting unexpected skills and competences' (p. ix). The most effective size for a small group seems to be three or four; five is a maximum, except for special tasks such as the preparation of a play. It is vital that pupils be seated facing one another.

Groups need to know exactly what they have to do. Usually group work of any length will be preceded by a whole-class planning session in which tasks are co-operatively defined and allocated to particular groups. Normally, too, it will be followed by some form of reporting back to the class as a whole: presenting findings, displaying the group collage, playing the group tape, and so on.

If the teacher is worried that group talk will stray too far from the point, each group can be asked to record its discussion on a cassette recorder. The presence of the cassette recorder (once the novelty has worn off) is a continual reminder to groups to press on with the task and serves to focus their talk.

For classes unused to group work, short tasks involving pairs or groups should be undertaken before extended group work is attempted. Even where it is intended that whole-class discussion will form the major part of a lesson, it is often advisable to place pupils in groups for five or ten minutes to try out their ideas on their peers. When this is done, both the length and quality of contributions to whole-class discussion improve.

Most Australian state education departments have produced booklets offering teachers advice on small-group work. Particularly good is *Small Group Work in the Classroom*, produced by the Curriculum Branch of the Education Department of Western Australia.

Reference

Douglas Barnes and Frankie Todd, *Communication and Learning in Small Groups*, London: Routledge & Kegan Paul, 1977.

SOCIOLINGUISTICS – The study of language in society, language as it affects relationships between people and the social implications of language. Sociolinguistics can be contrasted with approaches to language study which concentrate mainly on the language competence of the individual, as if he or she were some kind of representative ideal speaker/hearer. Students of sociolinguistics are not concerned with the ideal but with actual people in society and the way they use their language or languages in interaction with each other. It is well known that the social context can have a strong influence on the kind of language being used, but the converse is also true: the choice of a particular kind of language helps to create the social context; formal language can establish the formality of the situation.

Many traditional aspects of language study have come to be included in the field of sociolinguistics and the underlying theme of language in relation to its social context has provided a new focus for them. Dialects, for example, are seen as part of a wider concept of language variation including regional and social dialects and also register variation. This in turn is related to bilingualism – including, for example, how different languages are used in bilingual families and communities, the extent of their use and their roles and functions. At the broader national level, questions of language policy arise, and these have many implications for education. In some countries the policy involves deliberate language planning by governments.

Many aspects of sociolinguistics are relevant to the work of the English teacher. One of these is social dialect variation – the way different social groups within the community use their language. The status of various social dialects and languages in a community is based on the attitudes which people have towards each other's language and to their own. One aspect of this is the question of standard and non-standard varieties of a language, which must be a central concern of the English teacher. Related to all these issues are the functions for which people use language and their competence to use the appropriate register or language for every purpose for which they need to use language. **(JC)**

See also DIALECT; REGISTER; STANDARD ENGLISH; NON-STANDARD ENGLISH.

References

R. T. Bell, *Sociolinguistics: Goals, Approaches, Problems*, London: Batsford, 1976.

M. Clyne (ed.), *Australia Talks: Essays on the Sociology of Australian Immigrant and Aboriginal Languages*, Canberra: Dept. of Linguistics, R. S. Pac. Stud., ANU, 1976.

M. A. K. Halliday, *Language and Social Man*, London: Longman, 1974.

R. A. Hudson, *Sociolinguistics*, Cambridge: Cambridge University Press, 1980.

P. Robinson, *Language and Social Behaviour*, Harmondsworth, Penguin, 1974.

P. Robinson, *Language Management in Education: The Australian Context*, Sydney: George Allen & Unwin, 1978.

P. Trudgill, *Sociolinguistics*, Harmondsworth: Penguin, 1974.

SOURCE BOOKS AND COURSE BOOKS – Sometimes a distinction is made between textbooks which offer a wide variety of stimulus material from which teacher and pupils select what interests them (source books) and those which are divided into units designed to provide a sequential series of lesson (coursebooks). As far as the latter are concerned, the sequencing is often more apparent than real, and unfortunately the most widely used course books are those which substitute decontextualized, dummy-run exercises for meaningful language activities.

A scheme for evaluating textbooks may be found in Ken Watson's *English Teaching in Perspective* (Milton Keynes: Open University Press, 1987).

SPEAKING *See* TALK; DEBATING; INTERVIEWS; ORACY.

SPEED READING *See* READING MACHINES.

SPELLING – Much recent language-based spelling research would seem to make the following principles the basis of a worthwhile spelling policy:

(1) Spelling only makes real sense if considered as being in the service of writing. Isolated 'spelling' (spelling-test) lessons which bear no relation to the writing which children are doing are a waste of time. If children are encouraged to see spelling as part of writing then they are on the path to spelling correctly so as to get their writing correct. The research of Donald Graves with invented spelling (q.v.) shows that children do learn to spell correctly the words they want to use – motivation comes with the need. More recently, Graves has argued that learning to spell while writing and learning to spell arbitrary lists may be different processes – an argument

arising from his studies of children who only learnt to spell through writing (Graves, 'The spelling process: a look at strategies', *Language Arts*, NCTE, April 1982). Other research indicates that most spelling knowledge is acquired unconsciously (D. M. Bennett, *New Methods and Materials in Spelling: A Critical Analysis*, Melbourne: ACER, 1967) and that there even seem to be developmental stages in learning to spell (C. S. and J. W. Beers, *Language Arts*, May 1981).

(2) Encourage children to widen their vocabulary in writing, to use new words and to make guesses (or leave gaps with an initial letter) at spelling unfamiliar words. In a classroom using the process approach to writing (q.v.), proof-reading will be encouraged and it is at this stage that spelling can be corrected, rather than interrupting the flow of thought to get spelling correct in the first draft. (Remember spelling is only the tool, not the finished article.)

(3) If spelling is acquired unconsciously, then wide reading will be a great aid to improved spelling (not, by the way, vice versa).

(4) Have children keep lists of their personal spelling 'demons' and learn *these* (written tests of these can be conducted by a partner). If you do prefer to conduct whole-class spelling tests of the same list of words, then make your list from words related to the unit of work currently being undertaken, most common errors of *your* class, and most requested words.

(5) Don't drill spelling rules – the exceptions are so numerous, as with phonic 'rules', that it is almost arbitrary as to what should be the rule and what the exception.

(6) As with reading, phonics (q.v.) is only one strategy for aiding spelling, and it is certainly not of primary importance – after all, English spelling is notoriously irregular with respect to sound. Sight is probably the most useful sense in spelling and the look-cover-write-check approach the most useful strategy for memorizing a new word.

(7) Encourage children to use a number of strategies for finding the correct spelling of a word – ask you, ask each other, look at signs, posters, charts in the room, check class books, consult a dictionary. (A word on this last strategy – remember it will only work if the child has a reasonable idea of how a word is spelt already and certainly she or he must know the first couple of letters. The frequent advice to children to 'go to a dictionary' to discover a word's spelling ignores the fact that you have to be able to spell a word in order to find it in the dictionary in the first place.)

(8) Study spelling errors to see what they reveal – a child who alters 'sayed' to 'sed' has done something positive and this needs to be recognized. Phonic misspelling shows a certain sense of the language, as does spelling irregular tense changes regularly (e.g. 'sayed'). Be more worried about those errors which make no sense.

(9) Be aware yourself of changes in spelling (and remember that in the history of English writing, spelling has only recently become regular). The teacher whose class's spelling errors consist of spelling, say, 'medieval' instead of 'mediaeval' has no spelling problems and should not create them.

See also INVENTED SPELLING.

References

Don Smedley, *Teaching the Basic Skills*, London: Methuen, 1983.

D. Stratford, 'Spelling', in K. D. Watson and R. D. Eagleson, *English in Secondary Schools: Today and Tomorrow*, ETA & NSW, 1977; and *Primary English Newsletter*, 36, PETA, 1982.

Mike Torbe, *Teaching Spelling*, London: Ward Lock, 1978.

SPLIT INFINITIVE *See* USAGE.

SQ3R – A system designed to aid pupils in their independent reading in textbooks in the content areas. SQ3R has five stages: survey, question, read, recite, review:

(1) Survey: In this initial stage the reader looks over the material to be read to try to establish what the topic is and what the reading demands are likely to be. It also involves the reader in taking stock of what she or he already knows about the topic.

(2) Question: The reader makes hypotheses or predictions about the text, or establishes questions that the text might be expected to answer. Such questions can often be formulated from sub-headings in the text.

(3) Read: The passage is read:
   (i) to find the answers to the questions asked;
   (ii) to locate other important information that the question stage did not predict.

(4) Recite: In the Recite stage, the reader answers the questions posed in the Survey and Question stages.

(5) Review: Answering the questions at a later time, say, within twenty-four hours of the initial reading.

The system does not suit everyone, but it is worth teaching to all so that they can try it out.

SRA READING LABORATORIES *See* READING LABORATORIES.

SSR *See* SUSTAINED SILENT READING.

STANDARD ENGLISH – The variety or dialect of English which is generally used by educated people in formal situations, especially in writing. It has a degree of prestige and acceptance in the community at large which distinguishes it from other social dialects of English. Its position is reinforced by the fact that it is the variety generally recorded in dictionaries and grammar books. There are slight differences in standard English from one English-speaking country to another but these are mainly differences of accent which are irrelevant to written English. Standard English is often popularly thought of as 'correct English', a view which used to be held and even encouraged by English teachers. However, each social dialect is a valuable means of communication and social cohesion in its own context and teachers are faced with the difficult task of accepting each child's own social dialect and at the same time helping each child to learn to use standard English in those contexts where it is appropriate. **(JC)**

See also DIALECT; NON-STANDARD ENGLISH.

References

R. Quirk *et al.*, *A Grammar of Contemporary English*, London: Longman, 1972.

M. Stubbs, *Language and Literacy: The Sociolinguistics of Reading and Writing*, London: Routledge & Kegan Paul, 1980.

STANDARDIZED TESTS – Tests which have been normed against a sample which is considered representative of the population as a whole. IQ tests (q.v.) and tests which yield a reading age (q.v.) are examples. They allow one to say whether an individual is performing better or worse than average in the population or in the age group. It must be stressed that these are crude measures. The standardized reading tests may be useful as a screening device to detect students 'at risk', but more data gathering is necessary before it can be said that an individual is a weak reader.

See also IQ TESTS; READING AGE.

STANDARDS – The 'declining standards' school of thought, which is evident in most English-speaking countries, usually carries that subjective folklore emphasis that characterizes the 'Why, in my day . . .' school of educational debate. But certainly there is much community concern and much academic confusion and argument over 'What standards?' and 'What do we mean by "declining"?' All we can hope to do here is to provide a few brief comments:

(1) One system of education cannot be judged in terms of standards or tests derived by another. The view of education and learning espoused, for example, by Britton (q.v.), Moffett (q.v.) and other theorists of the 'new English' certainly strives for well-rounded excellence in skills such as reading, writing, speaking and listening, but not necessarily in ways susceptible to testing by a battery of formal, external, standardized examinations. Raising of real, worthwhile standards in these skills may not necessarily reduce to easily measured numerical figures.

(2) The argument is not helped by the 'decline school's' simplistic assumptions about definitions of 'literacy' and 'illiteracy'. The British Ministry of Education in 1950 stated that 'most definitions of illiteracy amount to this: that [she/he] is illiterate who is not as literate as someone else thinks [she/he] ought to be'. This is not to avoid facing the question of any illiteracy which does exist but it does point to the 'decline school's' assumptions about these concepts. Literacy is, and should be seen as, a continuum on which different people stand in different places just as they would if we were measuring a national standard of cricketing or athletics ability. (How many kids ever say 'I can't run'? and yet how many say 'I can't write'? But surely there are fewer Olympic athletes than there are illiterate adults.) Probably only contextual assessments of literacy are valid anyway – everybody's competence depends on the situation, though some are more competent in more situations than others. There is no objective global skill called 'literacy' which is easily examinable to determine a set of standards.

(3) Attempts to objectify 'literacy' and measure it lead only to the most narrow and miserable definitions with predictable results for education: increasingly objective measurement leads to increasingly minimal definitions of literacy with increasingly minimal aims for education. Many US school

districts have minimal competency standards and, as these are what is tested and thus what is taught, minimal competency could very well be what they get, (*see* Graham Little, 1977). In *Coming on Center*, Moffett (q.v.) reports that in parts of the United States, writing has been replaced by dummy-run exercises in punctuation and grammar because these are objectively measurable. Thus the 'standards' debate has fuelled the 'back to basics' (q.v.) movement. Any consequent decline in writing standards will, ironically, be the fault of the 'back to basics' movement.

(4) The 'decline school' and the 'back to basics' movement deplore the movement away from the study of grammar and mechanics. This begs at least two questions: How many schools have in fact 'moved away'? Just how 'basic' are grammar and mechanics? In answer to the latter, it can be stated quite categorically that the teaching of a grammatical system has no observable effect on one's ability to write or to speak and that surface mechanics are learnt most effectively in the context of language programmes that value language use for real, varied purposes and real, varied audiences. (*See* GRAMMAR AND WRITING; PUNCTUATION, TEACHING OF.)

(5) The 'decline school' rests, by definition, on an assumption of a golden age of literacy. No such age has existed. In Australia, for example, any comparison of New South Wales public examiners' comments from the 1910s to the 1960s reveals much the same comments about students' inability to cope with grammar, punctuation and spelling in times when these were the prescribed staple diet of English lessons and English examinations:

- 'Only a small minority of examinees know how to punctuate, and in hundreds of cases the punctuation was disgraceful.' (1915)
- 'Punctuation . . . unsatisfactory. Very many candidates were content with the occasional full stop. Spelling was not good.' (1917)
- 'Deplorable English . . . ungrammatical stuff.' (1919)
- 'any kind of English is good enough, no matter how full it may be of errors, vulgarisms and mispronunciations.' (1943)
- 'Spelling still weak.' (1950)
- 'Spelling and grammar are lost arts.' (1961)

The Bullock Report (q.v.) makes reference to the Newbolt Report of 1921 in which Messrs Vickers Ltd reported 'great difficulty in obtaining junior clerks who can speak and write English clearly and correctly, especially those aged from fifteen to sixteen years'. Messrs Lever Bros Ltd said, 'our young employees are . . . hopelessly deficient in their command of English'; and Boots Pure Drug Co. remarked that 'teaching of English in the present day schools produces a very limited command of the English language'. When was the 'golden age' of literacy?

(6) The few large-scale objective surveys that have been done suggest that, in terms the 'decline school' should accept, if anything standards are rising. Perhaps the best-known survey in this area is that conducted by Judith Goyen of Macquarie University reported in the *Newsletter of the National Committee for Teaching English* (March, 1976). Goyen used an ANOP

sample to survey 2,000 people over 16. The aim was to test 'functional literacy', defined as the ability to score 80 per cent on a forty-four item test by everyday survival skills such as form-filling. Among native speakers, the functional illiteracy rate was 12 per cent for those over 60 (schooled in the 1920s or before), reducing to less than 2 per cent for the under 30s (schooled in the 1960s and 1970s). There was a high illiteracy rate (60 per cent) among older migrants, but this reduced to 3 per cent for those with some schooling here, a further encouraging finding.

Graham Little (November 1978) suggests that further important evidence is the fact that authorities responsible for the verbal IQ testing of New South Wales schoolchildren at Years 4 and 6 have had to adjust the scaling so that all IQs were lowered by four points to bring the average back to the theoretical 100. This is a relevant standard because whatever value IQ tests may or may not have, it is certain that a score above chance level is dependent on being able to read for meaning, and kids had been scoring too high.

Other direct attainment tests during the 1960s and 1970s in a number of states also failed to detect any decline and the examiners' reports at matriculation level show no evidence of decline. In fact, in the last three years of the external School Certificate examination in New South Wales, for example, English examiners consistently commented upon the rising standards of written expression, particularly at Modified Level and in 1977 examiners of the 2-Unit NSW Higher School Certificate English paper commented that a considerable improvement had taken place over the previous two years.

As the dates of our quotations in this entry indicate, 1976 was a particularly loud year for the 'decline school' after the publication of the first ACER survey on levels of literacy. But the pessimism and gloom that was extracted from *Australian Studies in School Performance* (1976) seems ill-founded. For one thing, the test items were highly questionable with students being asked among other things to be able to understand headlines that contained typically mixed metaphor journalese. There was very little analysis of the concept of 'literacy' and the findings on criterion-referenced absolute standards are at best questionable. In terms of relative standards, the survey did find that Australian children were performing comparably with their peers in England and the United States (though not as well as New Zealanders); and, even in the absolute testing, the amount of illiteracy even as defined by the survey, was less than 1 per cent among 14 year olds. A subsequent ACER survey in 1980 found that in general standards of achievement had risen since 1976.

See also ASSESSMENT OF PERFORMANCE UNIT; BASICS; MINIMAL COMPETENCY TESTING.

References

P. Brock, 'Thunder without Enlightening', *English in Australia*, 53, AATE, Sept. 1980.
S. Doenan, *Have School Standards Declined?* (published by the author, 11 Rosemont Avenue, Pennant Hills, NSW 2120, 1981).
ETANSW, 'Back to the basics?', *ETANSW Newsletter*, ETANSW, Sept. 1978.

G. Little, 'Back to the basics in the USA', *English in Australia*, 40, AATE, May 1977.
G. Little, 'Literacy: the great non-debate', *The Teaching of English*, 35, ETANSW, Sept. 1978.
G. Little, 'Standards', *English in Australia*, 46, AATE, Nov. 1978.
J. Moffett, *Coming on Center*, Montclair, NJ: Boynton Cook, 1981.
R. Parker, 'Are our standards slipping?' *English in Australia*, 40, AATE, May, 1977.
K. Watson, *English Teaching in Perspective*, Milton Keynes: Open University Press, 1987.

STORY BOX (Rigby Aust.) or STORY CHEST (UK) – A literature-based Reading Programme designed for the infant grades, first published in Australia in 1982. This programme is based on the premise that children learn to read best through reading and rereading highly motivating and highly predictable literature in different styles and on various topics. It is comprised of sets of most attractive large books for group shared reading activities with matching sets of small-sized books in the same titles, and extra sets of small books for independent or small group reading.

The Story Box (Rigby) teacher's manuals provide excellent ideas and guidance for the teacher in how to use the programme most effectively and encourage an integrated whole-language approach. **(MRT)**
See also SHARED BOOK.

STORY GRAMMARS – Analyses of story structure, largely carried out by cognitive psychologists for experimental purposes. Experiments usually revolve around recall of stories and elements of recall are identified by the 'grammar'. Story grammars usually divide into 'episodes'. It is generally the case that story grammars are concerned only with elements of plot and lack the more sophisticated approaches of narratologists (see NARRATOLOGY) such as Genette (q.v.) or Chatman (q.v.). It is also generally true that the stories described by the grammars and used for experimental purposes are extremely bare and simple, giving no concession to the complexities of narrative understanding of which children are capable.

STREAM OF CONSCIOUSNESS – A style of writing in which the writer attempts to capture unrestrained the ebb and flow of a human consciousness by presenting a character's thoughts in no particular order other than that in which they occur. Interior monologue and free, random association are important elements of the method, whose most famous modern exponents are probably James Joyce and Virginia Woolf. The method can be echoed in school writing (e.g. in journals) by free association writing of 'what-ever comes into your head'.
See also INNER SPEECH.

STREAMING OR TRACKING – The practice of placing pupils in classes graded on ability. It is now generally acknowledged that streaming, if undertaken at all, should be delayed as long as possible. Certainly there is no reason for grading pupils in primary and lower secondary school, and if grading is undertaken at these levels, it is likely to do grave injustice to the late developer. The arguments against streaming are summarized in the entry on mixed-ability classes (q.v.).
See also IQ TESTING; MIXED-ABILITY TEACHING.

STRUCTURAL APPROACH TO ESL TEACHING – In this approach, English is broken down into its components, ordered into a pedagogic sequence, and then fed to the learner, who is drilled in correct patterns. It gives students a knowledge of the formal structural patterns of language, but it offers form without meaning. A typical structural text is *Situational English*, published by Longman. **(MG-S)**

See also FUNCTIONAL/NOTIONAL APPROACH.

A valuable article by Ian Pringle, outlining the Canadian experience in ESL teaching, draws attention to the theory of second-language learning formulated by the American linguist Stephen Krashen, who makes a distinction between 'learning' a second language and 'acquiring' it:

> Second-language 'learning' is due to direct teaching; for example, to direct instruction in the grammar of the second language. Second language 'acquisition', however, is due to comprehensible input – that is, it is due to an unconscious understanding of language which grows when the student's attention is focused not on the language but on its meaning. Krashen hypothesizes that these two processes are largely independent. He also hypothesizes that what is 'learnt', in his sense, can be assessed for linguistic performance only when certain very narrow conditions are met: the students must have enough time to think of the rules they have been taught; they must in fact do so (this does not necessarily follow from fulfilment of the first condition); and they must not be in an emotional state which prevents them from doing so. These conditions can be met in test situations; however, they cannot normally be met in situations where the use of language is normal (as it is not in test situations).
>
> In normal situations, learners have to fall back on what they have acquired on the basis of what Krashen calls 'comprehensible input'. According to this hypothesis, second-language learners acquire a working knowledge of the structure of the target language by focusing not on form, but on meaning.

Reference

Ian Pringle, 'English as a world language – right out there in the playground', in R. Arnold (ed.), *Timely Voices*, Melbourne: Oxford University Press, 1983, pp. 200–1.

STRUCTURAL GRAMMAR – An approach to grammatical description which was developed in the 1940s and 1950s especially in the United States. It differed from traditional grammar in several important ways. For example, it was not based on the written literature of the languages to which it was applied but rather on the spoken language which was regarded as the primary mode. This was partly because it was developed and extensively used in the study of non-European languages and many of these had no written form. The description in structural grammar was based on the forms of the words without taking account of the meaning. Words and other elements were classified in terms of the formal features they displayed (such as grammatical endings) and where they could occur in relation to other words. The structural approach to grammar was essentially descriptive; these grammarians carefully avoided making prescriptive judgements about the language features they were describing. If some feature or structure occurred in the usage of many speakers then it was treated as part of the language on that basis alone. **(JC)**

References

C. C. Fries, *The Structure of English*, New York: Holt, Rinehart & Winston Harcourt Brace, 1952.

J. Sledd, *A Short Introduction to English Grammar*, Chicago: Scott, Foresman, 1959.

B. M. H. Strang, *Modern English Structure*, 2nd edn, London: Arnold, 1968.

STRUCTURALISM – Once characterized, somewhat unfairly, by Richard Kostelanetz (*Twenties in the Sixties*, Westfort, Conn. and Sydney: Greenwood Press, 1979) as 'Parisian Bullshit', structuralism has provoked, and still provokes, intemperate antipathy or partisanship. The controversy is not clarified by the fact that some commentators use 'structuralism' as a shorthand for 'semiology', 'formalism', 'narratology', and even 'post-structuralism' – all of which are foreign/French/American, but definitely not Cambridge – a vice found on all sides of the controversy. See, for example, an anti-structuralist work, in many ways excellent, by Geoffrey Strickland, *Structuralism or Criticism?* (Cambridge: Cambridge University Press, 1981), which sets Leavis (sanity) against Barthes (structuralism) much to the disadvantage of the latter – convincingly at certain points, I feel, particularly when Strickland explores 'Thoughts on How We Read'.

Yet the fact is that there are insights and procedures in structuralism of use to the English teacher, wrapped as they often are, however, in a forbidding terminology taken from Saussurean linguistics, and expressed as they often are by critics like Roland Barthes who are only structuralists some of the time and make a virtue of shifting ground.

If ever you have asked your students to consider what other words than those present in a text *may* have been used, you have, perhaps without knowing it, been committing structuralism – exploring paradigmatic relationships.

Structuralism is essentially about relationships within a system. It conceives of language as self-contained and self-referential. The 'signification' of the linguistic 'sign' (which, in Saussure (q.v.), is the relation of an arbitrary 'signifier' to a socially and linguistically determined 'signified', the 'signified' not being the 'referent' or 'thing signified', but a mental concept) can only be understood/described by plotting it in relation to other items in the total system, and that is in the system as it is now ('synchrony') rather than as it has evolved ('diachrony'). Because the structuralists claim to be concerned with the structures that underlie 'literature', rather than with the meanings of individual literary works, they thus further claim that their methodology is ultimately a 'theory of reading'. They claim to be formulating a comprehensive theory of literary discourse, so that study of particular structures in any text illuminates not only that text, but also delivers 'a sense of how to read'.

It is the implications of this claim that may make their approach relevant to the classroom.

This essentially linguistic viewpoint has been developed to deal with other kinds of 'signs' and 'codes', in the study of narrative, of film, of advertisements, of poetic forms, of rhetoric, of dress, of food, and so on. Hence it shades into 'semiology' (q.v.). How valid such extensions are, and how deleterious struc-

turalism's inherent a-historicism and formalism, are matters of controversy. More serious still are allegations that the linguistics on which structuralism is based is itself inadequate. **(NJW)**
See also SAUSSURE; SEMIOLOGY/SEMIOTICS; POST-STRUCTURALISM.

References
R. Barthes, *Mythologies*, London: Paladin, 1973.
R. Barthes, *Barthes* by *Barthes*, New York: Hill & Wang, 1977.
R. Barthes, *Image–Music–Text*, London: Fontana, 1977.
J. Culler, *Structuralist Poetics*, London: Routledge & Kegan Paul, 1975.
J. Culler, *The Pursuit of Signs*, London: Routledge & Kegan Paul, 1981.
Roger Fowler, *Literature as Social Discourse*, Bloomington: Indiana University Press, 1981.
M. A. K. Halliday, *Language as Social Semiotic*, London: Arnold, 1978.
T. Hawkes, *Structuralism and Semiotics*, London: Methuen, 1977.
F. de Saussure, *Course in General Linguistics*, London: Fontana, 1974.
Geoffrey Strickland, *Structuralism or Criticism?* Cambridge: Cambridge University Press, 1981.
J. Sturrock (ed.), *Structuralism and Since*, Oxford: Oxford University Press, 1979.

STUDY SKILLS – A useful book on teaching study skills, one which incorporates insights gained from the major United Kingdom project 'Teaching of Study Skills', is Ann Irving (ed.), *Starting to Teach Study Skills* (London: Edward Arnold, 1982).
See also SQ3R.

SUBJUNCTIVES *See* USAGE.

SUB-TEXTING – Sub-texting is a process of making explicit the meanings, motivations and functions of a dramatic text in order to understand fully the meaning. In everyday life a simple greeting like 'Hello' can convey many different meanings depending on the context and the relationship between the speakers. Part of that meaning will be conveyed by the speakers' tone of voice, pitch, pace and gesture. The meaning will also be understood in the light of the implicit and shared understandings of the speakers of their relationship.

In a drama text the range of acceptable interpretations of a script will be circumscribed by the text as a whole and by the plausibility of the interpretation in terms of the relationships between characters.

In the classroom the initial purpose of sub-texting a script can be to elicit the underlying meanings the reader/speaker brings to the text in order to work towards some fuller understanding of the complex messages carried by the dialogue. A reader coming to the script for the first time may use only his or her intuitive understandings of dialogue and relationships, but it is important that students recognize that such understandings are important in the ways we interpret any language situation. Once the reader's interpretations are explicated, they can then be tested against the emerging patterns in the script and the unfolding relationships between characters.

A drama script is notoriously difficult to read alone and it is rare for students to persevere with a solitary reading. The following method can be used even if students have only a very rudimentary knowledge of the script.

Select a part of the play which reveals some significant details of characters' motivations – the first act of a Shakespeare play is usually effective – and ask each reader in turn to read a number of lines of the original (take enough lines to make sense of the meaning). The reader then returns to the beginning of his or her piece and, in the first person – speaking as the character – explains as fully as she or he can what she or he is feeling, thinking, wishing and wanting in saying the words in the dialogue. At this initial stage readers should be encouraged to say as much as they can and to interpret as freely as possible. At first students can be intimidated by the fear of saying something incorrect, so it is important that whatever they say at this point is accepted, even if it is clearly a misinterpretation of the script. What usually happens is that over the process of reworking the script, serious misinterpretations tend to be dropped naturally. The teacher needs to know at this stage what is influencing the readers' interpretations and what further insights the readers need in order to make full sense of the script. The readers need to know that they can and do bring prior knowledge of the functions of language to their reading of even new contexts. They also need to know that the meaning of the script lies within its language, not within the teacher's head or the abstruse pages of some literary crib. The ultimate aim of sub-texting is to move to the stage where the readers can say the original lines of the script with a rich sense of the multiple functions or simple function a line might carry.

Sub-texting is not a method alien to students' experience. From very early childhood we all engaged in interpreting quickly and fairly accurately the meanings conveyed in speech. What is inhibiting for some students unused to relying on their own intuitive abilities in the classroom is the fear of making a mistake in interpretation. This can be overcome if the teacher resists strongly the temptation to pre-empt, correct or analyse prematurely the early interpretations given by the readers. It is important that readers be given the chance to self-correct. It usually happens within a group situation where each member contributes his or her understanding of the text that some cohesive group interpretation emerges naturally. Once the students have gained confidence in their abilities to make meaning from the script, discussion about reasons for choices can take place. Furthermore, the teacher who presumably knows more about the script than the students, can offer illuminating comments and answer questions raised by the students. Obviously, some general résumé of the context of a dialogue can be helpful if students are completely new to the play. If the teacher wants the students to make explicit and refine their understandings of the script to the point where the original sounds like the reader's own words, then the process will have served its purpose. **(RA)**

SURVIVAL READING *See* FUNCTIONAL LITERACY.

SUSTAINED SILENT READING – A classroom technique for all grade levels whereby at a set time each day every pupil and the teacher read silently an individual selection for a substantial period of time without interruption. The successful practice of SSR involves complete freedom of choice of reading material by each pupil. Consequently, a wide variety of interesting reading materials accessible to the children needs to be provided. This material includes magazines, fiction and non-fiction and should cater for the differing levels of reading development within the class. Children may need guidance initially in choosing materials, as the value of SSR is destroyed if children are permitted to merely browse, or to spend the set time on several pieces of material rather than in the sustained reading of one selection.

It is imperative that the teacher reads with the class both to reinforce the value of the activity and to provide a good model of interested, sustained silent reading. Most teachers find that once the practice has been established, children will happily sustain silent reading for twenty-five minutes or more. The teacher's praise of pupils' efforts at the end of a SSR session will assist in establishing the practice. There should be no requirement that children report on their reading in any way, although teachers find that once SSR becomes a habit, children are eager to share their responses to reading through discussion, drama, writing, art and other media. **(MRT)**

References

Robert A. McCracken, 'Initiating sustained silent reading', *Journal of Reading*, 14, 8 May 1971: 521–4.

Robert A. McCracken and Marlene J. McCracken, 'Modelling is the key to sustained silent reading', *The Reading Teacher*, 31 (4), January 1978: 406–8.

Peter Sloan and Ross Latham, *Teaching Reading Is . . .* , Sydney: Nelson, 1981.

SWANN REPORT – The Report of a Committee of Inquiry into the Education of Children from Ethnic Minority Groups, chaired by Lord Swann, published in March 1985 (London: HMSO). The Committee originated in a concern expressed by the West Indian community during the late 1960s and early 1970s about the academic performance of their children. In setting up the Committee the government decided that the inquiry should be concerned with the needs of pupils from all ethnic minority groups with priority being given to children of West Indian origin.

The Committee was established in 1979 with the following terms of reference:

> Recognizing the contribution of schools in preparing all pupils for life in a society which is both multi-racial and culturally diverse, the Committee is required to:
>
> review in relation to schools the educational needs and attainments of children from ethnic minority groups taking account, as necessary, of factors outside the formal education system relevant to school performance, including influences in early childhood and prospects for school leavers;
>
> consider the potential value of instituting arrangements for keeping under review the educational performance of different ethnic minority groups, and what those arrangements might be;
>
> consider the most effective use of resources for these purposes; and to make recommendations.

In carrying out its programme of work, the Committee is to give early and particular attention to the educational needs and attainments of pupils of West Indian origin and to make interim recommendations as soon as possible on action which might be taken in the interests of this group.

NB: The Committee's terms of reference relate only to England.

SYLLABIC VERSE – A type of verse in which the number of syllables to each line is the same. An example is Thom Gunn's 'Considering the Snail'. Students can be set the task of writing poetry within these limits, or of varying the concept by:

(1) alternating the number of syllables per line, for example seven syllables / six syllables repeated;
(2) writing poems in which the number of syllables per line increases at a fixed rate (1–2–3–4) and perhaps reaches a crescendo to die down (1–2–3–4–3–2–1).

See also HAIKU.

SYMBOL/SYMBOLISM – The use of expressions or objects to represent certain ideas or figures. The notion of symbolism is easily introduced to students through the symbols that they see around them everyday – for example, symbols of political and religious groups such as the hammer-and-sickle, Star of David, the cross and so on. There is also a corpus of conventional literary symbolism, much of it from classical mythology (e.g. Cupid's darts as symbols of love) to which students could be introduced as a next step. As with any literary device, symbolism should be 'studied' in context and these preliminary steps are suggested only as a way in to looking at the structure of symbolism in a particular work under consideration. Unfortunately, a certain critical arbitrariness often creeps into the study of the symbolic structure of many works: Hemingway's old man and his fish have been seen as representing everything from a post-Freudian ego–id conflict through a representation of the political crises of the 1930s to the struggle of humans with their essential destiny. Melville's Moby Dick has suffered a similar fate. The most coherent symbolism is that which accrues its own meanings from its own context. This is demonstrable in much commonly studied school literature. Fire in *Lord of the Flies* symbolizes much that is both positive and negative because of the uses to which it is put in the novel itself. Blood in *Macbeth* symbolizes much that is negative, but also much that is positive, and the transformation echoes that in Macbeth himself, or more especially in the way he is perceived. Even the silver sword of Serraillier's children's novel gains a symbolic aspect in this way.

SYNTACTIC INFORMATION –

Syntactic information refers to an intuitive understanding of how one's language functions. It can be described as a feeling for the flow of language. It is what enables us to recognise the first of the following series of words, but not the second, as a meaningful sentence.

The bus is down the street.
Be will soon here it.

(Parker, 1983)

Syntactic information is one of the three major types of non-visual information (q.v.) that a reader uses in the process of comprehending print. **(MRT)**
See also VISUAL INFORMATION; NON-VISUAL INFORMATION; SEMANTIC INFORMATION; GRAPHO-PHONIC INFORMATION.

References
R. Parker, 'Towards a model of the reading process', in D. E. Burnes and G. M. Page (eds), *Reading: Insights and Strategies for Teaching*, Sydney: Harcourt Brace Jovanovich, 1983.
F. Smith, *Reading*, Cambridge: Cambridge University Press, 1978.

SYNTAX – That part of grammar which is concerned with the structure of word groups, phrases, clauses and sentences and with the occurrence of various classes of words in these structures. Syntax may be contrasted with morphology (*see* MORPHEME) which is concerned with the forms of words themselves, grammatical endings and other modifications to words. Syntax is the major part of the grammar of languages like Modern English in which formal modification of words has a fairly limited role. **(JC)**

SYSTEMIC GRAMMAR – A description of the grammatical resources of a language in which the meanings that can be expressed in that language are presented as networks of systems. A system is a set of choices between several possible meanings within a related area, together with the language forms by which those meanings are expressed. A very simple system could be:

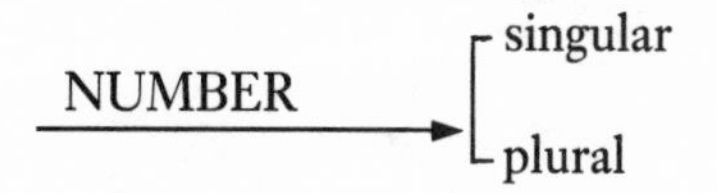

A language can be shown to consist of networks of interrelated systems; a term in one of the general systems might be the entry point for one of the more specific systems. The most general systems show the choices that are available at very general levels of meaning or function. These lead into more specific systems of choices in which more detailed aspects of the grammar are handled. Here is an example of part of a network:

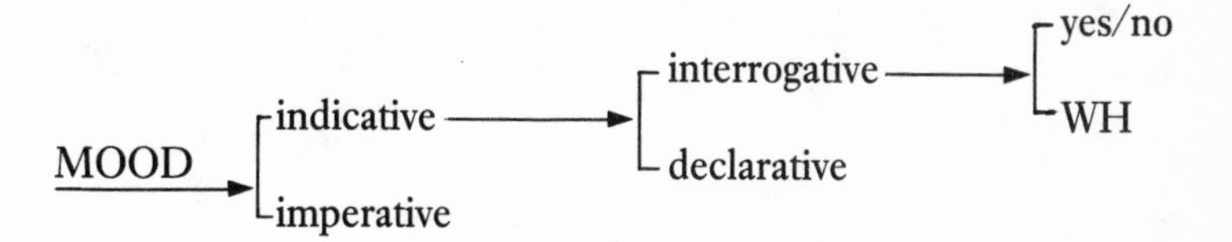

At the ends of these networks (though not shown in the above example) are the actual linguistic forms, the word, endings, structures and so on by which the specific meanings are expressed. **(JC)**
See also FUNCTIONAL GRAMMAR.

References
M. Berry, *Introduction to Systemic Linguistics*, London: Batsford, Vol. 1, 1975; Vol. 2, 1977.

M. A. K. Halliday, *System and Function in Language*, Oxford: Oxford University Press, 1976.
M. A. K. Halliday and J. R. Martin (eds), *Readings in Systemic Linguistics*, London: Batsford, 1981.
G. D. Morley, *An Introduction to Systemic Grammar*, Basingstoke: Macmillan, 1985.

t

TALK – The 'new English' emphasizes the centrality of talk. Talk is, as James Britton has said, 'the sea upon which everything else floats': talk is the main means by which we come to terms with new experiences and the main means by which language development occurs. The English classroom, then, must provide plenty of opportunity for talk: the tentative, exploratory talk that occurs as students try out their ideas in pairs and small groups (*see* SMALL-GROUP WORK), and the more consciously shaped talk that occurs in role play (q.v.), in the class forum, in individual presentation (e.g. where the student with some specialist knowledge – and it is surprising how many have an area of special interest – takes on the role of expert explaining something to the class), in debating (q.v.). As in writing, it is vital that the students have the opportunity to speak for different audiences (*see* AUDIENCE). Unit planning (q.v.), then, should take into account the need to provide opportunity for different kinds of talk, and especially the talk that enables students to sort out ideas and to shape tentative understandings.

See also DEBATING; INTERVIEWS.

TAPE RECORDER, USES OF – The following are some of the ways in which audiotapes can be used in the classroom:

(1) Recording small-group discussions. (The presence of the tape recorder acts as a powerful means of focusing discussion and preventing idle chatter.) The teacher can later analyse the discussion.
(2) Taping performances: radio plays, speeches, news and documentary broadcasts.
(3) Listening exercises: analysing arguments, tone, bias and so on.
(4) As a way of demonstrating sound effects, by showing how background sounds can make a difference to the quality of presentation.
(5) Stimulus for the writing of radio plays and radio programmes.
(6) Playing music/songs/speeches as stimulus for writing/performance.
(7) Small-group simulation games such as *Humanus* (Del Mar, California: Simile 2).
(8) Background music/sounds for drama work.
(9) Keeping a record of students' progress in speaking, for example compar-

ing a speech now with one made earlier in the year; building up records of reading-aloud performance.

(10) Taping an interview.

(11) Recording a panel discussion.

See also IMAGINATIVE RE-CREATION; INTERVIEWS.

TAUTOLOGY – Unnecessary repetition of words or ideas. Alex Buzo's two collections, published by Penguin, provide entertaining examples. Students can be encouraged to listen for them. A good example from a former minister of the crown: '[Union disruption is] a real threat to Australia's economic situation both domestically and at home . . . I find it difficult to say it again without repeating myself' (Tony Street).

TEACHER WRITING WITH CLASS – This is one of the important tactics advocated as part of the process-conference approach to writing. It can consist of:

(1) Sustained private writing by the teacher in front of the class, as in a journal session.

(2) A short period of private writing by the teacher followed by movement into conference sessions with the students.

(3) Public writing by the teacher on an overhead transparency, blackboard or large sheet to demonstrate the thinking-writing-revising-thinking process in action.

See also WRITING: PROCESS-CONFERENCE APPROACH.

Reference

Donald H. Graves, *Writing: Teachers and Children at Work*, Exeter, New Hampshire: Heinemann Educational, 1983.

TEACHING ENGLISH – The journal of teachers of English in Scotland, published three times a year by the Centre for Information on the Teaching of English, Moray House College of Education, Holyrood Road, Edinburgh EH8 8AQ.

TEAM TEACHING – Team teaching has been defined as 'a form of teaching organization in which two or more teachers have the responsibility, working together, for all the teaching of a group of pupils in some specified area of the curriculum' (Lovell). As far as English teaching is concerned, the major book is Anthony Adams' *Team Teaching and the Teaching of English*, Oxford: Pergamon, 1970.

Reference

K. Lovell, *Team Teaching*, Leeds: Institute of Education, 1967.

TELEVISION – The study of television as part of work on the media ought to aim not only at looking at the techniques of production, but more especially at helping students to become critical viewers. We would therefore suggest the following activities as being valuable:

(1) A study of the violence on television – particular shows could be selected for study. Questions to focus on would include the amount of violence, the degree and credibility of violence and the values behind it (does the programme show that violence solves problems?). A class survey of the number of violent acts they can count in a particular night's viewing could lead to a discussion of the effects of all this exposure.
(2) Survey the class's viewing habits as to favourite programmes and amount of hours watched, especially compared to other activities.
(3) Study the programming trends of TV stations – what kinds of shows are on when and why? What products are advertised at particular times and why?
(4) Close study of a particular TV programme with discussion of plot (cliché situations? standard formula?) characters (two-dimensional? stereotyped?) values (who are 'successful' people?).
(5) Debate the impact that television has had on our lifestyle – what would life be like without TV?
(6) Compare TV news presentations across the dial – what are the gimmicks of presentation? How much out-of-studio reporting is there and what is its style? What things are part of the programme that are not really 'current news' items (e.g. consumer reports, police files) and why are they there?
(7) Study TV critics for evidence of bias (what papers support what programmes?).
(8) Using class surveys of favourite programmes, have groups plan a programme format for a channel wanting to attract their age group for a particular time slot.
(9) Have the class 'produce' particular programmes which can be videotaped.

References

S. N. Judy and S. J. Judy, *The English Teacher's Handbook*, Cambridge, Mass: Winthrop, 1979.
L. Masterman, *Teaching About Television*, Basingstoke: Macmillan, 1980.
L. Masterman, *Teaching the Media*, London: Comedia Publishing Group, 1986.

TENSE – Problems with tense sequencing bedevil writers young and old. Thus one grammatical notion that does seem important for young writers is the distinction between present and past tense. (The future tenses do not seem a problem, at least for mature speakers.) There is no need to confuse students by drawing their attention to the various kinds of past and present tense. Checking sequence of tense is a task appropriate for the revision stage of writing.

THAN *See* USAGE: AS . . . AS/THAN.

THAT/WHICH *See* USAGE: WHICH/THAT.

THESE KIND/THESE SORT *See* USAGE.

TONE – The concept of 'tone' is not an intrinsically difficult one, but it is an important one which often causes problems for students.

'Tone' may be defined simply as 'an attitude conveyed'. Confusion often arises when we try to be more specific than this, but can be avoided if we are simply precise about *whose* attitude and towards *what.*

We can, for example, distinguish between a writer's attitude towards his or her subject matter and towards his or her audience. Students should be able to characterize the tone conveyed towards the reader in the opening chapters of each book of *Tom Jones*, or towards the addressed person in Coleridge's 'Conversation Poems'. They should be helped to precisely distinguish this kind of tone from the tone created by a writer's attitude towards his or her subject.

Lowell's immediate attitude towards his grandfather is easily defined in this extract from 'Grandparents':

> Never again
> to walk there, chalk our cues,
> insist on shooting for us both.
> Grandpa! Have me, hold me, cherish me!

But any student of *Life Studies* will need to contrast this tone to other revealed attitudes to his grandfather or to the complex tone of pity – tolerance – disgust he displays towards his father:

> Father
> bronzed, breezy, a shade too ruddy,
> swayed as if on deck-duty
> under his six pointed star-lantern –
> last July's birthday present.
> He smiled his oval Lowell smile,

The letters-to-the-editor columns of magazines and newspapers can be an endless source of material on 'tone':

> The latest barbarous Israeli attacks against the civilians in Southern Lebanon remind me of the true face of the aggressive, militant Israelis whose real intent is to kill the innocent. . . .

Moreover, as can be seen, such material can also be used for leading into useful discussion of connotation (q.v.) and emotive language.

In a poem like Robinson's 'Richard Cory', the very 'lack' of tone can be used to make a point – in this case, a point about the narrator's attitude, Cory's life and Robinson's skill in creating a shock effect:

> And Richard Cory, one calm summer night,
> Went home and put a bullet through his head.

Thus we need to distinguish with our students between different kinds of tone and the effects of these, and to be precise about which attitudes towards what we are discussing.

Other distinctions too need to be clear to the students – such as that between the writer's tone and that of the characters/personae/narrator(s). Of course, this opens up the whole area of problems that students often have in such distinctions generally, and it is not an area we need to enter here. Suffice it to say that students need to be made aware of the ways writers may use tone to capture the attitudes of their characters – for example, the ways in which Eliot characterizes Prufrock by his tone:

> I should have been a pair of ragged claws
> Scuttling across the floors of silent seas

or Austen uses Lady Catherine de Burgh's attitudes towards Elizabeth and her family to characterize Lady Catherine.

This question of 'whose attitude?' may often itself provoke lively discussion in class. For example, if we regard the *Ancient Mariner*'s 'He prayeth best who loveth best / All things both great and small', as somewhat trite and a 'cheat' (and we may not regard it as such, of course), then whose triteness is it? Coleridge's or the Mariner's?

So much of literary awareness depends on an awareness of the tone of a piece that time must be devoted to the concept. Apart from other reasons, the notion is vital to so many other areas that commonly trouble students such as satire (q.v.) or irony (q.v.). Many of the problems which students have with satire depend on their lack of background awareness of what is being satirized, but much also stems from problems with tone. A student who has never heard of Pierre Cardin would still appreciate the satire of the following passage because the tone of sarcasm is easily seen:

> M. Cardin does, as we all know, not lend his name to just any old product. So far he has restricted his imprimatur to shoes, ties, bags, frocks, umbrellas, shirts, suits, underpants, scarves, belts, chocolates, handkerchiefs, stockings, sweaters . . . tinned food, plates, knives, forks, lamps, napery and decorator accessories. So the Pierre Cardin Designer Collection for Feltex is really big news.
>
> (Leo Schofield, *Sydney Morning Herald*, 1982)

But they will not appreciate the irony and satire of Jane Austen's 'It is a truth universally acknowledged that a single man in possession of a good fortune must be in want of a wife' without an appreciation of the tone of such words as 'truth', 'universally' and 'must be' – and this latter arises from guided discussion of 'tone' as much as of the position of women in eighteenth-century provincial society.

Classroom Ideas

(1) Many language-in-literature resources: set literature, literature outside the texts set for study, language-in-literature resource books, articles from newspapers and magazines (especially editorials, letters-to-the editor and headline stories from the more sensational dailies).

(2) Provide a vocabulary in which to describe tone: hysterical, sarcastic, pitying, despairing and so on.

(3) Apart from class discussion, group work and so on, on the above, a number of writing exercises may be useful:

   (i) Pupils can write their own articles in which they adopt a stance on some particular issue of current importance. This could then be contrasted with an article of a more neutral nature. Tone could also be varied by varying the audience: audience already persuaded to your view /

audience who holds the opposite view; remote audience / close friend; someone familiar with the issue / someone who knows very little about it.

(ii) They could also be asked to rewrite a passage they have studied in class in order to vary the tone. The new attitude towards the subject could be either nominated by the teacher or left 'open', to be determined (and conveyed) by the student. Of course, the teacher could also have students vary the audience of a studied piece in order to vary its tone.

TOPIC SENTENCE – Close study of writing, in the expository mode, has revealed that the tendency to use topic sentences is not as widespread as we would have our students believe. Richard Braddock found that only 13 per cent of the paragraphs in his sample began with a topic sentence, and only 55 per cent had a topic sentence at all.

Reference

Richard Braddock, 'The Frequency and Placement of Topic Sentences in Expository Prose', *Research in the Teaching of English*, Vol. 8, Winter, 1974.

TRACKING *See* STREAMING.

TRADITIONAL GRAMMAR – The grammar which stems from the European tradition of grammatical studies and which has until comparatively recently been an important part of English teaching in schools. Its origins lie with Greek and Roman grammarians of classical times. It was applied to English first in the seventeenth and eighteenth centuries, though often in ways which were more appropriate for Latin and Greek since they were thought to represent the ideal of grammatical organization. Moreover, the grammar was thought to be of universal application and if a language did not easily fit the grammar, the language was thought to be at fault, not the grammar. The belief in the universality of traditional grammar is implied in the argument that children should be taught grammar (by primary or English teachers) to equip them for learning other languages.

The mainstay of traditional grammar is classification. Words are classified as 'the parts of speech' and there are classifications of phrases, clauses and sentences. Some aspects of this illustrate the inappropriateness of Latin categories when applied to English. There is virtually no need for the concept of grammatical gender in English and our verb forms are not easily described in terms of traditional grammar's tenses which are more appropriate for Latin. Because traditional grammar is based on written and especially literary texts, it does not deal adequately with grammatical features which are mainly evident in speech, nor with non-standard grammatical features which, if mentioned, are simply dismissed as errors. However, despite these limitations, much of traditional grammar is quite adequate as a description of English and much of it has been absorbed into the modern grammars in one way or another. It has often been taught in a prescriptive way, endorsing standard English (q.v.) and discouraging non-standard (q.v.), but this prescription is really a matter of the way the grammar has been taught. The teaching always included much that was descriptive and traditional grammar could be used simply to describe the language, without the prescriptive teaching with which it is usually associated.

The term 'traditional grammar' is a modern one coined to distinguish traditional grammar from other approaches to English grammar which have emerged over the last few decades. Prior to that, it was generally believed that grammar was grammar and that was the end of the matter. **(JC)**

Reference

J. C. Nesfield, *Manual of English Grammar and Composition*, Basingstoke: Macmillan, 1988.

TRANSACTIONAL LANGUAGE *See* LANGUAGE, FUNCTIONS OF.

TRANSACTIONAL THEORY OF READING *See* READER-RESPONSE CRITICISM.

TRANSFORMATIONAL OR GENERATIVE GRAMMAR – Either of these two forbidding terms may be used to refer to this approach to grammar, or both terms can be used together: *transformational/generative grammar* (TG for short). It emerged in the late 1950s in the United States and was clearly a powerful force in language studies during the 1960s under the inspiration of Noam Chomsky.

The grammar is presented as a series of logical rules which explain how each specific sentence in the language is related to the general concept of a sentence. The starting point is the general notion and the rules lead by successive stages through the major components of the sentence towards all the various possible specific sentences which the language could have. It is called generative because the rules in a sense generate sentences. The most basic rules embody the most basic sentences, but a further series of rules can lead to several different types of sentences by reordering, combinations, additions, deletions and other changes. The rules by which these changes are made are known as transformational rules. They enable the grammar to show relationships between different kinds of sentences, such as between a negative sentence and its affirmative equivalent, or between active and passive equivalents, and they constitute a large and important part of this kind of grammar.

A generative grammar will include rules which show how sentences emerge as spoken utterances and also rules which relate the words and structures to their meanings.

Many of the categories of traditional and structural grammar are found in TG but in it they are incorporated into a comprehensive and logically presented theory of language competence.

TG continued to develop vigorously throughout the 1960s and more recently. Not surprisingly there have been several different versions and, latterly, some divergent developments. Its significance has been more for our understanding the nature of language and how people learn it initially rather than for classroom teaching.

This kind of grammar is seen not merely as a description of a language but as a theory which accounts for the competence of each speaker to be able to produce virtually any sentence in that language. **(JC)**

References

R. Fowler, *An Introduction to Transformational Syntax*, London: Routledge & Kegan Paul, 1971.

H. A. Gleason, *Linguistics and English Grammar*, New York: Holt, Rinehart & Winston, 1965.

N. Smith and D. Wilson, *Modern Linguistics: The Results of Chomsky's Revolution*, Harmondsworth: Penguin, 1979.

O. Thomas and E. R. Kintgen, *Transformational Grammar and the Teacher of English*, 2nd edn, New York: Holt, Rinehart & Winston, 1974.

T-UNIT – A measure of syntactic maturity developed by Kellog Hunt. A t-unit is one main clause plus any subordinate clauses attached to it. Hunt argued that as students' writing matures, their t-units increase in length. He did not, however, make any distinction between kinds of writing. Harold Rosen has since found in the writings of a sample of 16 year olds a greater mean difference in the length of t-units between kinds of writing than Hunt found between grades 8 and 12. This suggests that the measure must be used with caution.

References

W. Kellog Hunt, *Grammatical Structures Written at Three Grade Levels*, Champaign, Ill.: NCTE, 1965.

John Pearce, 'Examinations in English language', in *Language: Classroom and Examinations*, Schools Council Program in Linguistics and English Teaching: Papers Series II, Vol. 4, 1974.

U

UNDER THE CIRCUMSTANCES / IN THE CIRCUMSTANCES *See* USAGE.

UNINTERESTED *See* USAGE: DISINTERESTED/UNINTERESTED.

UNIT PLANNING – If we are to offer students a rich, varied, integrative and imaginative experience in English, we need to find ways of structuring our teaching that allow for *continuity of experience* for students, and allow them to *develop a feeling for the interrelatedness of language modes.* We want our students to see – intuitively and consciously – that listening, speaking, reading and writing are naturally interlinked. A necessary condition for this is the creation of an interest in ideas, in the force of the imagination, and in the complexity of human feeling. Students need to be alive to their own intellectual, emotional and imaginative energies. Without this, English can be a pretty drab business where everything appears as a tedious exercise. When students are excited by, and interested in, their own qualities and those of other people, then there is a desire to use language. Of course, the process is interactive: as ideas, feelings and imagination develop, so does interest in language (that is, in using language); and as language is used more and more, so intellectual, emotional and imaginative qualities further develop. When we provide structures for the teaching of English that help this interactive process along, then we are working in the most positive way possible. Some of the structures that are available are described below. There are other possibilities. None of the categories are necessarily mutually exclusive, nor does one have to be adopted as the only approach. It would seem best, in fact, to adopt a particular structure in response to the needs and interests of a specific group of students, and to vary the structure to suit changes in those needs and interests.

Themes

Thematic approaches are based on the exploration of a concept or area of interest, such as 'Animals', 'Places of Historical Interest', or 'Prejudice'. The theme should be appropriate to the ability of the class, and should be designed to suit their anticipated duration of interest. A variety of resource materials will be used to explore the theme, and where possible students should be encouraged to draw on their own resources and experiences. As part of the activities of the theme, students will engage in a variety of language use, and the theme is the device that links these language activities together, providing the intellectual, emotional and imaginative energy that keeps them going. When that energy fades, the theme has probably lost its value and should be quickly finished off.

Once a theme has been started, it should be continued more or less non-stop until you feel that there is a clear need to finish it. However, this does not mean that every period will be spent in discussion of the central idea or interest in the theme. This idea or area of interest is a core that runs through the various activities. If you were exploring the theme of 'Prejudice' in Year 9, for example, you could start with a reading of *Nobody's Family Is Going to Change* (prejudice against blacks and children) in which there would be an exploration of a variety of issues, and then move on to look at some of the ways in which discrimination seems to operate against children in Australia. You could then expand the theme to examine ways in which Aborigines have experienced prejudice, and an excellent resource here would be the film *Lousy Little Sixpence* (or a number of other excellent films about Aborigines) which could stimulate a great deal of research and writing – writing of both a factual/historical and an imaginative nature: 'Is the film a factual account?'; 'Imagine yourself to be one of the women in the film and describe how you felt on your first night away from your mother'. The possibilities of what to do, of what directions to take, are really wide open. The key role for the teacher is to keep the theme going without wearing it out prematurely. It needs to be used as a linking and integrative device, and it needs to be emphasized that the theme is a *means* to the end of language development and not an end in itself. It is possible that students might become so absorbed in the theme that they and the teacher lose sight of language development. Of course, if the theme really takes hold, it is likely that language development will take place. What really needs to be avoided is turning the theme into a set of information that will subsequently be tested. The content of the theme is – in the end – not important. What is important is the language activity that flows out of the exploration of the theme.

Once a theme has been completed it is probably best to work in some other way for a while, so that another theme can have a chance of emerging naturally from the work being done. Theme approaches have been abused in the past, with students working on one theme after another with no sense of connecting logic, and no variety. With structures, as with strategies, variety is a basic principle, and for that reason alone we should try to avoid doing an uninterrupted succession of themes. When themes are done well, they are a powerful means of providing unity and purpose to English activities, and can be very satisfying to students.

Units based on core texts

These differ from themes in that they are usually based on one or two texts (print and/or visual). Many of the activities that are appropriate to themes are also appropriate to such units. A unit of work might, for example, be based on the novel *Children on the Oregon Trail* and might involve pupils in imaginative re-creation (q.v.) and also in reading and discussing poems and factual accounts of pioneering days in the American West.

Workshops
The idea here is that a certain amount of time is given to a particular activity. This could be writing, reading, drama, films, poetry, television, everyday language, and so on. The activity would be similar to the theme in that it would act as a linking device, but an important difference would be that one would hope that students would learn a great deal about the activity. For example, if one were to have a writing workshop that ran for six weeks and which gave students experience in writing for many different purposes and audiences, then a central aim would be that students would learn quite a lot about the writing process. The same applies, for example, to drama. One would hope that by the end of a workshop, students would know more than when they started about acting and plays. As with other structures, it is essential that students experience a reasonable balance of language activities. In a workshop on writing, for example, there is no reason that students should not do quite a bit of reading (poems, short stories, newspaper extracts, etc.) as part of a general stimulus for writing. Much of their writing will also be surrounded by talk of a constructively critical nature. When this happens, the workshop cannot be seen as a narrow pursuit of a particular interest, but the use of that interest to open up students once again to the interrelatedness of the language modes.

Productions
Here, a certain time is allocated to the creation of a product. This may take the form of – to use a few examples – a class newspaper, a school magazine, a play for presentation to the rest of the school, a radio programme, a short film or videotape, a collage of sounds and words that expresses an experience or idea, and so on. These productions can be done as a whole class or by groups, whichever is appropriate. As with workshops, the productions will involve students in a wide variety of language activities, and it is a key role for the teacher to ensure that this happens. Productions that will 'go public' have a strong motivational quality, but ones that will have only the class as their public are also strongly engaging for students.

Courses
In this structure there is an exploration of a particular idea, interest, sequence of events, or period in time. Examples are 'Images of Women in Contemporary Australian Novels' or 'The Production of Animated Films' or 'TV Soap Operas'. Unlike a theme, the material is less open; there aren't so many possible directions for a teacher to take. The focus is more narrow. But there is no reason for students not experiencing many language activities.
See also INTEGRATION **(PJ)**

USAGE – There are still many textbooks that attempt to impose a single standard of correctness on users of the English language. Their authors seem to believe, to quote Fred Flower, 'that there is somewhere laid up in Heaven an ideal English, the Queen's English, in which all concords are kept, no infinitives are split, and prepositions stand inevitably and invariably before the words they govern'. The notion of absolute rights and wrongs in language is, of course, misguided: the criterion for acceptability of a given usage will be its *appropriateness to the situation*, and at the bottom this is a social matter, not a matter of some 'rule' of grammar. As such, it is subject to change – a point which we have stressed in many of the entries on particular items of usage.

In an interesting article on the subject, W. H. Mittins shows the faultiness of much that has been written on the subject. The criterion of analogy, for example, cannot be pressed too far. Bishop Lowth, the eighteenth-century grammarian, argued, on grounds of analogy, for *her's*, *our's*, *your's*, and another eighteenth-century writer insisted on *hisself* and *theirselves* to parallel *myself* and *ourselves*. As Mittins notes, we accept analogy when it suits us and ignore it when it doesn't. We accept 'The sun had *shone*', but reject 'He had *wrote*'; we insist on 'He had *written*' and reject 'The sun had *shinnen*'. Nor is the criterion of logic any more reliable: it would require *amn't I?* instead of *aren't I?*, and 'He couldn't bear the sight of *his self*' instead of *himself*. As for the criterion of derivation, often cited by those deploring the use of *aggravate* for 'annoy' or *decimate* for 'destroy a great number or part of', this would mean using *silly* only in the sense of 'blessed' and insisting that *dilapidated* apply only to stone houses.

Mittins goes on to note that there are those who advocate as a standard some notion of the *best* usage, the usage of the best speakers and writers. He goes on to point out, however, that many of the usages outlawed in textbooks are to be found in the writings of the best authors, and quotes some interesting examples:

Shakespeare:	'These kind of knaves'
	'All debts are cleared between you and *I*'
Milton:	'At least try *and* teach the erring soul'
Dickens:	'Nobody will miss her *like* I shall'
Charlotte Brontë:	'A *very* unique child'
Hardy:	'*Who* are you speaking *of*?'

Mittins urges teachers to abandon notions of correctness in favour of *appropriateness*, to free themselves of their linguistic prejudices, and to face up to the facts about the multifarious character of language. This means

> defending clarity and precision to an appropriate degree but not to excess. It means not fighting battles that have already been lost, against, for instance, adverbial *due to* or the singular *data*. It means recognising that the job is to encourage a confident and resourceful flow of words, not to inhibit it. It means acknowledging that over-insistence on one allegedly 'correct' form may have unforeseen consequences elsewhere, as when 'you and *me*' in the position of subject is so energetically attacked that it feels wrong everywhere and we all end up saying 'Between you and *I*'. It means reasonable tolerance of alternative usages where no issue of comprehensibility is involved. . . . Above all, it means accepting that language changes and that change is not corruption.

Reference

W. H. Mittins, 'What is correctness?' *Educational Review*, 22 (1), Nov. 1969.

AND – One of the myths about writing that English teachers persist in passing on to their pupils is that one cannot begin a sentence with *and*. A glance at the King James version of the Bible will show how false is this dictum; if a more recent example be required, consider the opening of Patrick White's *Voss*:

'There is a man, here, miss, asking for your uncle,' said Rose. And stood breathing.

AS . . . AS; THAN – The case of pronouns after *as . . . as* and *than* is the source of some confusion. Textbook writers often offer for correction sentences such as 'He is as tall as me' and 'He is taller than me', and insist that in both cases *I* must be used instead of *me*, on the grounds that *as . . . as* and *than* are conjunctions introducing new clauses with verbs that are understood – 'He is taller than I (am)'. In this they have the somewhat qualified support of Fowler. We found, however, that among our sample of university graduates there was a wide tolerance of the former usages, and there is no doubt that a case can be made for their acceptability.

Such a case was, indeed, made by the eighteenth-century grammarian Joseph Priestley who, as Sterling Leonard has noted, stood alone amongst the eighteenth-century writers on language in his appreciation of the force of usage. Priestley argued that *as . . . as* and *than* have, in such sentences, the force of prepositions, so that '*greater than me*' will be more grammatical than '*greater than I*'. He was supported by his contemporary, Philip Withers, who pointed out the lack of logic in the insistence of Bishop Lowth and others that a construction is understood after *than*: 'the Instance adduced by Lowth to corroborate this Hypothesis unfortunately subverts it – *thou art wiser than I am WISER.*'

As for the claim that adherence to the view that *as . . . as* and *than* are conjunctions avoids ambiguity, this ignores the force of context. It may be true that, taken out of context, one of Priestley's examples from Smollett – 'Tell the Cardinal that I understand poetry better than him' – is possibly ambiguous, but any ambiguity disappears when the text as a whole is read.

Reference

Sterling Leonard, *The Doctrine of Correctness in English Usage, 1700–1800*, Madison: University of Wisconsin, 1929, pp. 191–2.

AS . . . THAN – 'He could write as well or better than most people.' This usage has wide acceptance in informal situations, according to surveys in the UK by Mittins and in Australia by Watson, but both surveys show that only a minority is prepared to accept it in the written form. Our more recent sampling of English graduates, however, suggests a growing acceptance of it in all situations, and even as far back as 1926 Fowler admitted that 'the offence does not seriously obstruct understanding'. In case any reader is wondering what all this is about, the sentence is an example of what Fowler called 'unequal yoke-fellows' – the failure to harness together two symmetrical items: *as well as* and *better than.* Omission of the second *as*, said Fowler, inflicts a 'passing discomfort on fastidious readers'!

References

W. H. Mittens *et al.*, *Attitudes to English Usage*, Oxford: Oxford University Press, 1970.
K. Watson, 'Teachers' attitudes to usage', in *Language in the Classroom*, Applied Linguistics Association of Australia Occasional Paper No. 2, 1978.

BETWEEN, AMONG – For about eighty years the *Oxford English Dictionary* and linguists like Fowler and Gowers have complained about the 'superstition' that *between* is used of two things and *among* of three or more, but inferior textbooks still offer it as a 'rule' of English (e.g. Sadler, Hayllar and Powell, *Language Two*, p. 177). As Walshe has pointed out, many of the best writers use *between* for three or more items, without loss of clarity, for example . . . 'my mind will, I fear, waver between dislike, exasperation, boredom and admiration' (T. S. Eliot).

BETWEEN YOU AND I/ME – Both Partridge in *Usage And Abusage* and Gowers in the second edition of Fowler's *Modern English Usage* are lenient on those who would say 'between you and I', while preferring 'between you and me' on the ground that *between*, being a preposition, takes the objective case in the same way as other prepositions (*after me*, *for you and me*). Partridge points out that while 'for you and me' means 'for you and for me', 'between you and me' does not equal 'between you and between me', and concludes that '*between you and I*, while indefensible grammatically, may be considered as a sense construction, and is often used by those who would never dream of saying *between he and I*.' Certainly there is no reason to assert, as J. B. Bremner does in *Words on Words*, that 'between you and I' is a barbarism; it is used at all levels of society in speech, though it is yet to gain acceptance in writing.

While most (85 per cent) of our university group were willing to accept *between you and I* in informal contexts, a substantial minority were unhappy about it in formal writing, even though the meaning is crystal-clear. Given their background as English graduates, this is not surprising; Peter Collins, surveying teenage college undergraduates, found that *between you and I* was regarded as considerably more acceptable than *between you and me* in formal contexts, perhaps because 'the use of *me* sparks off in the speaker's mind a half-remembered notion that *me* is "uneducated and wrong" in a number of constructions'.

Reference

Peter Collins, *Elicitation Experiments on Acceptability in Australian English*, Speech and Language Research Centre Working Papers, Vol. 2, No. 4, July 1979 (Macquarie University).

CAN, MAY – It can be stated quite emphatically that the distinction, first made by Dr Johnson, between *can* and *may* (that *can* expresses power to act, while *may* expresses permission to act) no longer applies in Australian English. Our studies have convinced us that *can* is used in both senses by the vast majority of Australians, including the most highly educated. Increasingly, *may* is being confined to expressions of possibility, as in 'Cabinet may announce its decision tonight'. As Walshe notes, the father who corrects his son's *Can I?* to *May I?* is likely then to say to his wife, 'I told him he *could*, if he asked properly' – and would be hurt if his wife then corrected his *could* to *might*.

CENTRE AROUND/ROUND – Partridge rejects these in favour of *centre on/in*, as does Gowers in the second edition of Fowler, though he adds: 'To reject idiom because it does not make sense if literally construed is to show oneself ignorant of the genius of the language.' Certainly many able writers use *centre round*: 'One group of apparent ironies [in *Moll Flanders*] centres round the deflation of emotional considerations by practical ones' (Ian Watt, *The Rise of the Novel*, p. 127).

COLLECTIVE NOUNS –

(1) Both Fowler and Partridge suggest that a collective noun will take a singular verb when unity is intended ('Parliament is sitting') and a plural verb when the idea of plurality is predominant ('The Government are divided on the issue'). One cannot say, 'The audience must be in its seat by 7.30.')
(2) Partridge provides, under the heading 'Group Terms', a number of humorous inventions which could stimulate pupils to coin their own: a dampness of babies, a bareness of bathers, a ledger of clerks, a grace of cricketers, a fleece of punters, a promise of MPs, a see-saw of surgeons, a wobble of cyclists, an unselfishness of school teachers.

CRITERIA – This is properly a plural noun (singular *criterion*) but, as with such words as *data* there is in both North America and Australia a growing tendency to treat it as singular e.g. '. . . the important criteria for a spy is the type of boredom which comes with English upper-class families.' (Susan Hely, *Sydney Morning Herald*, 6/8/83.)

The distinction between the singular and plural forms tends, however, still to be maintained in standard British usage.

DATA – *Data* comes from the Latin, where it is plural (singular *datum*), but while some people still insist in treating it as such ('The data are set out . . .') the vast majority of our sample of English graduates preferred to treat it as singular. In other words, *data* is going the same way as *agenda* and *stamina*.

DIFFERENT FROM/TO/THAN – In spoken English, 'different than' has become almost universal in the last ten years. (One of the editors has made its use in academic circles his special study. He found that in 1973–4 it was used about 50 per cent of the time, with 'different from' preferred to 'different to' in most other instances; by 1979 it was used in 96 per cent of recorded instances.) In written English 'different from' is still preferred by most writers, but 'different than' is creeping in, as in this example from the *Sydney Morning Herald:* 'Surprisingly enough, the question was based on a somewhat different premise than most of the Opposition's points' (Jenni Hewett, 28/10/82). Partridge, who prefers 'from' to 'to', has this to say on the case of 'different than': 'Evidently the comparative sense of the word rather than the fact of its positive form may govern the syntax. Whether this is regrettable is a matter of taste.' Certainly there is no justification for drilling pupils in 'different from'.

DISINTERESTED, UNINTERESTED – The efforts of generations of English teachers to preserve the distinction between *disinterested* and *uninterested* (that *disinterested* means 'impartial' and *uninterested* means 'not interested') have ended in failure. Of our sample of English graduates, 85 per cent use the two words interchangeably.

DOUBLE NEGATIVE – While double negatives abound in the works of writers like Shakespeare, they are now regarded as non-standard, except in sentences like 'I shouldn't wonder if it didn't rain'. Generally, the effect of the double negative is to give emphasis; it is foolish to assert, as some do, that the laws of mathematics apply and that two negatives make a positive.

DUE TO – Purists often object to *due to* in the sense of 'because of', in such sentences as, 'Due to an industrial dispute, train departures from Sydney to country areas have been cancelled' (Notice on Sydney's Central Railway Station). They say that a prepositional force of *due to* is inadmissible; that *due to* can only be used adjectivally, as in, 'The cancellation was due to a strike.' Almost all of our sample of English graduates did not make this distinction, and of a smaller sample of school teachers and university teachers, 57 per cent of the former and 88 per cent of the latter were prepared to accept *due to* in a prepositional position.

Reference

Ken Watson, 'Teachers' attitudes to usage', in *Language in the Classroom*, Occasional Papers No. 2, Applied Linguistics Association of Australia, 1978.

EACH OTHER / ONE ANOTHER – Fowler, noting that some authorities have recommended that *each other* be used of two persons or things, and *one another* for three or more, states that 'this differentiation is neither of present utility nor based on historical usage'. In modern British and Australian usage, the two phrases are interchangeable.

EITHER . . . OR; NEITHER . . . NOR – The problem of number and person after *either . . . or* and *neither . . . nor* has provided the authors of traditional English textbooks with endless opportunities for dummy-run exercises, all seeking to instil the 'rule' that the verb agrees with the second subject in both person and number. This rule works well enough when both subjects are singular and in the third person ('Neither Bill nor John was present'), but even here it must be noted that the plural seems to be preferred in common usage. The OED cites Dr Johnson ('Neither search nor labour *are* necessary') and John Ruskin ('Neither painting nor fighting *feed* men'), and sentences such as 'Neither Mr Hawke nor Mr Hayden *were* available for comment' are readily found in our newspapers and heard on the ABC. But, as Fowler points out, complications occur when the subjects differ in person and/or number: a sentence like 'Neither eyes nor nose *does its* work' sounds odd, to say the least. One must agree with the authors of *Watch Your Language* that 'most people probably [prefer] "Neither he nor I *are* able . . ." and the number who would wince at that is (or are) becoming fewer as time goes by.' Certainly the evidence from our sample of university graduates suggests that the textbook writers need to revise their notions of standard English.

ENQUIRY, INQUIRY – Fowler suggests that *enquire* and its noun should be considered a formal word for *ask*, and *inquiry* used for an investigation (as in *Court of Inquiry*), but it must be admitted that in both British and Australian English the two words are interchangeable.

EVERYONE, ANYONE, EACH, EVERYBODY – The problem of what pronoun to use after these words is a difficult one, especially since the use of *his* is likely to lay one open to the charge of sexism. 'Everyone chose his or her own books' sounds too pedantic; in everyday speech we normally opt for 'Everyone chose their own books', albeit with guilty feelings as a result of youthful acquaintance with the textbooks of Ridout or Allsopp and Hunt. This solution has the support of some good writers (e.g. John Ruskin: 'I am never angry with anyone unless they deserve it.'), and since the authorities are divided on the question, one must agree with Walshe that 'everyone should follow their own preference confidently!'

GOT – There are, regrettably, still some English teachers who frown on the word *got*, and the survey of secondary and tertiary teachers referred to elsewhere in this book there was little acceptance of it in writing and only reluctant acceptance in formal speech. There seems no reason for the general antipathy to *got*, except in cases where it is clearly being overused. Curiously, some teachers tell their pupils that *got* must be avoided because it is 'an ugly word'; as Walshe notes, this makes about as much sense as claiming that *God* is an ugly word!

IMPLY/INFER – These two words are frequently confused. To *imply* something is to hint or suggest it; to *infer* is to take the hint, or to conclude something from evidence. A recent example of the confusion of the two words comes from the letter columns of the *Sydney Morning Herald* (28/7/83): 'The letter from Dr Spigelman inferred that the reason for the lack of Aboriginal doctors was difficulty of entry into the medical course' (Prof. W. R. Pitney, University of NSW). Interestingly, the Macquarie Dictionary accepts *infer* for *imply* in colloquial usage.

ISE/IZE – This remains a vexed question and one where different publishers have different house styles. One cannot go wrong, however, by spelling all words with *-ise*, *-isation*, *-ising* (not *-ize*) when these are suffixes. Note, however, that the following words require *-ize* where it is not a suffix: apprize (in the sense of value), prize, size, seize. (The publishers of this book point out, however, that this advice is contrary to their own house style; itself a nice illustration of the vagaries of English usage!)

ITS/IT'S – The apostrophe is used for this word to replace the missing letter only in the phrase 'it is'. The possessive form of 'it' takes no apostrophe. The parallel is with the other pronouns: her/hers, him/his.

LEND, LOAN – *Loan*, once only a noun, is increasingly appearing as a verb in place of *lend*: 'His public relations machine had persuaded him to loan money on the project.' (*National Times*, 1/1/83.)

LESS/FEWER – *Less*, we are told in books on usage, refers to quantity; *fewer* to number. Thus we may speak of 'less milk' but not of 'less people'. But *less* is occurring more and more as an adjective of number: 'Do not vote for less than five or more than ten candidates.' (Instruction on University of Sydney Senate ballot paper, 1982.) Certainly, there are some sentences where *less* sounds better than *fewer*:

The cost is less / fewer than five dollars.

While our sample of university graduates preferred *fewer* for number, it is clear that tolerance of *less* for number is growing. Thus Australian English is harking back to the situation which existed in English before the prescriptive grammarians of the eighteenth century got to work.

LIE, LAY – In the standard dialect, *lay* ('put down'; past tense *laid*) is transitive, and *lie* ('recline'; past tense *lay*) is intransitive. Thus:

I lay / laid the book on the table.

I lie / lay down on the bed.

A typical non-standard usage is, 'Go and lay down for a while'. This is becoming so widespread that it may well be part of the standard dialect in twenty years' time; in the interim, there is no need for teachers to correct it in informal speech situations, though they may wish to do so in more formal contexts.

LIKE – There are still textbooks on the market which assert that *like* can never be used as a conjunction. As Burchfield points out, however, modern writers regularly use this construction. He quotes Graham Greene: 'Some girls change their lovers like they change their winter clothes.' In this example, *like* is used instead of *as*. The authors of *Watch Your Language!* consider the use of *like* in place of *as if* less defensible, deploring such a sentence as: 'It now looks like the bomb threat against Queen Elizabeth II is a hoax.' Such a usage is, however, becoming increasingly common amongst speakers of Standard English, and it would be hard to argue that there is any loss of clarity.

MEDIA – The authors of *Watch Your Language* notwithstanding, *media* in Australian English, particularly in the collocation *mass media*, has gone the way of *data* (q.v.) and is commonly treated as singular.

MILITATE, MITIGATE – These two words are frequently confused. Knowledge of the derivation of each can serve as a reminder of the distinction. Burchfield tells us that *militate* is from the Latin *militare*, 'to serve as a soldier', and *mitigate* from the Latin *mitigare*, 'to moderate, lighten, alleviate'. Hence *mitigate* means 'to make less intense or serious'; *militate* means 'to serve as a strong influence' as in 'Several factors militated against the success of our plan'. Shakespeare, despite having little Latin and less Greek, got it right when he had Portia say to Shylock:

I have spoke thus much
To mitigate the justice of thy plea

(Merchant of Venice)

Malcolm Fraser got it wrong when he said 'The mere fact that wages at the same time remain constant will not mitigate against it' (*Financial Times*, 14/4/77).

OFF/FROM – Many of our sample of English graduates objected to *off* in such a sentence as 'He bought some tomatoes off a barrow-boy', asserting that it was ambiguous, but the majority were prepared to accept it in informal contexts.

PRACTICABLE/PRACTICAL – Two words that are occasionally confused. *Practicable* means 'possible, feasible'; *practical* means 'sensible, businesslike, down-to-earth'.

PREPOSITION, PLACEMENT OF – There are still some who insist that a sentence cannot end with a preposition. (There is even one teacher in a Sydney school who teaches that a sentence cannot *begin* with a preposition!) Dryden seems to have been the first to put forward this 'rule', on mistaken analogy with Latin. Winston Churchill tried to kill the notion by sending a sharp note to some bureaucrat who had been insisting on it: 'This is the sort of arrant pedantry up with which I will not put!'

PROGRAM, PROGRAMME – *Program* is standard usage in North American English and is becoming increasingly so in Australia. The OED points out that *program* was the regular spelling until the mid-19th century (cf *anagram*, *diagram*); *programme* seems to have arisen in the mistaken assumption that the word was a French borrowing. There is a sound argument, then, for preferring *program*, although the alternative spelling is still more common in standard British usage.

There has recently been introduced into British English a further useful distinction in that *program* in the sense of 'computer program' is always spelt in this way. This may give continuing currency to the spelling *programme* when used in other senses.

REASON . . . BECAUSE or WHY . . . BECAUSE – Both Fowler and Partridge frown on this usage as redundant, preferring 'the reason . . . is that. . . .' The usage is, however, to be found in the works of such good writers as Patrick White.

SHALL/SHOULD/WILL/WOULD – One can still find textbooks (and teachers) who try to perpetuate the myth that *shall* is used with first person pronouns ('I shall') and *will* with second and third person pronouns ('You/He will'). This distinction, first offered by the prescriptive grammarians of the eighteenth century, has no basis in modern Australian usage, except occasionally in imperatives and when a question is asked ('Shall we go now?'). *Will* (and *would*) is favoured by Australian speakers in almost all contexts. *Should*, as Walshe notes, is now chiefly used for *ought to*.

SPLIT INFINITIVE – As Burchfield notes, infinitives have been split since at least the fourteenth century. We should follow Fowler's dictum that it is better to split the infinitive than to be ambiguous or artificial.

SUBJUNCTIVES – As long ago as 1917, in his famous book *The Play Way*, Caldwell Cook argues that English no longer had a subjunctive mood. The subjunctive mood, according to the OED, denotes 'an action or a state as conceived (and not as a fact), and (expressing) a wish, command, exhortation, or a contingent, hypothetical or prospective event'. Fowler agrees that it is moribund except in a few easily specified uses, among which he lists:

Come what may . . .
Be that as it may . . .
If he were here now . . .
I move that Mr Smith be appointed Chairman.

At least one of these uses is fast disappearing in Australian English, as the following heading for an article by Buzz Kennedy (*The Australian*, 13/11/82) shows: 'If Only There Was Time, I Could Be Just *So* Organised.'

THESE KIND / THESE SORT – When Shakespeare wrote 'these kind of knaves' he was using a construction since deplored by many textbook writers, but, rather surprisingly, condoned by both Fowler and Partridge, at least in everyday speech. It is a usage much favoured by our politicians.

UNDER THE CIRCUMSTANCES / IN THE CIRCUMSTANCES – Fowler declares roundly that objection to *under the circumstances* is 'puerile', pointing out that *under the circumstances* is not of recent invention (1665 in OED), 'and until the grammarians started telling us it was wrong was far more often heard than *in the circumstances*'.

VERB AGREEMENT – While the 'rule' that the verb and its subject should agree in number seems straightforward enough, problems occur in sentences like: 'Labor's long years in Opposition was a major factor in its downfall' (Editorial, *Sydney Morning Herald*, 4/12/82). Here it seems that the singular complement overwhelms the nominal subject. Less easy to account for are the following: 'Smoking, drinking and junk food is out' (*Australian Women's Weekly*, 15/12/82); 'Research and writing is what members of the Fine Arts Department do besides teaching' (notice in Fine Arts Dept, University of Sydney). It seems, however, that 'research and writing' is seen as a single activity, and 'smoking, drinking and junk food' as a single indulgence.
See also COLLECTIVE NOUNS.

WHICH, THAT – Partridge declares that *which* refers to things only; *that* to things and persons. He clearly has never heard Professor Harry Messel on TV ('The students which we teach . . .').

WHO, WHOM – In spoken English *whom* is almost defunct. Even amongst the most erudite, such usages as 'Who did you want?' and 'Who did you speak to?' are almost universally accepted. In writing, the distinction trips up so many able writers that it is surely not worth spending time trying to eradicate the alleged misuse of the two words. For example, Alexandra Hasluck, in *Portrait in a Mirror* writes: 'The religious head of it was Sister Vera, a tiny little old lady whom we all somehow knew had been born in Russia, while her father was

British Ambassador there, but we never knew her real name'. J. I. M. Stewart, a Professor of English who writes detective stories under the name of Michael Innes, is cited by Partridge as another who finds the distinction (that *who* is always nominative and *whom* objective case) too difficult to handle: 'To say nothing of the two men, whom he declared were spies of his rival' (*The Daffodil Case*). If English professors can err in this regard, why worry if schoolchildren do likewise? There is no loss of meaning. We confidently predict that in writing as well as in speech *whom* will be an archaism by the end of the century, except possibly where preceded by a preposition, as in 'He wondered to whom he had to report'.

USE OF ENGLISH, THE – The oldest of the UK journals for English teachers, founded by Denys Thompson. Three issues a year. Subscription information: Scottish Academic Press (Ref. U/E), 33 Montgomery St, Edinburgh EH7 5JX.

USSR *See* SUSTAINED SILENT READING.

. . . no teachers, whether of sciences, or languages or mathematics, or history or geography must be allowed to evade their own heavy responsibilities. They must not say 'our business is to teach science or mathematics or French, not English'. That is the great fallacy of 'subject teaching'. It is very definitely their business to teach English; and their failure to recognise it as their business is a cause of the evil they deplore. In a sense the function of history, geography, science and so forth in school is to provide material for the teaching of English. The specialist teacher defeats his own purpose precisely to the extent to which he neglects the language of his pupils.

(George Sampson
English for the English)

V

VALIDITY AND RELIABILITY – In educational measurement, a test is *valid* if it measures what it sets out to measure; it is *reliable* if it measures accurately each time it is used.

VARIANCE, ANALYSIS OF *See* ANALYSIS OF VARIANCE, COVARIANCE.

VERB AGREEMENT *See* USAGE.

VERSE SPEAKING *See* POETRY, SUGGESTIONS FOR TEACHING.

VERTICAL GROUPING – A form of organization often found in infants and lower primary schools, in which a 'family' class is made up of children in a two- or three-year age range. P. H. Hills, in his *Dictionary of Education* (London: Routledge & Kegan Paul, 1982) notes that one of the main advantages of vertical grouping is that 'younger children imitate and are stimulated by the work of older children, who in turn consolidate their own learning by demonstrating to the younger children what they can do'.

VIDEO CONTROL FACILITY – As an aid in the teaching of the language arts, videotape can be used in two principal ways: appreciation and production. A major focus of these functions can be found in the Video Control Facility. This is a whole-school system emanating from a secure location and preferably controlled by one operator who is able to direct video and television programmes to approximately eight remote locations.

The advantages of such a system are:

(1) The possibility of limiting the number of people handling delicate equipment.
(2) Centralized taping, filing and maintenance are more efficient, particularly if this can be done by one teacher's aide.
(3) Teachers using hand-held remote control devices can stop, start, freeze-frame or rewind footage without need to contact the system operator by intercom.
(4) A variety of equipment types (old and new) can be installed in the unit.

These include (BW)VTR, (Colour) U-matic and VHS VCR as well as studio model and portable cameras.

(5) Time can be saved in presenting videotapes of texts set for senior classes to several classes in different locations simultaneously.

(6) In schools where video equipment either does not exist or is insufficient for school needs, the installation of a centralized system allows efficient access to expensive equipment without undue duplication.

Basic to any system are:

(1) One commander console unit.
(2) One VCR (a VHS system is the best to buy if starting from scratch).
(3) Colour monitors cabled from the control room to as many locations as a school can afford, as well as a studio monitor (which may be black-and-white).
(4) One colour antenna.

Appreciation

In the classroom the VCF is useful in the input mode. Conventional uses of film and TV programmes on videotape can be easily achieved by on-line equipment. The software is cheap and easily controlled. The freeze-frame on most modern colour equipment allows technical and critical comment to be made at the appropriate time. The advent of three-hour format machines, together with the rise of video movie clubs, allows cheap and ready access to TV and film material. (*See* FILM STUDY; TELEVISION.)

Production

In the active role the VCF can operate as a complete study for video work. A central location has the advantage of permanent security for hardware and software while work is in progress. Work can be interrupted and returned to at will. This provides a better use of allocated class time and develops a useful routine. Such things as lights, sound boom, suitably painted studio corners (matt black is useful) credit rollers, camera tripod and dolly, as well as cables, powerboards and small items of hardware are permanently on hand. It is also possible to connect a video camera to the console to show live programmes in remote classrooms. This is the 'publication' dimensions of polished video work.

(LB)

VIDEO IN THE CLASSROOM – Modern video equipment can be of considerable use in assisting learning in English. Video production, like writing, emphasizes planning and process rather than simply the product. Video-making in the classroom allows cheap and easy experimentation and encourages the editing and polishing of unfinished work. Furthermore, successful video work requires detailed planning, involving purposeful talk and writing in small groups. Some obvious applications include:

(1) Impromptu and scripted video drama.
(2) Imitating common programme formats, for example news, current affairs, panel games, commercials, sportscasts, soap operas.
(3) Recording lesson activities in other faculties, for example experiments in science, musical performances, debating.

(4) Recording local issues for discussion starters, for example transport, entertainment, environment.
(5) Recording excursions for later follow-up work in the classroom.
(6) Production of school information tapes, for example routines and procedures, 'What to do if. . . .'

The basic equipment for such work includes:

(1) One colour portable video camera.
(2) One portable video cassette recorder (VCR).

Most states have the VHS format VCR on government contract. The VHS format has the advantage over the older U-matic format in that tapes available run for up to four hours and a three-hour tape can be purchased for less than a one-hour U-matic cassette.

Equipment of this type provides portable sound-equipped colour recording, and instant black-and-white playback in the camera. This removes the need for difficult editing. Automatic focus and zoom lens permit even greater flexibility. Units are commonly powered by both battery and mains and thus can be used in the studio or in the field.

A group using such equipment in a VCF/classroom or exterior location would comprise: camera operator, VCR operator, sound recordist (music over / voice over), boom assistant, director, and assorted helpers are required.
See also VIDEO CONTROL FACILITY. **(LB)**

VISUAL DISCRIMINATION – This term describes training in discriminatory tasks using work book activities. The tasks involve discerning differences and similarities between pictures or shapes or letters. This is done in the belief that reading is primarily a visual act and that these discriminatory tasks prepare the kindergarten child for better print processing.

However, the bulk of independent research indicates that almost all 5 year old children have these skills already (Paradis, 1974), and that visual discrimination exercises have no direct relationship with the development of reading ability (Church, 1974; Jacobs *et al.*, 1968; Rosen, 1966). **(MRT)**
See also READING READINESS; PRE-READING; VISUAL AND NON-VISUAL INFORMATION.

References

M. Church, 'Does visual perception training help beginning readers?' *Reading Teacher*, 27, 1974: 361–4.
J. N. Jacobs *et al.*, 'A follow-up evaluation of the Frostig visual-perceptual training program', *Educational Leadership Research Supplement*, 4, 1968: 169–75.
E. E. Paradis, 'The appropriateness of visual discrimination exercises', *Journal of Educational Research*, February 1974: 276–8.
C. Rosen, 'An experimental study . . . in first grade', *Perceptual and Motor Skills*, 22, 1966: 979–86.

VISUAL INFORMATION – The term 'visual information' is widely used in psycholinguistic accounts of the reading process to describe the information a reader derives directly from the page. Competent readers use only part of the total range of visual information which is available to them.

Many aspects of traditional approaches to teaching reading have wrongly emphasized the role of visual information reading. Such aspects include the development of sight vocabulary, the use of flashcards, training in visual discrimination and the repetitious presentation of core words in basal readers. When the use of visual information is so emphasized, the reader's ability to process print efficiently is reduced, and comprehending is impaired.
See also PSYCHOLINGUISTICS; NON-VISUAL INFORMATION.

Reference

Frank Smith, *Understanding Reading*, 3rd edn, New York: Holt, Rinehart & Winston, 1982.

VOCABULARY DEVELOPMENT IN READING – Vocabulary development occurs most effectively in the context of meaningful reading experiences where the child is able to make use of knowledge derived from the broader learning context as well as from the surrounding text. **(MRT)**
See also CONTEXT.

VYGOTSKY, L. S. – Russian psychologist whose work has become very influential, especially through its mediation through the writings of James Britton (q.v.). Vygotsky was responsible for the development of the concept of 'inner speech' (q.v.) and for consideration of the relationship between external (or 'social') speech, inner speech ('speech for oneself') and thought.

Vygotsky sees them as related in the following way:

> Inner speech is not the interior aspect of external speech – it is a function in itself. It still remains speech, i.e. thought connected with words. But while in external speech thought is embodied in words, in inner speech words die as they bring forth thought. Inner speech is to a large extent thinking in pure meanings. It is a dynamic, shifting, unstable thing, fluttering between word and thought, the two more or less stable, more or less delineated components of verbal thought. (As quoted in James Britton's *Language and Learning*, London: The Penguin Press, 1970.)

Reference

L. S. Vygotsky, *Thought and Language*, Cambridge, Mass.: MIT Press and New York: John Wiley, 1962 (translated by Hanfmann and Vakar).

W

WHICH, THAT *See* USAGE.

WHO, WHOM *See* USAGE.

WHOLE-CLASS DISCUSSION – Whole-class discussion is the preferred method of secondary English teachers throughout the English-speaking world, and one suspects that this is also true of teachers at upper primary levels. What passes for discussion is often, however, question-and-answer of the most restrictive kind (*see* QUESTIONING). It seems essential that English teachers not only make greater use of small-group discussion (q.v.) as an alternative, but endeavour to improve the quality of whole-class discussion. Some ways of achieving this include: arranging the class in a circle; having ten or fifteen minutes of small-group talk on a topic before whole-class discussion of that topic begins; encouraging students to develop their answers; gradually relaxing the teacher's control of the discussion to the point where students feel free to respond to one another's contributions without waiting for the teacher to say something.

Reference

Ken Watson, 'Improving whole-class discussion', in R. D. Walshe *et al.*, *Teaching Literature*, Sydney: PETA, 1983.

WIDE READING – An essential part of any English programme in both primary and secondary school. In the primary classroom there should be a reading corner or class library in constant use. In the secondary classroom, at least up to the point where the pressures of external examinations begin to be felt, there should be a wide reading programme which is given a weekly time allocation. Pupils should also understand that when, as individuals or groups, they finish work ahead of the rest of the class, they are to go on with their wide reading. This solves the perennial problem of what to do with those who finish an activity ahead of time.

Follow-up activities should not be burdensome, as the central aim of a wide reading programme is to promote enjoyment in reading. Insisting on follow-up book reviews is likely to be counter-productive. Generally, it is easy enough to gauge how much reading is being done by engaging pupils in conversation about the books they have read. Once pupils have read three or four books, it may be fruitful to ask them to select one on which they would like to do something further, and then offer a range of imaginative re-creation (q.v.) activities from which they can choose.

See also RIB-IT; SUSTAINED SILENT READING.

WILL/WOULD *See* USAGE: SHALL/SHOULD.

WORD ATTACK – The term 'word attack' has been used to include such strategies of word identification as analysis of words into their constituent letters and accompanying sounds (i.e. sounding out), structural analysis (i.e. breaking a word up into pronounceable units), use of context clues, use of dictionary skills.

While all of these strategies have their place in reading, an emphasis on any of them may lead a pupil to the erroneous conclusion that proficient reading is a matter of the accurate identification of every word on the page. It is essential that developing readers recognize that prediction of meaning is central to comprehending, and that such laborious methods of word identification as those listed above should be used only as a last resort. **(MRT)**

WORD GAMES –

For juniors

The King's Game – The answer to each clue is a word ending in -king, for example 'A king worn on the feet' is *stocking*.

(1) A king found at an information bureau (asking).
(2) A king coming from a horn (honking).
(3) A king of words (talking).
(4) This king is like a jelly (shaking).
(5) This king bets (backing).
(6) This king shuts one eye (winking).
(7) This king is humorous (joking).
(8) This king is not blind (seeking).
(9) This king imitates (mimicking).
(10) This king is destructive (breaking).

The Asses' Game – The answer must be a word beginning with 'ass' or 'as' pronounced 'ass'.

(1) An ass which helps (assistant).
(2) This ass is a variety of asses (assortment).
(3) This ass is surprised (astonished, astounded).
(4) This ass is a rising ass (ascending).
(5) This ass studies the stars (astronomer).
(6) This ass is a murderer (assassin).
(7) This ass attacks people (assailant).
(8) This ass has been lost (astray).
(9) This ass is a Zulu weapon (assegai).
(10) This is a society of asses (association).

The Ice Game – The answer is a word ending in '-ice'.

(1) This ice keeps trying (practice).
(2) This ice is found in tennis (service).
(3) This ice will hold (vice).
(4) Some ice lost their tails (mice).
(5) This ice concerns ropes (splice).
(6) This ice feeds us (rice).
(7) This ice tells us what it costs (price).
(8) This ice is thrown (dice).
(9) This ice guards the streets (police).
(10) This ice is still learning (apprentice, novice).

NE (1) 4 IOS? (Anyone For Tennis?) – There is a dialogue which is written entirely in letters of the alphabet. The scene is a restaurant; the characters are a waitress and a diner. The waitress approaches the diner:

He (to waitress):	F U NE X?
She:	YS V F X.
He:	F U NE M?
She:	YS V F M.
He:	OK L F M N X.

A translation of the last line should make everything clear – if you read it very fast: Okay, I'll have ham and eggs.

A Little More Sophisticated

Alphabetical Adjectives – The first pupil announces an adjective–noun combination in which the adjective begins with 'a' and the noun with any letter of the pupil's choice (except 'x' or 'z'). The next pupil must give an adjective beginning with 'b', and a noun beginning with the same letter as before – and so on around the class. For instance: able basketballer, bouncing baby, contented bovine, dangerous bull.

Hanky Panky – The teacher gives the class a definition for a meaningful pair of rhymed words, both of either one, two or three syllables. The number of syllables involved is indicated by saying 'hank-pank' (i.e. two words of one syllable), 'hanky-panky' or 'hankady-pankady'. For example, overweight rodent – fat rat; unhappy father – sad dad.

Hank-Panks:	a lotion for the hands – palm balm
	a wise thermometer – sage gauge
	an easy arrest – cinch pinch
	a torn teepee – rent tent.
Hanky-Pankies:	a fish doctor – sturgeon surgeon
	a cheap trumpet – frugal bugle
	a trumpet teacher – tooter tutor
	under-age ore digger – minor miner
Hankady-Pankadies:	a wicked preacher – sinister minister
	ineffective Sherlock Holmes – defective detective

Other ideas for playing with words can be gleaned from the various collec-

tions of *New Statesman* competitions edited by Arthur Marshall and from the following:
Willard Espy, *The Game of Words*, London: Wolfe, 1971.
Gyles Brandreth, *Word Play*, London: Severn House, 1982.

WORK-REQUIRED ASSESSMENTS *See* GOAL-BASED ASSESSMENT.

WRITING, ASSESSMENT OF – The assessment of writing continues to be a major worry for the English teacher, especially since (despite syllabuses which emphasize oracy (q.v.) as well as literacy) most Australian states continue to have written public examinations as the main form of end-of-school assessment. But assessment should be a concern in any case if we are to diagnose what any child can do and what next steps are needed to improve his/her ability.

Assessment may be criterion-referenced or holistic. Holistic evaluation which attempts to describe what a young writer has done in much the same way as one would analyse a piece of 'literature' seems a more useful method than setting up predetermined criteria either of language-mechanics (syntax, spelling, usage) or other features (sequencing, author's role, etc.). Criterion-referenced assessment can tell you what a young writer has not done in this piece of writing; holistic-impression-description evaluation can tell you what the same child can do as a writer and about his/her stage of development in language use.

A 'middle way' between descriptive marking and criterion-referenced evaluation has been achieved by important research studies on students' writing over the last few years which have looked at students' writing, described what has been in it and then graded these features into what seem to be increasing degrees of maturity in language use. These graded features *then* become the criteria for assessing other pieces of writing. Most important among these is the work of Leslie Stratta and John Dixon, whose series of booklets *Achievements in Writing at 16+* (Southern Regional Examination Board, 1981–4) look at writing in various modes. As a result of their study of narratives based on personal experience, for example, they make a tentative hypothesis about 'staging points' in writing against which personal narratives may be assessed. In order of ascending development these staging points are:

(1) Writing which has many of the characteristics of spoken English: simple clauses, simple conjunctions, central verbs.
(2) Writing which has much of (1) but also definite paragraph structure with episodes, more detailed commentary and some interpretation of motive and action. This is the 'transitional' stage.
(3) 'The literary model: early phase': variety of simple and complex sentences, greater use of dialogue to further action and indicate character.
(4) 'Towards a mature literary model': more complex patterning of events, more depth of characterization, broader perspective on events and more sensitive use of language.

The Crediton Project reported in A. Wilkinson *et al.*, *Assessing Language Development* (Oxford: Oxford University Press, 1980), is another most important look at assessment. The Crediton team looked at writing as manifesting certain levels of a child's growth in four areas: cognitive, moral, affective and stylistic development. Each of these areas is subdivided into what again amount to 'staging-points' in a child's linguistic psychological maturity.

The difference between such research-based, descriptive 'staging-points' approaches to assessment and the take-it-up-give-it-a-mark-hand-it-back approach lies in that the latter makes isolated judgements about one piece of writing, while the former *uses* pieces of writing as themselves evidence for judgements about the linguistic competence (and, in the case of Crediton, psychological maturity) of the writer.

Apart from these attempts at objectifying assessment on individual pieces, James Moffett and Betty Jane Wagner have provided a 24-point growth sequence for discourse generally, against which a child's development over time can be assessed. Some of their points include:

- tending towards more general and differentiated audiences;
- towards increasing sensitive judgement about when explicitness or implicitness is more appropriate in composing and comprehending;
- from emphasis on the present to past to timelessness;
- toward increasing versatility in constructing sentences, exploiting more nearly the total resources in modifying, conjoining, reducing and embedding clauses.

Brian Johnston has been engaged in important work in South Australia making distinctions between judgemental and non-judgemental assessment and demonstrating ways of making the latter viable. Johnston's important book, *Assessing English* (Milton Keynes: Open University Press, 1987) discusses useful ways of monitoring students' writing through activities such as:

(1) 'showing how you read' – by keeping a tape-recorded response to students' writing as you are in the process of reading it.
(2) 'more processed reader reactions', such as discussing students' writing with them by focusing on three key questions:
   (i) What do I find as the key idea or centre of gravity of the piece?
   (ii) Can I see a pattern in the writing which indicates how the elements in the piece relate together?
   (iii) Did the writer lead me to appreciate the centre and how the elements of the story relate to it?

He also suggests that continuity in assessment can be provided by developing the habit of responding to students' writing by filling out columns of comments such as 'Need to Learn / Can Do' or 'Strengths/Goals'. This also aids the development of student self-assessment.

See also ASSESSMENT; PEER ASSESSMENT; SELF-ASSESSMENT BY STUDENTS.

References

Brian Johnston, *Assessing English*, Milton Keynes: Open University Press, 1986.
J. Moffett and B. J. Wagner, *Student Centered Language Arts and Reading K-13*, Boston: Houghton Mifflin, 1976.
Andrew Wilkinson *et al.*, *Assessing Language Development*, Oxford: Oxford University Press, 1980.

WRITING CONFERENCE *See* WRITING: PROCESS-CONFERENCE APPROACH.

WRITING, OWNERSHIP OF – Researchers into the writing process (q.v.) continually stress the importance of keeping control of the writing in the hands of the child – control, for example, of the editing process by being taught how to become a self-editor. They also stress the importance of ownership of the topic and the importance of the child becoming a self-originator of his/her own topics. 'Nothing influences a child's attitude to writing more', writes Donald Graves, 'than the choice of topic. If the child has chosen it and if the teacher shows genuine interest in it, then there's no limit to the effort the child will make' (Walshe, November 1981, p. 9).

Among other ideas, Walshe suggests the following as ways of helping the child become a self-reliant originator of topics:

(1) Encourage the keeping of a journal from which topics will arise.
(2) Keep all draft writings – topics may later be found in these.
(3) Keep a continually growing list of 'possible topics'.
(4) Each term, put up a 'Top 20' chart.
(5) Arrange writing partners, from whom topics can be culled.
(6) Provide opportunities to publish (Walshe, March, 1981, pp. 64–5).

See also WRITING: PROCESS-CONFERENCE APPROACH.

References

Donald H. Graves, *Writing: Teachers and Children at Work*, Exeter, New Hampshire: Heinemann Educational, 1983.
R. D. Walshe, *Every Child Can Write!* Sydney: PETA, November, 1981.
R. D. Walshe (ed.), *Donald Graves in Australia*, Sydney: PETA, March, 1981.

WRITING PARTNERS – A number of scholars – Britton (q.v.), Martin, Graves and Moffett (q.v.) – advocate the advantages of students sharing their work in progress or at completion with a peer, usually someone readily available in the process of writing. Teachers involved in developing their own writing abilities in courses such as the Bay Area Writing Project (q.v.) make use of writing partners to develop confidence and awareness of audience response to writing. The conference approach to writing development also makes use of writing partners. There are obvious advantages to the approach provided the partners are empathetic and positive in their response to each other's writing. There needs to be a sense of co-operative relationship between the partners. In the classroom it may take some time for writers to develop the constructive responsiveness necessary for the method's effectiveness.

Another form of writing partners can involve writers sharing their writing even though they have never met. In one research project an exchange of letters was arranged between two groups of case study pupils in different secondary schools, (Arnold, in progress). In this project the writing partners established rapport through their letters and provided strong mutual motivation for reciprocal writing. While the writing partners in this situation rarely commented specifically on aspects of each other's writing, the letters increased the writers' positive self-concept as writers and encouraged the kinds of reflection and thinking important for the development of authentic writing.

There is considerable scope for the development of the method across school classes, regions, even countries. The core of the method's success is the mutual involvement of the partners. Where each partner experiences a sense of a responsive reader to whom the writing can be addressed, confidence increases and risk-taking with new forms of writing is more likely to occur. Because of the reciprocal relationship which develops between writing partners, there is often a deep investment in the continuation of the writing process. This in itself can extend the range of authentic writing tasks beyond those of the regular classroom, with its pupil-to-teacher writing. **(RA)**

See also WRITING: PROCESS-CONFERENCE APPROACH.

WRITING: PROCESS-CONFERENCE APPROACH – A broad approach to the teaching of written expression. Two well-known contributors to the theory and practice of the approach are Donald H. Graves for the infant-primary area and Donald M. Murray for the tertiary area.

Graves' research has established that children can write at 5–6 years old, that they enjoy doing so, and that at this stage they can make the most rapid and delightful growth in writing of their entire lives. (*See* his *Writing: Teachers and Children at Work*, London: Heinemann, 1983. A highly successful Australian trial of the approach by twenty-seven teachers is reported in *No Better Way to Teach Writing*, ed. Jan Turbill, Sydney: PETA, 1982.)

At the beginning level, the five main features of the approach are analogous to the way an infant learns to talk. The 5- to 6-year-old child begins 'writing' by making marks on a page, using '*invented spelling*' (q.v.) which can be compared to an infant's early chatter. The *conferences*, meaning brief discussions of the writing between individual child and teacher, can be compared to the function of parents and others in listening to the infant's chatter. Through *ownership*, meaning the child's choice of topic and full control of the writing, there is a parallel with the infant's choice and control of early utterances. The *process* of writing, including drafting and revising, compares to the infant's efforts at making speech-meaning clear. And the classroom affords *writing time*, to practise daily – to learn to write by writing – which compares with all the time spent by an infant in learning to talk by talking abundantly. The process-conference approach flourishes under a teacher who is able to turn away from traditional instructional methods of teaching writing and develop a form of classroom management which has the children working individually or in pairs or small groups while the brief teacher–child 'conferences' are taking place. The young writers are invariably stimulated by the prospect of some form of 'publication' of their work within the classroom, often small typed and illustrated books. **(RDW)**

Writing Conference

A 'conference' is a conversation that takes place between child and teacher about a piece of writing that the child is doing or has done. Donald Graves, popularizer of the 'conference approach', argues that the core of the conference is for the child to teach the teacher about the subject of the writing. Thus comments on the writing should be specific and questions asked by the teacher should be aimed at the meaning of the piece. Surface mechanics can all be taught at the point of need in a conference, but conferences, as with any other process of editing, should be seen primarily as an opportunity to manipulate meaning and enliven the text and should not become an exercise in 'Where should the full stops be?'

Variations on the teacher–pupil conference approach for more experienced classes are the group conference (in which a group reads and comments on each of its members pieces of writing) or peer editing (in which students conference with a writing partner as part of their editing process).

Works which explain the theory of the conference approach and attest to its success are: Donald H. Graves, *Writing: Teachers and Children at Work* (Exeter New Hampshire: Heinemann Educational, 1983); R. D. Walshe, *Every Child Can Write!* (Sydney: PETA, 1981).
See also WRITING PROCESS, MODELS OF; WRITING, OWNERSHIP OF.

WRITING PROCESS, MODELS OF – The last few years have seen a resurgence of interest in the writing process. In that time a number of models of the writing process have been put forward. Probably the most well-known are those of:

(1) Donald Murray: The writer is trying to integrate 'four primary forces': collecting (ideas), connecting them (the 'craft' of writing), writing and reading (both as proofreader and in the place of his potential audience). Murray stresses the recursiveness of the process: 'We write/read or read/write'. Donald M. Murray, 'Writing as process: how writing finds its own meaning', in J. R. Donovan and B. W. McClelland (eds), *Eight Approaches To Composition Teaching* (Urbana, Illinois: NCTE, 1980).
(2) Donald Graves. Graves stresses that the process is different according to stages of development, but that basically it follows a pattern of selection, rehearsal, composition, reading. As the writer develops, the process repeats itself to take account of revision, redrafting and a desire of publication. Thus selection, rehearsal, composition, reading, selection, composition, reading. . . . (Donald H. Graves, *Writing: Teachers and Children at Work*, Exeter New Hampshire: Heinemann Educational, 1983).
(3) R. D. Walshe: Walshe's model includes pre-writing, writing and post-writing stages. The pre-writing stage includes growth of intention to write resulting from some experience or problem and often activities such as reading, research, reflection or discussion. The writing stage includes draft writing, revising, editing and proofreading. The post-writing stage includes publication, readers' response and the writer's attitude to this whole experience (R. D. Walshe, *Every Child Can Write!* Sydney: PETA, 1980).

The terms used above in these three models are self-explanatory, so we will confine our commentary to trends. The emphasis on pre-writing in each of these three models is in the tradition of Britton (q.v.) and his advocacy of the need for talk as part of the writing process. The main impact of models like these in the early 1980s seems to be in the areas of revising and editing and publication. More and more classrooms are implementing revision and editing (including teaching children to be self-editors) as part of their normal writing practice. Publication, too, is seen as an important incentive in encouraging redrafting (*see* AUDIENCE) and also provides an important extra reading resource for the classroom. The increasing use of microcomputers (q.v.) with word processors may be an important future incentive in encouraging children to manipulate text.

Further, despite their description in a 'stages' presentation here, none of the models are in fact linear or lock-step. This has already been seen with Murray but all these writers stress the recursive, interactive nature of the writing process and present their models as two-dimensional representatives of what they acknowledge as a complex process. An important attempt (but too complex to reproduce here) at a three-dimensional diagrammatic model which takes account of other factors and also of the recursive, interactive nature of the process is Garth Boomer's 'Towards a model of the composing process in writing', paper presented at the ANZAAS Conference, Adelaide (May, 1980). *See also* WRITING: PROCESS-CONFERENCE APPROACH.

WRITING, TEN IDEAS FOR –

(1) 'Business cards'

Give each pupil a card and ask them to illustrate themselves in words or pictures. Cards should not bear pupils' names. Cards are collected by the teacher and then handed out to other pupils, who guess the identity of the writers/artists.

(2) Finishing stories

Read three-quarters of Guy de Maupassant's *The Necklace* (widely anthologized) to the class, and then have them finish the story. Compare pupils' versions with the real ending. Suitable for Years 8, 9, 10.

Two stories which leave the reader up in the air are Frank Stockton's *The Lady or the Tiger?* (also widely anthologized, particularly in collections of American short stories) and Price Warung's *Lieutenant Darrell's Predicament* (from his collection *Convict Days*. Read these and ask pupils to provide a more 'satisfying' ending. *The Lady or the Tiger?* is suitable for able Year 9, Year 10; *Lieutenant Darrell's Predicament* is for Year 8 upwards.

(3) Class books

Make a series of class books, each book based on some particular theme, for example 'Stories from Primary School' / a handbook for incoming new pupils / book of instructions, directions, recipes and so on / book of topics on which individual kids are experts or have some interest.

(4) Theme days

At the beginning of the year, allot a particular day of the year to a student who has to research the background of the day and write a piece based on the day's theme (e.g. any Friday the 13th, St Patrick's Day, Anzac Day) for presentation on or near the day itself.

(5) Books for younger children

Have the class write storybooks for younger children in the school or for a class at the local primary school; but first obtain a class list from the younger class's teacher and have students incorporate the younger students' names into their stories.

(6) Picture stimulus

A useful variation on simply using a picture for a stimulus to creative writing is to have different sections of the class write about it from a different viewpoint; for example, a beautiful landscape could be written about from the viewpoints of a property developer, a tourist, a botanist, a conservationist, an architect and so on.

(7) Theme-card packs

Make card packs based on a particular theme, for example a set of cards each of which has on it a book title, or another set each of which has on it a clue from a whodunnit. Separate packs can be given titles ('Book Titles', 'Whodunnits'); the number of packs is endless and they become a rich source of writing stimuli. See *English Journal*, September 1977, for ideas for other themes.

(8) Given situation

Set up a given scenario with the class and negotiate a range of writing topics that arise naturally from it. For example, 'Our local area has just been ravaged by bushfires and the school is one of the few buildings left standing. The Civil Defence people want to use the school to house people for three to four weeks.' Writing activities that arise from the scenario would include taking inventories of what facilities the school has for such things as washing, cooking, eating and drinking and what reserve facilities could be used; planning how the school will be used (areas for sleeping, serving food, care of the sick and so on); interviewing heads of departments about what special contributions of resources their department could make; an infinite number of imaginative writing topics (interviews with victims, scenes of dialogue between civil defence people and the principal/victims, newspapers articles about the fires, script for a show put on as entertainment within the school, etc.).

(9) Class newspaper

Make a class newspaper with different groups in the class taking responsibility for different sections of the paper. This can be an ongoing activity based on 'real' news around the class or school or local area or a unit within itself. If the latter is chosen, you may wish to branch out into other areas, perhaps based on current units of work, for example a Second World War newspaper, a newspaper from the year AD 3000, a Middle-Earth newspaper, and so on.

(10) Time capsule

Make a time capsule which consists entirely of writing that would give people a picture of 'these kids at this school in this year'. Entries in the capsule could include: descriptions of the school and local area, poems and short stories perhaps modelled on those studied in class, diary extracts and so on. A variation on this activity which could ensure audience feedback is to make it a 'space' capsule which could be sent to a school interstate or even overseas in return for a capsule from them.

See also IMAGINARY ISLAND; OBITUARIES.

y

YOUNG ADULT LITERATURE – Since the Second World War the Western world has seen the cultivation of the adolescent market as a new, separate and profitable area for the attention of the manufacturer and advertiser. The publishing industry has been no exception, and the last twenty years has seen the appearance (and sometimes disappearance) of such imprints as Peacock (now called Puffin Plus), Puffin, Collins Armada, Cascades and Fontana Lions, Bodley Head's Books for New Adults and Macmillan Topliners, to name but a few.

All of this publishing activity has provided exciting new material for the English teacher as the best of young adult literature offers a chance for us to push out all the frontiers of the adolescent's reading experience. Most obviously, this kind of literature offers the possibility of a deepening exploration of such themes and issues as relationships and conflict with parents and family (William Mayne, *A Game of Dark*), encounters with authority (Robert Cormier, *The Chocolate War*), establishing one's own identity and directions in life (Stanley Watts, *The Breaking of Arnold*) and the whole delicate area of developing sexuality (Ursula Le Guin, *A Very Long Way from Anywhere Else*; Aidan Chambers, *Dance on My Grave*; Deborah Hautzig, *Hey, Dollface*). These personal concerns widen out into a whole range of socio-cultural issues confronting adolescent life. A really useful summary of some of the material available can be found in Chris Kloet's 'An A–Z of fiction for teenagers' in Peter Kennerley's collection (listed below). To look for challenging, relevant, well-written material which can touch the reader's life does not mean subscribing to the American notion of bibliotherapy (q.v.) in adolescent fiction where the acts of reading and response are seen solely as aids to solving some personal or social problem.

In addition to these thematic developments, some writers have experimented with form and style in this field. Select examples would include the psychological intensity achieved by the dislocation of narrative in Robert Cormier's *I Am the Cheese*, the sense of the flux of time and its effects on relationships and individual perception in *Goldengrove* and *Unleaving* of Jill Paton Walsh, while Aidan Chambers in *Breaktime* uses the adolescent novel as a vehicle for an examination of the nature of fiction and the functions of various narrative styles. Perhaps the most original and complex example in the whole field is Alan Garner's *Red Shift*.

Increasingly, substantial and satisfying material is available for use in the senior classroom and it offers the possibility of its being used as a bridge for the gap between fiction in the junior school and the demands made on adolescents by the kind of adult literature studied in the last years of secondary school.

(WF)

References

K. L. Donelson and A. P. Nilsen, *Literature for Today's Young Adults*, New York: Scott, Foresman, 1980.

Peter Kennerley (ed.), *Teenage Reading*, London: Ward Lock, 1979.

Z

ZEUGMA – A figure of speech where two ideas are yoked together, e.g. 'Kill the boys and the luggage!'

In zeugma, the two ideas are not grammatically in accord. Thus, in the above example, the verb 'plunder', or some equivalent, has to be inserted in order to fill out the sense.

The authors of this book do not recommend the teaching of such figures of speech but found this one necessary to complete the alphabet!

Reading Lists

What follows is not intended to constitute a full bibliography on the teaching of English. In any case many of the entries in this book have their own lists of readings attached to them. These lists simply indicate some of the books that have been found especially helpful by the editors across a wide variety of entries. Except in a few cases of exceptional importance the list has been confined to books that are internationally available and in print at the time of going to press.

General Books for the English Teacher

Author	Title	Publisher
Ros Arnold	*Timely Voices*	Open University Press
John Dixon	*Growth Through English*	Open University Press
Tricia Evans	*Teaching English*	Croom Helm
David Jackson	*Continuity in Secondary English*	Methuen
Stephen Judy	*The ABCs Of Literacy*	OUP
Richard Knott	*The English Department in a Changing World*	Open University Press
Martin Lightfoot & Nancy Martin (eds)	*The Word for Teaching is Learning*	Heinemann
Robert McGregor & Marion Meiers	*English Teaching in Practice: Talking With Teachers*	St Clair
Gordon M. Pradl (ed.)	*Prospect and Retrospect: Selected Essays of James Britton*	Heinemann
Leslie Stratta, John Dixon & Andrew Wilkinson	*Patterns Of Language*	Heinemann
Stephen Tchudi (ed.)	*Language, Schooling and Society*	Boynton/Cook
Ken Watson	*English Teaching in Perspective*	Open University Press

Books on Children's Literature

Author	Title	Publisher
Bruno Bettelheim	*The Uses Of Enchantment*	Penguin
Dennis Butts	*Good Writers For Young Readers*	Hart-Davis
Nancy Chambers (ed.)	*The Signal Approach to Children's Books*	Kestrel
Geoff Fox *et al.*	*Writers Critics And Children*	Heinemann
Walter McVitty	*Innocence And Experience*	Nelson
Margaret Meek *et al.*	*The Cool Web*	Bodley Head
John Rowe Townsend	*A Sounding Of Storytellers*	Kestrel
John Rowe Townsend	*Written for Children*	Penguin

See also the in-service training package, 'Children, Language and Literature', published by the Open University Press

Books on Language Acquisition and Development and Language Across the Curriculum

Author	Title	Publisher
Douglas Barnes	*From Communication To Curriculum*	Penguin
Douglas Barnes, James Britton & Harold Rosen	*Language, The Learner And The School*	Penguin
James Britton	*Language And Learning*	Penguin
A. Cashdan *et al.* (eds)	*Language in Education*	Routledge & Kegan Paul
F. D. Flower	*Language And Education*	Longmans
Michael Halliday	*Learning How To Mean*	Edward Arnold
Brian Johnston	*Assessing English*	Open University Press
A. R. Luria & F. la Yudovich	*Speech And The Development Of Mental Processes In The Child*	Penguin
James Moffett	*Teaching The Universe Of Discourse*	Houghton Mifflin
John Richmond	*The Resources of Classroom Language*	Edward Arnold
Connie & Harold Rosen	*The Language Of Primary School Children*	Penguin
Mike Torbe (ed.)	*Language across the Curriculum*	Ward Lock
Andrew Wilkinson	*Language And Education*	Open University Press
Andrew Wilkinson *et al.*	*Assessing Language Development*	Open University Press

Books on Writing

Author	Title	Publisher
James Britton *et al.*	*The Development Of Writing Abilities 11–18*	Macmillan
T. Dunsbee & T. Ford	*Mark My Words*	Ashton
Eldonna L. Evertts	*Explorations In Children's Writing*	NCTE
Donald H. Graves	*Writing: Teachers And Children At Work*	Heinemann
Nancy Martin	*Writing And Learning Across The Curriculum 11–16*	Ward Lock
James Moffett	*Active Voice*	Boynton/Cook
	Coming On Center	Boynton/Cook
James Moffett & Betty Jane Wagner	*Student-Centered Language Arts And Reading K-13*	Houghton Mifflin
Robert Protherough	*Encouraging Writing*	Methuen
Frank Smith	*Writing and the Writer*	Heinemann
Morag Styles	*Collaboration and Writing*	Open University Press
Andrew Wilkinson	*Assessing Language Development*	OUP

See also the publications arising out of the UK National Writing Project (*q.v.*) to be published in 1989 by Nelson

Books on Reading

Author	Title	Publisher
Dorothy Butler	*Babies Need Books*	Penguin
Marie Clay	*Reading: The Patterning Of Complex Behaviour*	Heinemann
Bill Corcoran & Emrys Evans (eds)	*Readers, Texts, Teachers*	Open University Press
Patrick Dias & Michael Heyhoe	*Developing Response to Poetry*	Open University Press
Kenneth S. Goodman	*Language And Literacy, Vols I and II*	Routledge & Kegan Paul
Yetta Goodman & Carolyn Burke	*Reading Strategies: Focus On Comprehension*	Holt Rinehart
David Jackson	*Encounters with Books*	Methuen

Eric Lunzer & Keith Gardner	*The Effective Use Of Reading*	Heinemann
Eric Lunzer & Keith Gardner	*Learning from the Written Word*	Ward Lock
Margaret Meek	*Achieving Literacy*	Routledge & Kegan Paul
Margaret Meek	*Learning To Read*	Bodley Head
Robert Protherough	*Developing Response to Literature*	Open University Press
Frank Smith	*Psycholinguistics And Reading*	Holt Rinehart
	Reading	CUP
	Understanding Reading	Holt Rinehart